The Art of Quick Breads

The Art of Quick Breads

Simple Everyday Baking

BY BETH HENSPERGER

PHOTOGRAPHY BY JOYCE OUDKERK POOL

STYLING BY AMY NATHAN

CHRONICLE BOOKS

SAN FRANCISCO

Printed in Japan.

LIBRARY OF CONGRESS
CATALOGING-IN-PUBLICATION DATA

Hensperger, Beth.
    The art of quick breads : simple everyday
  baking / by Beth Hensperger ; photography
  by Joyce Oudkerk Pool.
        p.   cm.
    Includes index.
    ISBN 0-8118-0540-9 (hc)
    ISBN 0-8118-0353-8 (pbk)
    1. Bread.   I. Title.
  TX769.H427 1994
  641.8'15--dc20   93-25599
                            CIP

Book and cover design: Gretchen Scoble
Composition: On Line Typography
Props: Carol Hacker

Distributed in Canada by Raincoast Books,
112 East Third Ave., Vancouver, B.C. V5T 1C8

10 9 8 7 6 5 4 3 2 1

Chronicle Books
275 Fifth Street
San Francisco, CA 94103

~ Table of Contents ~

Acknowledgments

~

I especially wish to thank:

Martha Casselman, for proving in countless

ways that she is a very special and remarkable literary agent.

Artist Michael Montfort for his discerning eye

and palate, encouragement, and support.

Bro Jim, Mary Jo Turek, and my Mom, my very own patrons of the arts.

Bill LeBlond, for his interest in my bread book projects.

Leslie 'hold that thought' Jonath, for answering every little

question with wit and wisdom.

Carolyn Krebs for her precise editing skills and many

excellent suggestions.

~ Inspiration in the Kitchen ~

Good quick breads are made from good recipes. This book contributes traditional-style recipes that bake to perfection and have an exceptionally pleasing taste. Breads of all types are blessed with the mystical ability to satisfy much more than mere physical hunger, and for a small amount of effort in the kitchen, they offer the reward of great eating pleasure. Quick breads in particular offer something that modern bakers value: ease of preparation. They are leavened not with the time-consuming demands of yeast, but with baking powder and soda, which respond immediately to moisture and the heat of the oven. All quick breads are so easy, they can be baked fresh for every meal.

Quick loaves (or tea breads), cornbreads, gingerbreads, pancakes, waffles, crêpes, popovers, and coffee cakes are "batter" breads, easy to spot because they do not hold their own shapes and are baked in molds of varying shapes and sizes. In most recipes of this type, liquid and dry ingredients will be in equal proportion. In contrast, biscuits, scones, soda breads, shortcakes, and cobbler toppings are known as "quick dough" breads, which are stiff enough to be hand-shaped and baked on flat pans. They have a higher percentage of dry ingredients to liquid than the batter breads.

Quick breads are very much like cakes in that they demand precise combinations of liquid, leavening, flour, fat, and flavorings. All the components are important and create a balanced chemical equation, making the home baker an alchemist of sorts. Professional bakers look at these components in a bit more scientific light: The liquids (water, milk, buttermilk, eggs, honey, syrups) moisten and lengthen storage time; dry ingredients (flour, dry milk) give the quick bread its body, bind all the ingredients together, and absorb and retain moisture; the tenderizers (fats, sugar, egg yolks, chocolate, sour cream, yogurt) give a soft, delicate texture; leaveners (baking powder, baking soda,

eggs) are added for volume and lightness; and, finally, the flavorings (chocolate, eggs, butter, citrus, coffee, nuts, salt, extracts) dictate and enhance the overall taste of the bread.

Old-fashioned quick breads may be served at any time of the day: toasted for breakfast, alongside egg dishes for brunch, with crisp fruit or vegetable salads, as a sandwich with a variety of spreads or meats, sliced and served hot for a snack, or for tea parties with fresh fruit or a bit of cheese. Most freeze beautifully, ready to be thawed and served at any time.

Quick breads are economical as well as easy to mix and bake. Once you master the basic techniques, you will be able to produce a staggering variety of batter or dough breads. Many of the recipes are executed in a few quick steps and are ready for the oven in under 15 minutes. Except for a few large-sized loaves and coffee cakes, all bake in under 1 hour.

Although all the recipes are written to provide the necessary information to produce a wonderful baked good, the end section titled "Notes from the Kitchen" gives extra helpful tips on techniques, ingredients and basic recipes, equipment, and extraordinary mail-order resources. Use it as a reference guide when baking of all types of quick breads for information as diverse as from where to mail order pure maple or cane syrups and how to make coconut milk, to techniques for adapting your recipes with light baking ingredients.

Although quick breads can be deceptively plain looking, whether free-formed or molded, they are deliciously rich, moist textured, and uncomplicated in flavor. The simple batters offer the perfect vehicle for showcasing seasonal ingredients. This genre of baking is a wondrous combination of improvisation, inspiration, and nostalgia— a simple pleasure for both experienced and beginning bakers.

Quick Batter Breads

~ Quick Loaves ~

Quick loaves rely exclusively on the power of chemical leaveners to make their batters light and fluffy. Before the invention of the baking powder mixture by a German inventor in the late 1800s, loaves were compact and dense, usually raised with yeast, naturally fermented starters, beer, or eggs. Early Americans used saleratus (an early form of bicarbonate of soda converted from sea salt), hartshorn (the ground antler of a male deer, the chief source of ammonia), cream of tartar, and pearlash (ashes from wood, seaweed, pea, or bean stalks) for leavening home quick breads, each with its own pronounced flavor. All of these forms of leavening were at times scarce and often worked unreliably in producing consistent-quality baked goods.

Because of the capricious nature of these leavenings, early cookbooks advised bakers to keep the oven shut during baking, to avoid drafts, to dissolve leavenings in water to prevent black spots, to beat batters laboriously by hand for long periods, and to never let a finished batter stand, as it would lose its slightly raised texture very quickly. Adding to the baker's difficulties was the fact that these loaves were often baked in wood cookstoves, known for their quick, intense, and uneven heat. Although some of these directions might still be included in a modern recipe, they are leftovers from another era and need not be heeded with today's reliable leaveners and consistent ingredients.

Modern baking powders are double acting, which means they begin to rise as soon as the leavening is moistened in the batter and again during the baking process. Most of the carbon dioxide produced will be released in the oven, making a stable batter that bakes into a high, light bread. This allows for batters to rest overnight in the refrigerator and still bake into an excellent loaf. Aluminum sulfate, a common ingredient in commercial baking powder, can often be tasted in quick breads by some people, so many bakers and recipes recommend nonaluminum baking powder, sold under the commercial name of Rumford. For more information on leavenings and how to make homemade single-acting baking powder, which makes a tender and flavorful baked good, see the Notes from the Kitchen, pages 112-13.

The modern quick loaf is a pure American product, with a taste and texture between a yeasted bread and a sweet cake. A large assortment of breads can be made by a simple variation in ingredients. They are delicious with added seasonal fresh or dried fruits or accented with luscious liqueurs, chunks of mellow nuts, creamy cheeses, aromatic herbs, and pungent exotic spices.

One of the most important techniques in baking quick loaves is beating the wet ingredients with a whisk or electric mixer to aerate and expand their total volume. The mixture will double, becoming thick and creamy at the same time. The dry ingredients are mixed separately, with all the leavenings evenly distributed. All intense beating is done while these two mixtures are separate. The dry and the wet ingredients are then mixed together with a quick and light hand (never beaten unless specifically directed to do so) to avoid activating the gluten in the flour. Most batters are immediately scraped or poured into greased pans to bake in a preheated moderate oven. All breads using baking powder improve in texture and flavor by rising for 15 to 20 minutes at room temperature before going into the oven.

Recipes need to be followed exactly, with the mixing done in the manner outlined in each recipe. The proper oven temperature is important for "oven spring," the final expanding of the dough when in contact with heat. Bake on the middle shelves with at least two inches of space between each pan to allow the heat to circulate. When baking on two shelves, make sure the pans are staggered for even baking. A quick loaf is finished baking when the top looks and feels firm and dry; when the edges pull slightly away from the sides of the pan; when it is evenly browned; and when a cake tester inserted into the center comes out dry. If the center is still gooey, continue to bake another 5 to 8 minutes. Immediately turn the loaf out of its hot pan onto a wire rack to cool on its side, allowing for air to circulate around it. Loaves that are more cakelike in texture can stand for 15 minutes to firm up slightly before being turned out of their pans.

Quick loaves are easier to slice if cooled completely beforehand, and their flavors and textures are best after standing overnight. Always use a good serrated knife for even slicing. To store, wrap in plastic, whether storing at room temperature, in the refrigerator, or in the freezer. The loaves store well at room temperature unless they contain chunks of cheese or other dairy products that can spoil easily, in which case they should be refrigerated. Properly stored, quick loaves will retain good flavor and texture up to one week. Quick loaves also keep perfectly up to 3 months if frozen in freezer bags or in plastic wrap and then foil, so often it is best to make double quantities to enjoy later. Let the wrapped loaves thaw to room temperature before serving.

The loaves are never frosted in the traditional manner of more elaborate cakes, although they are sometimes drizzled with a thin sugar glaze or shiny coating of sweet counterpoint flavor. For a pretty finish, try dusting the loaves with a mist of sifted plain powdered sugar or your own homemade Scented Powdered Sugar (page 113). Serve tea loaves plain or with butter or cream cheese spreads, alongside fruit or vegetable salads. They also make excellent sandwiches with seafood, meat, and poultry. Savory loaves are good with light meals and are wonderful toasted.

Batter breads can be made in a variety of appealing fluted molds, as well as rectangular loaves, because their batter is too liquid to retain its own shape. Unique alternatives to the traditional rectangular loaf shapes are mini-bundt or tube pans (small patterned ring molds), charlotte molds, and half-loaf pans, reminiscent of the ridged, half-moon European *rehrücken* loaf pan or guttered mold. Using the correct pan size and filling it only one-half to two-thirds full is important to allow the batter to climb as it rises and to dome attractively. A recipe containing 2 cups of flour will bake perfectly into a rectangular 8- or 9-inch loaf, a 6-cup mini-bundt pan, a full pan of 12 muffins, an 8-inch charlotte mold, or three 5- or 6-inch loaf pans.

TROUBLESHOOTING QUICK LOAVES

Soggy Texture with a Sunken Middle:
—Too much liquid in proportion to the dry ingredients in the recipe
—Too little total leavening or leavenings not potent
—Batter left too long before baking

Crack Along the Center of the Top Surface:
—Characteristic of a good quick loaf, indicating expansion during baking
—To eliminate the crack, let the batter rise slightly at room temperature for 20 minutes before baking

Coarse, Crumbly Texture:
—Too much fat in proportion to the other ingredients in the recipe
—Too much leavening

Greasy with Crisp Edges:
—Too much fat in proportion to the other ingredients

Thick, Porous, and Overly Browned Crust:
—Too much sugar in proportion to the other ingredients
—Oven temperature too high

Tough-Textured:
—Overhandling of the batter during the mixing
—Oven temperature too high

Bitter or Soapy Aftertaste:
—Too much baking powder or baking soda

Amaretto Nut Bread

~

Amaretto Nut Bread is my basic all-purpose nut loaf. It has a firm texture that makes it slice perfectly, a moist crumb, and a flavorful, buttery essence of nuts infused into the bread during baking. The addition of almond-flavored liqueur gives the loaf a subtle quality that complements the nuts rather than over-powering them. I tend to make nut breads most during the cool fall and winter months, and stash lots of loaves in the freezer for unexpected visitors and for gifts. As with all quick loaves, wrap tightly in plastic wrap and let rest overnight before slicing, to develop flavor and texture.

YIELD: One 9-by-5-inch loaf or three 6-by-3-inch loaves

2 cups unbleached all-purpose flour
2½ teaspoons baking powder
½ teaspoon baking soda
½ teaspoon salt
1½ teaspoons ground mace or nutmeg
1¼ cups (6 ounces) chopped walnuts, pecans,
  hazelnuts, or any combination
¼ cup vegetable oil
1 cup light brown sugar
2 eggs
1½ teaspoons pure vanilla extract
1½ cups sour cream
½ cup amaretto liqueur

1. Preheat the oven to 350°F. Combine the flour, baking powder, baking soda, salt, and spice in a medium bowl. Add the nuts and stir until evenly distributed.

2. In another bowl, with a whisk, or in the workbowl of an electric mixer, beat together the oil and brown sugar until fluffy and light colored. Add the eggs and vanilla extract.

3. Add the flour mixture to the creamed mixture in three equal portions, alternating with the sour cream and liqueur. Beat until smooth after each addition. The batter will be thin.

4. Pour the batter into one 9-by-5-inch loaf pan or three 6-by-3-inch loaf pans, greased and floured. Bake in the center of the preheated oven, 40 to 45 minutes, until the top is firm, the loaf pulls away from the sides of the pan, and a cake tester inserted into the center comes out clean. Cool in the pan 10 minutes. Remove from the pan onto a wire rack to cool completely. Wrap tightly in plastic wrap and chill overnight or up to 3 days before serving.

Dried Apricot~Pecan Bread

~

Dried Apricot–Pecan Bread is incredibly delicious served in plain, thin slices or spread with sweet butter to accompany tea or coffee. I also serve it often for picnics and holidays, sandwiching paper-thin slices of smoked turkey and Black Forest ham. An equal amount of orange brandy may be substituted for the orange juice, if you prefer a more sophisticated flavored loaf. The combination of dried fruit and rich nuts produces one of the most complementary of culinary pairings.

YIELD: Two 7¼-by-3½-inch loaves

1½ cups dried apricot halves
1 cup boiling water
3 tablespoons unsalted butter
1 cup sugar
2 cups unbleached all-purpose flour
1½ teaspoons baking soda
½ teaspoon salt
½ cup whole-wheat flour
1 cup (4 ounces) chopped raw pecans
2 eggs
½ cup orange juice, fresh or frozen

1. Coarsely chop the apricots by hand or in a food processor. Place in a large bowl and add the boiling water, butter, and sugar. Mix well and set aside to cool to lukewarm.

2. Combine the unbleached flour, baking soda, and salt. Add to the apricot mixture and stir to combine. Add the whole-wheat flour, pecans, eggs, and orange juice. Beat well to make a batter that is evenly combined but slightly lumpy. Do not overmix.

3. Pour the batter into two 7¼-by-3½-inch greased and floured loaf pans. Preheat oven to 350°F. Let the loaves rest at room temperature 15 minutes before placing in the center of the oven to bake for 55 to 60 minutes. When done, the tops will be firm to the touch, the loaves will pull away from the sides of the pans, and a cake tester inserted into the centers will come out clean. Remove from the pans and cool completely on a rack. Wrap tightly in plastic wrap and chill overnight or up to 5 days before serving.

Papaya-Macadamia Nut Bread

~

A fragile fruit, the papaya is imported to American produce markets from lands below the Tropic of Cancer: Hawaii, Florida, the Bahamas, and Latin America. Check for ripe fruit by feel (there should be a bit of give), rather than by smell or sight. Puréed fresh papaya has a luxurious texture and perfumed flavor that enhances baked goods, such as this quick bread. One large papaya yields about 1 cup purée.

YIELD: One 9-by-5-inch loaf

1 large ripe papaya
½ cup sugar
3 cups unbleached all-purpose flour
1 tablespoon baking powder
1 teaspoon salt
½ cup chopped raw unsalted macadamia nuts
Grated zest of 1 orange
2 eggs
1 cup milk or fresh coconut milk, page 116
1 teaspoon pure vanilla extract
3 tablespoons unsalted butter, melted

1. Peel and seed the papaya. Mash well with a fork or purée the pulp in a blender or food processor to equal 1 cup. With a whisk, combine the pulp with the sugar in a small bowl. Let stand 10 minutes. Meanwhile, preheat the oven to 350°F.

2. Combine the flour, baking powder, salt, nuts, and orange zest in a medium mixing bowl. Add the eggs, milk, vanilla, and butter to the papaya pulp. Stir to combine. Make a well in the dry ingredients and pour in papaya mixture. Stir just to combine. The batter will be a bit lumpy.

3. Pour the batter into a greased 9-by-5-inch loaf pan and bake in the center of the preheated oven until the top is firm to the touch and a cake tester inserted into the center comes out clean, about 50 to 60 minutes. Turn the loaf out onto a rack to cool completely. Wrap in plastic wrap and let stand at room temperature until serving.

Cranberry-Orange Tea Bread

~

Cranberries, called *sassamanesh* by northeastern Native Americans, range in color from a lusty, deep pink to a deep crimson, appearing in time to announce the arrival of the fall harvest. The cranberry is, surprisingly, a member of the rhododendron and heather families. Grown mostly in New England and Canadian bogs, the raw fruit has a definite astringent, yet refreshingly tart taste. In combination with other ingredients, sweetened and cooked, the fruit is a boon to creative cooks because of its delightfully tangy flavor. Cranberries can be frozen in bags and used unthawed in recipes calling for fresh, any time of year. Serve this bread thinly sliced, with sweet butter or whipped cream cheese.

YIELD: One 8-by-4-inch loaf

1½ cups whole fresh cranberries
1 cup sugar
2 cups unbleached all-purpose flour
1 tablespoon baking powder
½ teaspoon fresh-ground nutmeg
¼ teaspoon ground ginger
¼ teaspoon salt
Grated zest of 2 oranges
½ cup raw walnuts, chopped
¾ cup fresh orange juice
2 eggs
1 teaspoon pure vanilla extract
4 tablespoons unsalted butter, melted

1. Preheat the oven to 350°F. Combine the cranberries and sugar in the workbowl of a food processor fitted with the steel blade. Pulse to coarsely grind. Set aside.

2. In a large bowl, combine the flour, baking powder, spices, and salt. Add the orange zest and walnuts. Toss to blend.

3. In a small bowl, combine the orange juice and eggs. Beat with a whisk until frothy. Add the vanilla extract and cranberry mixture. Stir to combine. Pour over the dry ingredients and drizzle with the butter. Stir with a large spatula just until moistened and cranberries are evenly distributed.

4. Pour the batter into an 8-by-4-inch greased and floured loaf pan. Bake in the center of the preheated oven 45 to 50 minutes, or until a cake tester inserted into the center comes out clean. The top surface should be crusty and golden. Turn the loaf out onto a rack to cool completely. Wrap tightly in plastic wrap and let stand at room temperature overnight before serving.

Lemon—Poppy Seed Bread
~

The aromatic poppy seed is a favorite crunchy addition to quick breads. Soaking the seeds before adding them to the batter accentuates their elusive flavor. Poppy seeds can range from a clear slate blue to blue-black in color, with a corresponding wide range of sweetness. In specialty stores, look for Dutch blue poppy seeds, as they are the highest quality and very sweet. Store seeds in the freezer to prevent rancidity because, like nuts, they have a high oil content. Lemon—Poppy Seed Bread is completely addictive, so you may want to double the recipe.

YIELD: One 9-by-5-inch loaf

3 tablespoons fresh poppy seeds
½ cup milk
5 tablespoons unsalted butter, room temperature
1 cup sugar
2 eggs
1½ cups unbleached all-purpose flour
1 teaspoon baking powder
Grated zest of 2 lemons
¼ teaspoon salt

LEMON SYRUP
¼ cup granulated sugar
¼ cup fresh lemon juice

1. In a small bowl, combine the poppy seeds and milk. Let stand 1 hour to macerate and meld flavors.

2. Preheat oven to 325°F. Cream the butter and sugar in the workbowl of an electric mixer. Add the eggs one at a time, beating well after each addition. Combine the flour, baking powder, lemon zest, and salt in a small bowl. Add the dry ingredients to the creamed mixture in three equal portions, alternating with the poppy seed milk. Beat just until smooth.

3. Pour the batter into a greased 9-by-5-inch loaf pan and bake in the center of the preheated oven until golden brown and a cake tester inserted into the center of the loaf comes out clean, about 55 to 65 minutes. Place the loaf in the pan on a cooling rack.

4. Meanwhile, to make the lemon syrup, combine the sugar and lemon juice in a small saucepan. Place over low heat just until the sugar dissolves. Set aside. Pierce the hot loaf about a dozen times to the bottom with a bamboo skewer, toothpick, or metal cake tester. Immediately pour over the hot lemon syrup. Cool 30 minutes before turning out of the pan onto a rack to cool completely. Wrap tightly in plastic wrap and let stand at room temperature overnight before serving.

LEMON—POPPY SEED BREAD
WITH SAFFRON

Add ⅛ teaspoon powdered saffron to the milk in Step 1. Continue to mix the batter, bake, and glaze as for Lemon—Poppy Seed Bread.

Cream Sherry-Pumpkin Bread
~

Pumpkins are the fruit of a large herbaceous plant with long, vinelike shoots and curling tendrils. They have a silky, bright orange pulp that adds a delicate flavor and moisture to quick breads. Use a fresh Sugar Pie pumpkin or other winter squash, such as a large Blue Hubbard, for the best flavor when making your own purée (page 123), although commercially canned pumpkin is also an excellent alternative.

YIELD: Three 8-by-4-inch loaves

2 cups granulated sugar
1¼ cups light brown sugar
3⅔ cups puréed fresh pumpkin, or one 29-ounce
*   can pumpkin*
4 eggs
1 cup nut oil, such as walnut, almond, or
*   sunflower seed*
4⅔ cups unbleached all-purpose flour
1 tablespoon baking soda
1½ teaspoons each ground cinnamon, cloves,
*   and coriander*
1 teaspoon salt
½ cup good-quality cream sherry

1. Preheat the oven to 350°F. In a large bowl, combine the sugars, pumpkin, eggs, and nut oil. Beat with a large whisk or an electric mixer until smooth, about 1 minute.

2. In another bowl, combine the flour, baking soda, spices, and salt. With a large spatula, combine the wet and dry mixtures and beat until smooth. Stir in the cream sherry. Vigorously beat until thoroughly blended, about 1 to 2 minutes. The batter will be thick and fluffy.

3. Scrape the batter into three greased 8-by-4-inch loaf pans, filling each no more than three-fourths full. Bake immediately in the center of the preheated oven 65 to 75 minutes, or until a cake tester inserted into each center comes out clean. The top surfaces will be crusty and have a long center crack. Let stand 5 minutes in the pans before turning the loaves out onto a rack to cool completely. Wrap tightly in plastic wrap and let set at room temperature overnight or up to 4 days before serving.

INDIAN PUMPKIN BREAD

Substitute 1⅓ cups fine-grind yellow, white, or blue cornmeal for an equal amount of unbleached flour in Step 2 to make the batter. Continue to mix and bake as for Cream Sherry–Pumpkin Bread.

Whole-Wheat Prune Bread with Orange Cream Cheese

The combination of nutty whole-wheat flour and moist dried prunes makes for one of the most popular quick loaves I have in my repertoire. When you serve this loaf, be prepared to give out the recipe; at least one person always asks. The Orange Cream Cheese is a sophisticated touch.

YIELD: Three 6-by-3-inch loaves

12 ounces moist pitted prunes
1 cup whole-wheat flour
¾ cup (3 ounces) chopped pecans
1 cup unbleached all-purpose flour
1 teaspoon baking soda
1 teaspoon ground cinnamon
½ teaspoon baking powder
¼ teaspoon salt
4 tablespoons unsalted butter, room temperature
¾ cup packed light brown sugar
1 egg
1 cup plus 2 tablespoons cultured buttermilk
Orange Cream Cheese, following (optional)

1. Preheat the oven to 350°F. In the workbowl of a food processor, combine the prunes and ½ cup of the whole-wheat flour. Pulse to coarsely chop. Remove from the workbowl. Add the pecans to the prune mixture. Set aside.

2. In a large bowl, combine the remaining whole-wheat flour, unbleached flour, baking soda, cinnamon, baking powder, and salt. Add the prune-nut mixture and toss to blend.

3. In another bowl, cream the butter and brown sugar until fluffy with a wooden spoon or an electric mixer. Add the egg and beat until well combined. Alternately add the flour mixture and the buttermilk to the creamed mixture in 3 equal portions. Beat just until smooth and evenly combined. The batter will be thick.

4. Scrape the batter into three 6-by-3-inch greased loaf pans and bake in the center of the preheated oven 40 to 45 minutes, or until a cake tester inserted into the center of each loaf comes out clean. Cool in the pans 10 minutes before removing to a rack to cool completely. Wrap tightly in plastic wrap and let stand at room temperature or refrigerate overnight before slicing. Serve with Orange Cream Cheese, if desired.

ORANGE CREAM CHEESE

YIELD: About 1½ cups

6 ounces fresh cream cheese
3 tablespoons sugar
3 tablespoons plain yogurt
Grated zest of 2 oranges
Fresh mint or pineapple sage leaves for
  serving, optional

Mix together all ingredients in a bowl, with a spoon, or in a food processor, until fluffy and evenly combined. Store covered in the refrigerator for up to 1 week before serving. Serve on a bed of aromatic leaves, if desired.

Pear Bread with Vanilla and Ginger

~

Vanilla is the strong-scented, dried pod of a tropical orchid native to Mexico, Madagascar, Tahiti, Java, and the Seychelles. It was introduced to Europe via Spain after the Mexican conquest. Ginger, a sturdy East Indian perennial whose root is spicy-hot, took the opposite route from Spain to the West Indies, where some of the finest ginger is cultivated today. Together with ambrosial fresh pears, this bread has a remarkable perfumed aroma and a variety of textures, with the ginger melting into pockets of sweetness throughout the loaf. Use red or green Bartlett, Winter Nelis, d'Anjou, Bosc, Seckel, or firm Comice pear varieties.

YIELD: One 9-by-5-inch loaf

½ cup (1 stick) unsalted butter, room
   temperature
1 cup sugar
2 eggs
1½ teaspoons pure vanilla extract
2 cups unbleached all-purpose flour
1 teaspoon baking powder
½ teaspoon baking soda
Pinch salt
Grated zest of 1 lemon
⅓ cup finely chopped crystallized
   candied ginger
¼ cup cultured buttermilk
1½ cups peeled, cored, and coarsely chopped
   fresh pears (about 2 to 3 whole pears), such
   as Bartlett, Winter Nelis, d'Anjou, Bosc,
   Seckel, or Comice

1. Preheat the oven to 350°F. In a large bowl, cream the butter and sugar with an electric mixer or by hand. Add the eggs one at a time, beating well after each addition. Add the vanilla extract and beat just until combined.

2. Combine the flour, baking powder, baking soda, salt, lemon zest, and crystallized ginger in a small bowl. Add the dry ingredients to the creamed mixture in three equal portions, alternating with the buttermilk. Beat just until smooth. Fold in the pears just until evenly distributed.

3. Scrape the batter into a greased 9-inch loaf pan and bake in the center of the preheated oven until golden brown and a cake tester inserted into the center of the loaf comes out clean, about 55 to 65 minutes. Remove the loaf from the pan onto a rack to cool completely before slicing.

Brandy-Glazed Zucchini Bread

~

Zucchini was the first vegetable I ever tasted that was used like a fruit in baking, making a moist, sweet bread. The smooth, cylindrical fruits of this annual herbaceous plant make a distinguished loaf flecked with green and white. Glazed with a good brandy or cognac, it can be served as a dessert as well as a tea bread.

YIELD: One 9-by-5-inch or three 6-by-3-inch loaves

¾ cup vegetable oil
1½ cups sugar
3 eggs
1 teaspoon pure vanilla extract
2 cups grated raw zucchini summer squash
2 cups unbleached all-purpose flour
1½ teaspoons baking soda
1 teaspoon baking powder
1 teaspoon each ground cinnamon and cloves
¼ teaspoon salt
1 cup (4 ounces) chopped walnuts, or drained,
   plumped golden raisins

BRANDY GLAZE
¼ cup granulated sugar
¼ cup good-quality brandy or cognac

1. Preheat the oven to 350°F. In a medium bowl, combine the oil and sugar. Beat hard with a whisk or electric mixer until light colored and creamy, about 1 minute. Add the eggs and vanilla extract and beat again until well combined. Fold in the grated zucchini and stir until evenly distributed.

2. Combine the unbleached flour, baking soda, baking powder, spices, salt, and walnuts or raisins. Add to the zucchini-egg mixture and stir to combine. Beat just until the batter is evenly combined and creamy in consistency.

3. Scrape the batter into one 9-by-5-inch or three 6-by-3-inch greased and floured loaf pans. Bake in the center of the oven for about 65 to 75 minutes for the large loaf and 40 to 50 minutes for the small loaves. When done, the tops will be firm to the touch, the loaves will pull away from the sides of the pans, and a cake tester inserted into each center will come out clean. Let stand 5 minutes at room temperature.

4. Meanwhile, prepare the brandy glaze: Combine the sugar and brandy in a small saucepan. Place over low heat just until the sugar dissolves. Set aside. Pierce the hot loaf to the bottom about a dozen times with a bamboo skewer, toothpick, or metal cake tester. Immediately pour over the warm brandy glaze. Cool 30 minutes in the pan before turning out onto a rack to cool completely. Wrap tightly in plastic wrap and chill overnight before serving.

Fresh Orange-Oatmeal Bread
~

Individual loaves of this moist, orange-spiked bread are excellent served warm accompanied with a Ricotta Cheese Heart (following) and steaming cups of Darjeeling tea.

YIELD: Eight 4-by-2½-inch loaves

1 cup rolled oats
1 cup cultured buttermilk
2 medium navel oranges or
*   4 Fairchild tangerines*
3 tablespoons orange liqueur

BROWN SUGAR STREUSEL
½ cup packed light brown sugar
⅓ cup unbleached all-purpose flour
4 tablespoons cold unsalted butter, cut into
*   8 pieces*

½ cup packed light brown sugar
2 tablespoons granulated sugar
3 tablespoons vegetable oil
2 eggs
1⅔ cups unbleached all-purpose flour
2 teaspoons baking powder
1 teaspoon baking soda
¼ teaspoon salt
Ricotta Cheese Hearts, following (optional)

1. In a bowl, combine the oats and buttermilk. Cover and refrigerate 1 hour. Meanwhile, grate the zest from the navel oranges or tangerines and set aside. With a small sharp knife, cut off the remaining outer white membranes. Cut or pull apart the navel oranges or tangerines into sections and coarsely chop, taking care not to lose too much of the juice. Place the chopped sections in a small bowl and add the zest and orange liqueur. Set aside at room temperature to macerate.

2. Meanwhile, make the Brown Sugar Streusel. Combine the brown sugar and the flour in a small bowl. Work in the cold pieces of butter with your fingers or a fork until coarse crumbs are formed. This can also be done with an electric mixer or food processor, if desired. Set aside. Preheat the oven to 350°F.

3. Add the sugars, oil, and eggs to the cold oat-buttermilk mixture. Beat with a whisk until combined. Stir in the macerated orange sections and all the juices. In a mixing bowl, combine the flour, baking powder, baking soda, and salt. Add the wet ingredients and stir with a large spatula just until combined. The batter will be lumpy.

4. Scrape the batter into the eight 4-by-2½-inch greased mini-loaf pans, filling the batter level to the tops of the pans. Sprinkle each loaf with a few tablespoons of the Streusel. Bake in the center of the preheated oven for about 30 to 35 minutes. When done, the tops will be firm to the touch, the loaves will pull away from the sides of the pans, and a cake tester inserted into each center will come out clean. Let stand 5 minutes at room temperature before removing from the pans onto a rack to cool. Serve sliced, along with a honey-drizzled Ricotta Cheese Heart for each whole loaf.

Ricotta Cheese Hearts

YIELD: 6 small hearts (about 1 cup cheese mixture)

1 cup whole-milk or low-fat ricotta cheese
3 tablespoons plain yogurt
1 tablespoon sugar or honey (optional)
½ teaspoon pure vanilla extract or liqueur flavoring, as desired
⅓ cup regular or spiced honey, preferably local, for drizzling, if desired
6 sprigs lemon balm, pineapple sage, or other edible sweet herb, for garnish

1. Combine the ricotta, yogurt, sugar, and vanilla in a food processor or small bowl and blend until just smooth and fluffy. Pulse no more than half a dozen times in the food processor, or use a wooden spoon if making by hand.

2. Divide the cheese among 6 individual *coeur à la crème* porcelain molds lined with 2 layers of rinsed cheesecloth. Fold the cheesecloth over the cheese and press gently. Place on a tray to catch the drips and cover with plastic wrap. Refrigerate overnight. The cheese can also be scraped into a serving bowl, covered, refrigerated, and served directly from the bowl.

3. To serve: Fold back the cheesecloth and gently turn each heart out onto a small plate. Heat additional honey, if desired, and drizzle a tablespoon over each heart. Top with a sprig of lemon balm or pineapple sage.

Whole-Wheat Bran Bread with Dates

~

Whole-Wheat Bran Bread is a coarse-textured, mildly sweet loaf made with no added butter or oil. Considering how economical the ingredients, the resulting flavor of this loaf is distinctive. Serve year-round, plain or toasted, with coffee, fruit salads, and soft cheeses.

YIELD: Two 8-by-4-inch loaves

2¼ cups whole-wheat flour
1¾ cups wheat bran
¼ cup packed light brown sugar
1½ teaspoons baking soda
½ teaspoon baking powder
½ teaspoon salt
1¾ cups cultured buttermilk
1 egg
⅓ cup molasses
⅔ cup chopped pitted dates

1. Preheat the oven to 350°F. In a large bowl, combine the flour, bran, brown sugar, baking soda, baking powder, and salt.

2. In a small bowl, combine the buttermilk, egg, and molasses. Beat with a whisk until frothy. Add the dates and stir to combine. Pour over the dry ingredients. Stir with a large spatula just until moistened.

3. Pour into two greased and floured 8-by-4-inch loaf pans. Bake in the center of the preheated oven 60 to 70 minutes, or until a cake tester inserted into the center comes out clean. The top surface will be crusty. Let rest in the pan 15 minutes. Turn the loaf out onto a rack to cool completely. Wrap tightly in plastic wrap and let set at room temperature overnight before serving.

Steamed Brown Bread with Dried Blueberries

~

Traditionally made by cooking in a tightly covered mold in simmering water to form a cylindrical-shaped loaf, brown bread is pure Americana. Developed during the colonial period to utilize native corn, along with small amounts of locally grown rye and molasses imported from the West Indies, the loaf perfectly complemented a big pot of savory baked beans. Use two 1-pound coffee cans topped with foil for the high loaf, or a European-style metal pudding mold with a clamp lid for a more decorative shape. Serve this ultra-moist bread sliced into rounds spread with natural cream cheese or tangy kefir cheese, available in natural foods stores. The slices are also great toasted.

YIELD: Two 1-pound loaves

1 cup dried blueberries (see Notes from the
  Kitchen, page 119)
3 tablespoons golden rum
1 cup yellow cornmeal, preferably stone-ground
1 cup graham or whole-wheat flour
1 cup unbleached all-purpose flour
2 teaspoons baking soda
½ teaspoon salt
2 cups cultured buttermilk
¾ cup light molasses, warmed slightly for
  easiest pouring
1 egg

1. In a small bowl, combine the blueberries and the rum. Let stand at room temperature 1 hour to macerate. Generously grease two 1-pound coffee cans and line the bottoms with a circle of parchment paper.

2. In a large bowl, combine the cornmeal, graham flour, unbleached flour, baking soda, and salt. In a 4-cup measure, combine the buttermilk, molasses, and egg. Stir with a whisk. Pour into the dry ingredients and add the plumped blueberries. Beat well until evenly moistened.

3. Scrape the batter into the prepared molds, filling each no more than two-thirds full. Cover tightly with a lid or with foil and thick rubber bands. Place on a rack in a deep kettle. Add boiling water to a depth of 1 to 2 inches up the sides of the molds. Cover pot and adjust heat to a low simmer. Steam 2 hours, or until a cake tester inserted into the center of each loaf comes out clean. Add more boiling water, if necessary, during the steaming if too much has evaporated.

4. Preheat oven to 400°F. When the breads are done, remove the lids and place in the oven no more than 5 minutes to dry slightly. Remove from the cans, peel off parchment paper, and cool loaves on their sides on a rack. Serve warm, sliced into rounds. Store wrapped in plastic wrap at room temperature for up to 3 days.

STEAMED APPLESAUCE BROWN BREAD

Substitute 1 cup of unsweetened applesauce for 1 cup of the buttermilk in Step 2. If the dough seems a bit dry, depending on the consistency of your applesauce, add a few more tablespoons of buttermilk. Continue to mix and bake as for Steamed Brown Bread with Dried Blueberries.

Note: Steamed breads also can be baked in a conventional 350°F oven for 40 to 50 minutes in two 8-by-4-by-3-inch loaf pans, but the consistency will be a bit drier and there will be a crusty top surface.

~ Gingerbreads ~

Along with dried clove flower buds, giant nutmeg seeds, ground cassia bark (cinnamon), and peppercorns, sacks of dried ginger originally came to Europe from remote islands in the Indian Ocean. A highly precious import utilized as a money standard, ginger and the other spices traveled via the Arab merchant land caravans and Venetian sea trade routes. The high demand for these Oriental spices inspired many sea voyages by Portuguese and English sailors, since they were literally worth their weight in gold.

Ginger root, also known as *singabera* in Sanskrit, is originally native to Bengal, India, and Southern China and transplanted easily to the warm climate of Southern Europe. The Spanish were the first to carry the lilylike plant to the West Indies, where it is now widely cultivated. Jamaican ginger *(zingiber)* in particular is highly prized throughout the world.

Looking clearly like the palm of a human hand with fingers, ginger holds a distinguished position in Western as well as Eastern medicinal lore, attributed healing powers whether used fresh, or dried and finely ground. The root of the perennial plant is dug up at about a year old, then simply washed and sun-dried before being ready for use.

Gingerbread is often called the oldest baked sweet in the world as it was baked in ancient Greece many centuries before Christ. Recipes for the spiced bread were preserved during the Dark Ages in monasteries. Known to early American bakers as "gyngerbredde," recipes arriving with the Pilgrims were adapted to a variety of native ingredients, such as dried pumpkin flour, cornmeal, and honey. Leavening was pearlash, a vegetable ash often made from pea and bean stalks, which was a common combination with molasses. Gingerbread could either be made with a thin boiling water-based batter that baked into soft and moist cakes, as we make it today, or made with a stiff batter that baked into firm and dry-textured cookies or breads, like the sturdy French *pain d'épices,* English parkin, and Dutch honey and rye *koeks.*

One of the great pleasures of baking gingerbread is the warm, intoxicating fragrance which pervades your kitchen while baking. Use plenty of fresh ground ginger (buy a new bottle every 6 to 9 months) for the best flavor. One tablespoon of ground ginger may be substituted with one 2-inch piece peeled and finely grated fresh ginger (to make about ¼ cup), but the flavor will be quite different, as the powdered ginger has a more concentrated, hot and fiery flavor.

Besides its blend of intensely aromatic spices, the true heart of good gingerbread is the molasses, which lends its characteristic flavor, color, and soft texture to the bread. Use the unsulphured "Barbados" variety rather than "blackstrap," which is bitter. English cookbooks call for dark or light treacle, which may be substituted with pure cane syrup or Lyle's Golden Syrup for a mellower flavor. In the making of white gingerbreads, substitute sugar, maple syrup, or honey for the molasses.

This is a cake you will rarely find in a bakery—it is a real homemade treat. It dresses up well with puréed fruit, sweet custard sauces, layers of good jam, chocolate glazes, fluffy lemon frosting, whipped cream, and cream cheese spreads.

Gingerbreads can be baked successfully into a moist, spongy, spicy loaf in a wide variety of shallow baking pans of metal, clay, porcelain, or glass. They can be eaten straight from an oven-to-table baking dish or turned out to free stand and drip with a glaze. Gingerbread's intense flavor mellows nicely after a day or two, but it is just as good eaten warm from the oven.

Pumpkin Gingerbread

~

Bake this stunning and moist cake in a square, rectangular, round, or even heart-shaped pan to showcase the crumb top. Adding cornmeal to the recipe (variation follows) makes a gently textured cake redolent of its New England roots. For an extra-special dimension, serve the warm cake topped with a cup of heavy cream that has been whipped to soft mounds with 3 tablespoons maple syrup.

YIELD: One 9-inch cake

2½ cups unbleached all-purpose flour
½ cup whole-wheat flour
1 cup sugar
1½ teaspoons ground ginger
1 teaspoon ground cinnamon
1 teaspoon fresh-ground nutmeg
¾ cup (1½ sticks) unsalted butter, cut into
  12 pieces
2 cups puréed fresh pumpkin (page 123), or
  one 16-ounce can pumpkin
2 eggs
½ cup light molasses
⅓ cup cultured buttermilk
1½ teaspoons baking soda

1. Preheat the oven to 350°F. In a large bowl, combine the flours, sugar, and spices. Cut in the butter pieces with your fingers, a pastry blender, or an electric mixer until the mixture makes coarse crumbs. Set aside ¾ cup of the crumbs for the topping.

2. In another mixing bowl, combine the pumpkin, eggs, molasses, buttermilk, and baking soda with a whisk. Make a well in the dry ingredients and pour in the pumpkin mixture. Stir just until moistened.

3. Pour the batter into a greased 9-inch square, round cake, or springform pan. Sprinkle evenly with reserved crumb topping. Bake in the center of the preheated oven until the top is firm to the touch and a cake tester inserted in the center comes out clean, about 40 to 45 minutes. Cool the cake in the pan on a rack. Serve warm.

PUMPKIN-CORNMEAL GINGERBREAD

Substitute 1 cup fine-grind yellow cornmeal for an equal amount of flour in Step 1. Continue to mix, bake, and serve as for Pumpkin Gingerbread.

Gingerbread with Lemon and Raspberry Sauces

~

For sophisticated diners, serve this English-style moist spice cake napped with the bright-flavored lemon and raspberry sauces, dollops of cold *crème fraîche,* and fresh tart berries. I make this recipe often for young diners and, in lieu of the sauces, serve it with hot, unsweetened applesauce. Cutting the large, thin bread into individual rounds is very convenient for serving the dessert to large groups.

YIELD: One 9-inch cake or twelve 3-inch cakes

2½ cups unbleached all-purpose flour
2 tablespoons instant espresso powder
1 tablespoon ground ginger
1 teaspoon ground cinnamon
½ teaspoon ground cloves
½ teaspoon fresh-ground nutmeg
¼ teaspoon ground black pepper
¼ teaspoon salt
Grated zest of 1 lemon
½ cup (1 stick) unsalted butter
½ cup packed light brown sugar
½ cup light molasses
½ cup pure maple syrup
2 large eggs
2 teaspoons baking soda
1 cup boiling water
Raspberry Sauce, following
Lemon Sauce, following
1 cup crème fraîche for serving
1 pint fresh raspberries for serving
12 mint sprigs for garnish

1. Preheat the oven to 350°F. In a large mixing bowl, combine the flour, espresso, spices, salt, and lemon zest. Set aside. In a small saucepan, combine the butter, brown sugar, molasses, and maple syrup. Stir constantly over low heat until the butter is melted. Remove from heat.

2. Make a well in the center of the dry ingredients and pour in the hot butter mixture.

Add the eggs and immediately beat with a wooden spoon or electric mixer until smooth. Combine the baking soda and boiling water. Pour over the batter and stir gently just until evenly incorporated.

3. For one large cake, pour the batter into a greased 9-inch square, round cake, or springform pan. Bake in the center of the preheated oven until the top springs back when touched and a cake tester inserted into the center comes out clean, about 35 to 40 minutes. For the individual cake rounds, spread the batter into a greased and parchment-lined 15-by-10-by-1-inch pan and bake for 25 to 30 minutes. Let the cake cool in the pan on a rack.

4. To serve: Place a spoonful of each fruit sauce on a dessert plate. Place a wedge, square, or round of gingerbread on top of the sauce. For individual cake rounds, cut out 12 rounds with a 3-inch round biscuit or other decorative cutter, saving the excess cake for snacks. Top with cold *crème fraîche,* fresh raspberries, and a mint sprig.

RASPBERRY SAUCE

YIELD: About 2 cups

*2 cups fresh raspberries or one 12-ounce
    package thawed unsweetened frozen
    raspberries*
3 tablespoons raspberry vinegar
¼ cup sugar or to taste

In a small bowl, sprinkle the berries with the vinegar and sugar. Let stand 1 hour at room temperature. Pass through a sieve to remove seeds. Refrigerate until serving.

LEMON SAUCE

YIELD: About 1⅓ cups

¼ cup fresh lemon juice
½ cup water
½ cup sugar
Grated zest of 2 lemons
1 tablespoon cornstarch
3 tablespoons unsalted butter

Combine the lemon juice, ¼ cup of the water, sugar, and zest in a medium saucepan. Heat just until sugar is dissolved. Dissolve the cornstarch in the remaining ¼ cup water. Add to hot lemon mixture. Stir constantly with a whisk over medium-high heat until mixture comes to a full boil, thickens, and becomes clear. Remove from the heat and stir in butter. Serve warm or at room temperature.

Chocolate Gingerbread with Bittersweet Glaze

⌒

This is the most decadent recipe in this collection, bringing the classic prim Puritan gingerbread into this century. Serve the dense chocolate gingerbread, which is glazed with a thin layer of bittersweet chocolate, cut into wedges with spoonfuls of Poached Ginger Prunes (following) alongside.

YIELD: One 9-inch cake

3 ounces unsweetened chocolate
½ cup light molasses
½ cup vegetable oil
4 tablespoons unsalted butter
2½ cups unbleached all-purpose flour
1 cup light brown sugar
*1 teaspoon each baking soda and
    baking powder*
1 teaspoon ground ginger
*¼ teaspoon each ground cinnamon, nutmeg,
    white pepper, and salt*
2 eggs
1 cup cultured buttermilk
1 teaspoon pure vanilla extract
Bittersweet Glaze, following
Poached Ginger Prunes, following (optional)

1. In a double boiler, place the chocolate, molasses, oil, and butter. Stir over low heat until the chocolate is melted and the mixture is smooth. Set aside.

2. Preheat the oven to 350°F. In a mixing bowl, combine the flour, brown sugar, baking soda, baking powder, spices, and salt. In a small bowl, beat the eggs with a whisk until foamy. Add the buttermilk and vanilla.

3. Make a well in the center of the dry ingredients and pour in the buttermilk-egg mixture. Stir to combine. Add the chocolate mixture. Beat with a wooden spoon or electric mixer until smooth.

4. Pour the batter into a greased 9-inch springform pan. Bake in the center of the preheated oven until the top springs back when touched and a cake tester inserted into the center comes out clean, about 35 to 40 minutes. Set the cake on a rack and remove the springform sides. Prepare the Bittersweet Glaze and pour over the warm cake, allowing the glaze to drip down the sides. Cool on a rack to set the glaze until serving time. Serve with Poached Ginger Prunes, if desired.

BITTERSWEET GLAZE

6 tablespoons unsalted butter
4½ ounces bittersweet or semisweet chocolate
1 tablespoon light corn syrup

In a double boiler, combine the butter, chocolate, and corn syrup over low heat, stirring with a whisk until the mixture is melted and smooth. Pour the glaze onto the center of the gingerbread and use a metal spatula to coat the cake in a few strokes.

POACHED GINGER PRUNES

YIELD: About 2 cups

12 ounces large pitted prunes
1 cup water
1 tablespoon minced crystallized candied ginger
2 strips fresh lemon rind
2 cinnamon sticks
½ teaspoon pure vanilla extract

1. Combine all the ingredients in a small saucepan. Bring to a boil, cover, and simmer 5 to 8 minutes, or until the prunes are soft. This can also be made in a microwave oven, if desired.

2. Remove and discard the rind and spices. Serve room temperature or chilled, alongside the Chocolate Gingerbread.

Fresh Apricot Gingerbread
~

This is strictly an early summer, country-style gingerbread, with a batter embellished with ripe fresh apricots. It is a marriage of spices and fruit that is quite unusual, but exceptionally complementary. Crystallized preserved ginger is classified as a confection rather than a spice and is available in gourmet food stores. Serve the cake on a platter decorated with a bed of fresh apricot or fig leaves.

YIELD: One 10-inch tube cake

1 cup sour cream
½ cup (1 stick) unsalted butter, softened
⅔ cup light molasses
½ cup sugar
2 eggs
3½ cups unbleached all-purpose flour
2 teaspoons baking soda
1 tablespoon ground ginger
1 teaspoon each ground mace and cinnamon
½ teaspoon cream of tartar
¼ teaspoon salt
12 ripe fresh apricots, halved, stoned, and each snipped into 4 pieces
½ cup chopped pecans
2 pieces crystallized ginger, finely chopped
Powdered sugar for dusting

1. Preheat the oven to 350°F. In a mixing bowl, combine the sour cream, butter, molasses, sugar, and eggs. Beat hard with a wooden spoon or an electric mixer until smooth and well blended, about 1 minute.

2. In another bowl, combine the flour, baking soda, spices, cream of tartar, and salt. Beat into the sour cream mixture until light and fluffy. Fold in the fresh apricots, pecans, and crystallized ginger with a large spatula.

3. Pour the batter into a greased 10-inch fluted tube or tube spring form pan. Bake in the center of the preheated oven until the top springs back when touched and a cake tester inserted into the center comes out clean, about 45 to 50 minutes. Let stand in the pan 10 minutes before turning out on a rack to cool completely before slicing. Dust with powdered sugar, if desired.

Peach Upside-Down Ginger Cake

Upside-down cakes have a reputation for being cloyingly sweet, which they need not be. Every summer I take advantage of the bounty of fresh fruit to make delicate cakes embellished with a variety of seasonal fruits. Many sophisticated restaurants like Spago in Los Angeles and Chez Panisse in Berkeley also serve these old-fashioned, seasonal cakes on their menus. The variations are endless. My favorite version was consumed at Eddy Jacks, a South-of-Market eatery in San Francisco. It was made with fresh figs and served in a pool of raspberry sauce. The baker said it was her grandmother's recipe, a source which I suspect many of these old-fashioned cakes can be traced back to. This cake, which uses fresh peaches, is also excellent made with fresh pineapple, papaya, apricots, or sweet cherries. Dress up this dessert with Amaretto Crème Anglaise (following), a delicate French custard sauce.

YIELD: One 9-inch cake

4 tablespoons unsalted butter
¾ cup light brown sugar
¼ teaspoon each ground cinnamon, nutmeg, and ginger
6 firm, ripe large peaches, peeled, pitted, and thick-sliced (2 to 3 cups)

GINGER CAKE BATTER

½ cup (1 stick) unsalted butter, room temperature
½ cup granulated sugar
2 eggs
3 tablespoons light molasses
1 teaspoon pure vanilla extract
1½ cups unbleached all-purpose flour
1½ teaspoons ground ginger
½ teaspoon each ground cinnamon and baking soda
¼ teaspoon each ground cloves, nutmeg, and salt
¼ cup boiling water
Amaretto Crème Anglaise, following (optional)

1. Preheat the oven to 350°F. Melt the 4 tablespoons butter in a 9-inch ceramic or metal cake or springform pan in the oven or over low heat. When melted, stir in the brown sugar and spices. Heat just until the brown sugar is melted. Remove from the heat and arrange the fresh peach slices in a single layer over the caramel. Set aside.

2. To make the Ginger Cake batter, in a mixing bowl, cream the butter and sugar. Beat in the eggs, molasses, and vanilla extract until fluffy. In another bowl, combine the flour, spices, baking soda, and salt. Stir into the creamed mixture alternately with the boiling water, mixing just until creamy. Do not overbeat.

3. Carefully spoon the batter over the peaches in the pan. Bake in the center of the preheated oven 30 to 40 minutes, or until a cake tester inserted into the center of the cake comes out clean. Cool the cake in the pan for 5 minutes before inverting onto a serving plate. Serve warm or at room temperature accompanied by Amaretto Crème Anglaise.

CRANBERRY-ORANGE UPSIDE-DOWN GINGER CAKE

Combine 2 cups of fresh cranberries and a fresh, whole seedless orange, peeled and cut into chunks, in the workbowl of a food processor. Pulse to just coarsely chop. Spoon the mixture in a single layer evenly over the caramel and sprinkle with ½ cup golden raisins in place of the peaches in Step 1. Continue to mix, bake, and serve as for Peach Upside-Down Ginger Cake.

AMARETTO CRÈME ANGLAISE

YIELD: About 3 cups

2 cups heavy cream
½ cup sugar
3 large eggs
¼ cup amaretto liqueur

In a saucepan or a microwave, scald the heavy cream. In a mixing bowl or food processor, combine the sugar and the eggs. Beat hard with a whisk or process until light colored and foamy. Whisking constantly, or with the food processor running, add the hot cream very slowly. Pour into a saucepan over medium heat. Cook the sauce gently, stirring constantly, until just slightly thickened. Pour into a bowl and stir in the liqueur. Cool slightly. Refrigerate, covered, until serving time.

Blueberry Gingerbread with Cinnamon Ice Cream

~

Fresh blueberry gingerbread is really special for a summer dessert when served with Cinnamon Ice Cream and additional fresh berries. This is one of my favorite cakes: moist, spicy, and fruity. With the ice cream, it is quite ethereal.

YIELD: One 8-inch cake

1½ cups fresh blueberries plus an additional
   2 cups (1 pint) fresh blueberries for serving
2 tablespoons sugar
3 tablespoons blueberry vinegar
1½ cups unbleached all-purpose flour
½ cup light brown sugar
1 teaspoon baking soda
2 teaspoons ground ginger
¼ teaspoon each ground cinnamon, ground
   mace, and salt
½ cup sour cream
½ cup (1 stick) unsalted butter, melted
2 eggs
2 tablespoons pure maple syrup
Cinnamon Ice Cream, following

1. In a bowl, gently toss the 1½ cups of the blueberries with the sugar and vinegar. Let stand at room temperature 1 hour.

2. Preheat the oven to 350°F. In a mixing bowl, combine the flour, brown sugar, baking soda, spices, and salt. Drain the berries, reserving the juices, and set aside. In another bowl, stir the reserved juices into the sour cream. Add the melted butter, eggs, and maple syrup, combining with a whisk. Add ½ cup of the flour mixture and beat until smooth. Add the remaining flour mixture and beat just until smooth and fluffy.

3. Spread two thirds of the batter into a greased 8-inch square or heart-shaped cake pan or an 8-inch springform pan. Arrange the macerated berries over the top. Spoon over the remaining batter, without completely covering the fruit. Bake in the preheated oven about 45 to 50 minutes, or until the top is dry and springy and a cake tester inserted into the center comes out clean. Cool on a rack until serving time. Serve cut into wedges with one or two small scoops of Cinnamon Ice Cream and additional fresh berries spooned over each serving.

CINNAMON ICE CREAM

YIELD: 1 quart

1 quart vanilla ice cream
2 tablespoons ground cinnamon

Let the vanilla ice cream soften slightly at room temperature for 10 to 15 minutes. With an electric mixer or by hand, beat the ice cream until just creamy. Add the cinnamon and blend until evenly distributed. Working quickly, scrape the ice cream back into the carton with a large spatula. Refreeze at least 6 hours.

~ Cornbreads ~

Originally a finger-sized wild plant native to the Mexican highlands, corn traveled northward to the United States by three main corridors, quickly growing immense seed heads over the centuries. The tropical route to Sonora and Southern Arizona produced the heat- and drought-resistant crops still grown there today. The Sierra Madre corridor produced corn, adapted to the highlands, with their subtropical rainy summers. An eastern corridor along the northeastern United States resulted in corn that became the base for hybridized dents in the 1920s, today our modern commercial corn crop known for the dimple that tops each kernel. Corn was already grown in a staggering number of varieties (food historians have isolated over a thousand pure strains) throughout the North and Central American continent when the Pilgrims landed on the New England coast.

In the Northeast, Native Americans taught European settlers and traders how to grow and prepare flint field corn, the hard corn that is ground into meals, from their own stockpiles. A milk was made from ground corn mixed with boiled chestnuts. Recipes adapted from the Indians became daily staples, including flat, dense *pones,* learned from the Algonquin, that were shaped and baked on platters of wood; long-lasting hot-stone johnnycakes; flat cakes baked in the ashes of a hearthfire; corn porridge called *suppawn,* sweetened with crushed green corn stalks, which would later be called spoon bread; whole dried corn boiled with ashes to form smoky-flavored *hominy;* and *nookik,* hoecakes with salt roasted on greased rake blades.

The rich yellow and white cornmeals of colonial and Yankee kitchens are still popular in the Northeast. With a sweetening of honey, sugar, molasses, or maple syrup, they were originally baked in a "spider," a black iron frying pan with legs used on an open hearth.

Yankee johnnycakes, originally an unsweetened, dense griddle cake baked on an iron hanging skillet, is still a favorite. Northeastern water-powered mills have been grinding local flint corn on their granite stones since the 1600s. Most early American mills, like Kenyon's and Gray's Grist Mill in Rhode Island, are still grinding and selling their quality products. Gray's has the distinction of grinding Narragansett Indian White Cap flint corn, the original delicious strain, often called "cow corn," grown when the Pilgrims landed.

The South stands by its pristine, unsweetened white corn-breads made from water-ground Boone County White dent corn grown in the southern Corn Belt, from Ohio to southern Tennessee. Distinguished southern cooks would never consider making their creamy coarse-ground grits, crusty corn sticks, corn dodgers, and fluffy spoon breads with northern corn. Classic recipes abound: Generations have enjoyed fritter cornmeal batters panfried into hush puppies alongside fish; Arkansas corn flapjacks are legendary; and in neighboring New Orleans, Cajun-Creole cooking features hot yellow cornbreads and Caribbean-style cornbreads made with fresh coconut milk. To supply the area with fresh cornmeals, several local water-powered mills dating from the Civil War era have been refurbished, such as the War Eagle Mill in Arkansas.

Midwestern country kitchens have used sweet, home-rendered lard to create blue-ribbon farm-style cornbreads and sugared muffins. During cattle drives or while traveling across the prairies, western pioneer chuckwagons incorporated lots of yellow cornmeal into bacon-flecked breads made in covered cast-iron pots that baked over an open fire.

For centuries, the Southwest has used its indigenous calico

blue, red, black, and speckled varieties of corn in making native breads and the tortillas learned from the Mexicans. Bakers and home cooks use yellow and white meals, often ground on native metate stone slabs or with wind-powered mills, for limey *masa* flour-and-baking powder cornbreads flavored with hot chiles and fresh corn kernels scraped off the cob. Since Native American religious beliefs include a reverence for local foods as the sustainers of life, corn is closely associated with tribal spiritual practices and their intense mythology.

Corn was also incorporated into the breads of Europe and beyond. Columbus brought the cultivated staple grain of the New World, *mahiz* (meaning the "stuff of life") back to Europe on his first voyage. The Portuguese and Spanish took an immediate liking to Indian corn. The lusty Basque, Gascony, and Bearn wine-producing provinces of southern France are known as maize country, having grown the hard field corn since its introduction in the sixteenth century to make a cornmeal bread known as *méture*. *Pain de mais de sac* is a rustic Basque country bread steamed over a kettle of water. The northern regions of Italy bordering on Austria, Lombardy, Veneto, and Piedmont grow and serve ground *gran turco* in the form of a dense yeasted *pain di mais* flavored with fruity olive oil. Corn traveled the sea trade routes to Africa, Turkey, and the Far East. It also followed the Ottoman Empire to Romania, where it is served today·as *malai,* a yeasted cornbread with cottage or feta cheese.

Not every cuisine favored breads made of corn. The Swiss, the Scandinavians, and the Dutch consider it exclusively an animal food and Britain depended on the cold weather grain crops such as barley and oats.

Although cornmeal was originally laboriously hand-ground between stones, American towns soon had their own municipal water-powered gristmills complete with heavy, imported French millstones. No one wanted to cook with grains from an unknown origin, so each farm grew its own grains, and then threshed and ground them at the local mill. Quality and purity was guaranteed. Today large commercial milling complexes grind kiln-dried hybrid corn grown on large corporate farms throughout the midwestern Corn Belt, although many bakers claim the meals lack the flavor, depth, and character of the now-rare varieties of stone-ground hominy, such as the northeastern Indian *tackhummin,* or southwestern adobe-oven roasted corns. These meals were made by grinding the entire kernel, rather than just the starchy endosperm, which is the method for modern degerminated meals.

All large-scale commercial cornmeals are now ground from the starchy-sweet hybrid dent corn. All types of cornmeal and corn flour can be used in quick breads. Baked goods made with cornmeal are crumbly in texture and a bit gritty. Because cornmeal is unique in flavor and texture, there is no substitute for it. The different grinds of cornmeal contribute to a variety of textures and crumb in the finished baked cornbread. The

packaged steel-cut cornmeals available on grocery shelves are usually a medium grind, very good in flavor, and keep fresh a long time, as they are degerminated. For an exceptional flavor, use very fresh, water-ground meals, which are crushed between heavy granite stones and retain flecks of the the flavorful germ. These meals are available from small local mills or natural foods stores. Stone-ground cornmeals are usually available in a variety of grinds, and now, after centuries of unpopularity, a variety of colors are reappearing. All colors of cornmeal are interchangeable in recipes as long as the grind is similar, but the flavor will vary slightly. Store your cornmeals in the refrigerator up to about 6 months and in the freezer up to a year. Fresh meals will always smell sweet, never sour or rancid.

The most popular method of baking cornbread is in an 8- or 9-inch square or round pan, but there is a long history of using a seasoned 9-inch cast-iron skillet, which produces the crispest crust (especially on the bottom) and a moist interior. Most households used these skillets as a staple kitchen utensil for use in open hearth and wood stove cookery. Southerners especially like the round skillets that are divided into eight wedge-shaped sections and the cornstick-patterned pans, which will serve 4 to 6 diners. For baking in cast iron, heat the pan in a preheated 425°F oven for 5 minutes, remove with a thick oven mitt to prevent burns, then swirl with a tablespoon of solid shortening or butter to grease, and pour in the batter. Immediately return the pan to the hot oven and bake until the top is dry to the touch and the bread separates from the sides. If you do not have a cast-iron skillet, substitute an 8-inch square or round pan, or a 9-inch pan for a thinner bread. Fourteen corn-shaped sticks or ten 3-inch muffins can also be made in the same manner.

Cornbreads are meant to be eaten fresh from the oven for the best flavor (once aptly described by food writer Richard Sax as tasting like "hot sunshine"), as they begin to stale quickly, but the leftovers are perfect for poultry stuffings. Cold, day-old cornbread is also good split, brushed with melted butter flavored with fresh garlic or crushed dried herbs, curry or chili powders, and broiled until lightly toasted. Wrapped tightly in plastic wrap and then foil, all cornbreads can be frozen up to 2 months. Consider contributing a large pan of your own cornbread for your next potluck supper, outdoor picnic, or barbecue.

Yogurt Cornbread
~

One of my favorite breakfasts is a wedge of day-old Yogurt Cornbread, heated well, slathered with butter, and drizzled with some pure maple syrup. Alternatively, by adding a few teaspoons of poultry herbs to the batter, you can create the perfect base for a stuffing. To prepare the cornbread for making into stuffing, crumble onto a flat pan or plate, cover loosely with a tea towel, and let air-dry overnight at room temperature before using.

YIELD: One 8-inch cornbread

1 cup fine-grind yellow or white cornmeal, preferably stone-ground
1 cup unbleached all-purpose flour
2 tablespoons sugar
½ teaspoon salt
½ teaspoon baking soda
Grated zest of 1 large orange
2 eggs
¼ cup cultured buttermilk
1¼ cups plain yogurt
4 tablespoons unsalted butter, melted, or
¼ cup corn oil

1. Preheat the oven to 425°F. Combine the cornmeal, flour, sugar, salt, baking soda, and orange zest in a large bowl.

2. In a small bowl, mix the eggs, buttermilk, and yogurt with a whisk. Add to the dry ingredients and pour the melted butter over the top of the batter. Stir just until all ingredients are moistened yet thoroughly blended. Take care not to overmix.

3. Pour the batter into a greased 8-inch springform or deep cake pan. Bake in the preheated oven about 20 to 25 minutes, until golden around the edges and a cake tester inserted into the center comes out clean. Let stand 15 minutes before cutting into thick wedges to serve.

MAPLE PAN CORNBREAD

Heat a seasoned 9-inch skillet in a preheated 425°F oven for 5 minutes, then swirl with a tablespoon of shortening or butter to grease. Immediately scrape in the Yogurt Cornbread batter. Sprinkle the surface with ½ cup (3 to 3½ ounces) coarsely chopped pure maple sugar candy. Return the skillet to the oven and bake as directed.

BACON CORNBREAD

In a medium skillet, cook 1 cup diced smoked bacon or Italian pancetta (about 4 to 5 slices) until crisp. Drain on paper towels and add to the Yogurt Cornbread batter in Step 2. Bake as directed.

BERRY CORNBREAD

Fold 1½ cups rinsed fresh raspberries, blueberries, or blackberries into the Yogurt Cornbread batter in Step 2. Bake as directed.

BLACK OLIVE CORNBREAD

Add 1 cup chopped California or imported black olives to the Yogurt Cornbread batter in Step 2. Scrape the batter into a 9-by-5-inch loaf pan. Bake about 35 to 40 minutes, or until bread tests done.

APPLE CORNBREAD

Add 1½ cups peeled, cored, and coarsely chopped tart cooking apples (about 2 whole) to the Yogurt Cornbread batter in Step 2. Bake as directed.

Rice Cornbread

Add 1 cup cold, cooked brown, wild, or white rice to the Yogurt Cornbread batter in Step 2. Bake as directed.

Green and Red Pepper Cornbread

~

A variety of chiles are essential to the cuisine of the Southwest, and they are often used in baking for unusual savory fillings. This bread combines sweet bright-red bell peppers with a thick-fleshed mild green chile and spikes it all with a dash of jalapeños in a rich sour cream batter. For a more authentic flavor, use *masa harina,* the cornmeal ground from hominy used for making tortillas, available in the flour section of supermarkets or ethnic grocery stores. Serve this hearty bread for a casual lunch with fresh tomato soup and a simple tossed green salad.
YIELD: One 8-inch cornbread

2 tablespoons corn oil
½ red bell pepper, cored, seeded, and cut into
*   thin strips about 1 inch long*
½ mild green chile pepper, such as Anaheim,
*   New Mexico, or poblano, cored, seeded, and*
*   cut into thin strips about 1 inch long*
½ small hot green pepper, such as a jalapeño,
*   cored, seeded, deveined, and minced*

¾ cup unbleached all-purpose flour
¾ cup fine-grind yellow cornmeal, preferably
*   stone-ground, or masa harina*
3 tablespoons sugar
2 teaspoons baking powder
½ teaspoon baking soda
½ teaspoon ground cumin
½ teaspoon salt
1 egg
1 cup sour cream
½ cup shredded Monterey Jack cheese

1. Preheat the oven to 400°F. Heat the corn oil in a small skillet and add the bell pepper and chiles. Cover and cook over low heat until tender, about 5 minutes. Remove from heat.

2. Combine the flour, cornmeal, sugar, baking powder, baking soda, cumin, and salt in a large bowl. In a small bowl, beat together the egg, sour cream, and cooked chiles with any excess oil. Mix into the dry ingredients just until evenly combined. Take care not to overmix. The batter will be lumpy.

3. Pour the batter into a greased 8-inch springform pan or pie plate or a 9-inch cast-iron skillet. Bake in the preheated oven for 15 minutes. Sprinkle with the shredded cheese and return to oven for about 10 minutes longer. When done, the cornbread will be golden around the edges and a cake tester inserted into the center will come out clean. Let stand 15 minutes before cutting into wedges to serve.

Sweet-Potato Cornbread with Orange Butter

~

Sweet potatoes add a lush texture and delicate color to traditional cornbread, although pumpkin purée may be substituted, if desired. A great way to use leftover baked "sweets," this bread is good with turkey or spicy black bean soup on a blustery day. Serve warm, dripping with Orange Butter.
YIELD: One 9-inch cornbread

1 cup unbleached all-purpose flour
½ cup fine-grind yellow or white cornmeal,
*   preferably stone-ground*
1 teaspoon baking powder
½ teaspoon baking soda
½ teaspoon salt
⅛ teaspoon each ground allspice and mace
2 eggs
1 cup puréed baked sweet potatoes or
*   ruby yams, cooled*
¼ cup corn oil
3 tablespoons pure maple syrup
½ cup cultured buttermilk
Orange Butter, following (optional)

1. Preheat the oven to 375°F. Combine the flour, cornmeal, baking powder, baking soda, salt, and spices in a large bowl.

2. In a small bowl, mix the eggs, sweet potatoes, corn oil, maple syrup, and buttermilk with a whisk. Add to the dry ingredients. Stir just until all ingredients are moistened yet thoroughly blended. Take care not to overmix.

3. Pour the batter into a greased 9-inch round springform or square cake pan. Bake in the preheated oven about 20 to 25 minutes, until golden around the edges and a cake tester inserted into the center comes out clean. Let stand 15 minutes before cutting into thick wedges. Serve with Orange Butter, if desired.

ORANGE BUTTER

YIELD: ½ cup

½ cup (1 stick) unsalted butter,
  room temperature
Grated zest of 1 large orange

In a small bowl with the back of a spoon, or in a blender or food processor, cream the butter and zest until fluffy and well combined. Store, covered, in the refrigerator for up to 1 week. Bring to room temperature before serving.

Maple Whole-Wheat Johnnycake with Blueberries

~

This is a northern-style cornbread using ground yellow cornmeal, gently sweetened and full of juicy, ripe berries. In comparison, southern-style cornbreads are characteristically white and contain no added sweetening in their batters. Whole-wheat johnnycakes are popular in Nova Scotia and New England, where maple sugar trees grow profusely. Locals say maple sweetenings are unequalled by any others in the world, and they are a common addition to cornbreads from that area. Serve for brunch with Maple Butter (following), fresh juices, and scrambled eggs, or for Sunday night supper with pumpkin soup. Cornbreads do not keep well, so plan to mix, bake, and serve your bread the same day it is made.

YIELD: One 9-inch cornbread

1¼ cups fine-grind yellow cornmeal, preferably
  stone-ground
1 cup whole-wheat pastry flour
1 tablespoon baking powder
½ teaspoon salt
2 eggs
¾ cup cultured buttermilk
¼ cup pure maple syrup
4 tablespoons unsalted butter, melted
1½ cups fresh or frozen, unthawed blueberries
Maple Butter, following (optional)

1. Preheat the oven to 400°F. Combine the cornmeal, flour, baking powder, and salt in a large bowl.

2. In a small bowl, mix the eggs, buttermilk, and maple syrup with a whisk. Add to the dry ingredients and pour over the melted butter. Stir with a wooden spoon just until all ingredients are moistened yet thoroughly blended. Take care not to overmix. With a rubber spatula, gently fold in the blueberries.

3. Pour the batter into a greased 8-inch springform or deep cake pan. Bake in the preheated oven about 20 to 25 minutes, until golden around the edges and a cake tester inserted into the center comes out clean. Let stand 15 minutes before cutting into thick wedges. Serve with Maple Butter, if desired.

MAPLE BUTTER

YIELD: ½ cup

½ cup (1 stick) unsalted butter,
  room temperature
3 tablespoons pure maple syrup

In a small bowl with the back of a spoon, or in a blender or food processor, cream the butter and maple syrup until fluffy and well combined. Store, covered, in the refrigerator for up to 3 days. Bring to room temperature before serving.

Cranberry-Walnut Cornbread

~

Cranberries and walnuts are one of my favorite fruit-and-nut combinations. Fresh cranberries arrive in the supermarkets late September, packaged in 12-ounce plastic bags. They can be frozen and used in baking year-round. Their tart, crunchy nature makes for a hearty cornbread with a delicate, fruity flavor.

YIELD: One 9-inch loaf

1 cup fine-grind yellow cornmeal, preferably
    stone-ground
1 cup unbleached all-purpose flour
¾ cup light brown sugar or granulated
    maple sugar
½ teaspoon salt
½ teaspoon baking soda
Grated zest of 1 large orange
1 cup fresh cranberries, coarsely chopped
1 cup (4 ounces) walnuts, chopped
2 eggs
1 cup cultured buttermilk
6 tablespoons unsalted butter, melted

1. Preheat the oven to 425°F. Combine the cornmeal, flour, brown or maple sugar, salt, baking soda, and orange zest in a large bowl. Add the cranberries and the walnuts.

2. In a small bowl, mix the eggs and buttermilk with a whisk. Add to the dry ingredients and pour the melted butter over the top of the batter. Stir just until all ingredients are moistened yet thoroughly blended. Take care not to overmix.

3. Pour the batter into a greased 9-by-5-inch loaf pan. Bake in the preheated oven about 35 to 40 minutes, until golden around the edges and a cake tester inserted into the center comes out clean. Let stand 15 minutes before cutting into thick slices to serve.

Country Whole-Wheat Cornbread

~

This is the recipe I use when making cornbread for a large crowd. Although it uses whole-wheat rather than unbleached flour, the bread bakes moist, light, and flavorful. Feel free to reduce or eliminate the brown sugar if your diet restricts sugar intake. Bake in a 12-inch round or 9-by-13-inch rectangular pan, or, for a thin bread, in a 13-by-16-inch sheet pan, which will serve ten hearty eaters. Serve hot for brunch with some Hazelnut Honey Butter (following) melting over the wedges. For dinner, split and fill, as for a shortcake, with creamed lobster in season and garnish with a sprinkle of paprika and lemon wedges.

YIELD: One 12-inch cornbread

3½ cups fine-grind yellow cornmeal, preferably
    stone-ground
2 cups whole-wheat pastry flour
½ cup light brown sugar or granulated
    maple sugar
2 teaspoons baking powder
1½ teaspoons baking soda
1 teaspoon salt
4 eggs
3 cups cultured buttermilk
¾ cup (1½ sticks) unsalted butter, melted
Hazelnut Honey Butter, following (optional)

1. Preheat the oven to 325°F. Combine the cornmeal, flour, brown sugar, baking powder, baking soda, and salt in a large bowl.

2. In a small bowl, mix the eggs and buttermilk with a whisk. Add to the dry ingredients and pour the melted butter over the top of the batter. Stir just until all ingredients are moistened yet thoroughly blended. Take care not to overmix.

3. Pour the batter into a greased 12-inch springform or deep cake pan. Bake in the preheated oven about 45 to 50 minutes, until golden around the edges and a cake tester inserted into the center comes out clean. Let stand 15 minutes before cutting into thick wedges. Serve with Hazelnut Honey Butter, if desired.

HAZELNUT HONEY BUTTER
YIELD: About 1 cup

¼ cup raw hazelnuts
½ cup (1 stick) unsalted butter,
    room temperature
⅓ cup mild honey

1. Preheat the oven to 350°F. Spread the hazelnuts in a baking pan and bake until lightly toasted, about 8 minutes. Place the nuts in the center of a clean kitchen towel, fold the towel over, and rub the hazelnuts to remove their skins. Let cool.

2. In a blender or a food processor fitted with the metal blade, blend all the ingredients until smooth, stopping as necessary to scrape down the sides of the container. Place in a covered container and store in the refrigerator for up to 1 week. For the best flavor, let stand 1 hour at room temperature before serving.

Blue Cornbread with Goat Cheese and Green Chiles

~

This sophisticated cornbread is ideal for serving to a discriminating group of diners. Laced with spicy chiles, it is not too sweet, with a buttery consistency and crumbly texture. The goat cheese creates delightful, creamy pockets of flavor. Serve with baked beans, corn on the cob, and a large mixed raw-vegetable salad with a tomato vinaigrette.
YIELD: One 10-inch cornbread

¾ cup (1½ sticks) unsalted butter,
  room temperature
¼ cup sugar
1 cup fine- to medium-grind blue cornmeal
  (harina de maís azul para tortillas)
4 eggs
1½ cups unbleached all-purpose flour
1 tablespoon baking powder
1 teaspoon salt
One 15-ounce can cream-style corn
1 poblano or Anaheim green chile, roasted,
  peeled, seeded, and minced, or
  one 4-ounce can diced green chiles
5½ ounces fresh goat cheese, such as chabi or
  French Montrachet, crumbled

1. Preheat the oven to 375°F. In a large bowl with an electric mixer, beat the butter and sugar until creamy. Add the cornmeal and beat until blended. Add the eggs, one at a time, beating until fluffy after each addition.

2. In another bowl, combine the flour, baking powder, and salt. Add to the cornmeal batter and beat well with the electric mixer. Fold in the corn, chiles, and crumbled goat cheese until evenly distributed.

3. Pour the batter into a greased hot 10-inch skillet, or a greased 10-inch springform pan or 9-by-13-inch baking dish. Bake in the preheated oven about 35 to 40 minutes, until golden around the edges and a cake tester inserted into the center comes out clean. Let stand 15 minutes before cutting into thick wedges to serve.

Italian Polenta Cornbread with Sun-Dried Tomatoes and Basil

~

Polenta is a coarse cornmeal that is a staple in Northern Italy. Indian meal traveled to Italy during the 1500s and rapidly became a popular, unpretentious peasant food also known as *gran turco,* the "Turkish grain." In Italy today, it is grown in yellow-, white-, and copper-colored varieties that are ground into polenta. This recipe makes a Tuscan-style, basil-scented, rustic *pane di polenta.* If you own a food processor, you can mince the *basilico* in it with ¼ cup of the flour. Sun-dried Roma tomatoes can be bought marinated in oil or as dehydrated slices. Use a good-quality, fresh, whole-milk mozzarella as the exquisite final touch.
YIELD: One 10-inch cornbread

2 ounces sliced sun-dried tomatoes, or ¼ cup
  marinated sun-dried tomatoes
1 large shallot, chopped
4 tablespoons unsalted butter or oil
  from tomatoes
1¼ cups unbleached all-purpose flour
¾ cup polenta or coarsely ground yellow
  cornmeal, preferably stone-ground
½ teaspoon salt
½ teaspoon baking powder
½ teaspoon baking soda
2 tablespoons minced fresh basil
¼ teaspoon ground cumin
3 eggs
½ cup sour cream
One 17-ounce can baby corn kernels, undrained
1 cup (4 ounces) coarsely shredded or
  diced plain whole-milk or smoked
  mozzarella cheese

1. Preheat the oven to 400°F. In a small bowl, soften the dried tomatoes in boiling water for 5 minutes. Drain and chop. If using marinated tomatoes, omit the softening, drain and reserve the oil, and chop. In a small skillet, sauté the shallot in the butter or reserved tomato oil until softened. Remove from heat and set aside.

2. Combine the flour, polenta or coarse cornmeal, salt, baking powder, baking soda, basil, and cumin in a large bowl.

3. In a small bowl, mix the eggs, sour cream, corn with its liquid, sautéed shallots and the butter, chopped dried tomatoes, and cheese with a wooden spoon. Add to the dry ingredients and stir just until all ingredients are moistened yet thoroughly blended. Take care not to overmix; the batter will be thin.

4. Pour the batter into a greased hot 10-inch skillet, a greased 10-inch springform pan, or a 9-by-13-inch baking dish. Bake in the preheated oven about 30 to 35 minutes, until golden around the edges and a cake tester inserted into the center comes out clean. Let stand 15 minutes before cutting into thick wedges to serve.

Fresh Corn Kernel and Cornmeal Bread

~

Use a fresh stone-ground cornmeal to make this exceptionally moist bread studded with plump, golden kernels of fresh corn off the cob. If you decide to make twenty individual corn sticks from this batter, preheat the greased cast-iron molds at 425°F while making the batter. Bake as for the individual Cornmeal Savarins (following), which are baked in miniature ring molds known as *savarin* or Mary Ann pans (a cupcake-like form with a small center bump that creates an indented center). Individual scalloped bundt pan molds, sold in connected sets of six, like muffin tins, and plain miniature tube pans will also work. The effect is stunning.

YIELD: One 8-inch tube cornbread

1 cup fine-grind white or yellow cornmeal,
*   preferably stone-ground*
1 cup unbleached all-purpose flour
¼ cup sugar
2½ teaspoons baking powder
1¼ teaspoons hot red pepper flakes
¼ teaspoon salt
2 eggs, separated
⅔ cup milk
⅔ cup heavy cream
½ cup (1 stick) unsalted butter, melted
2 cups fresh or frozen baby white or yellow
*   corn kernels*

1. Preheat the oven to 375°F. Combine the cornmeal, flour, sugar, baking powder, red pepper flakes, and salt in a large bowl.

2. In a small bowl, mix the egg yolks, milk, cream, butter, and corn kernels with a whisk. Add the egg yolk mixture to the dry ingredients. Stir with a wooden spoon just until all ingredients are moistened yet thoroughly blended, taking care not to overmix. The batter will be lumpy. With an electric mixer, beat the egg whites to soft peaks in a small bowl. With a spatula, gently fold the whites into the batter, just until there are no more streaks.

3. Scrape the batter into a greased 8-inch heavy-gauge aluminum tube or bundt pan. Bake in the preheated oven about 45 to 50 minutes, until golden around the edges and a cake tester inserted into the center comes out clean. Invert out of the pan onto a rack to cool. Let stand 15 minutes before cutting into thick slices to serve.

CORNMEAL SAVARINS

YIELD: 16 individual cornbreads

Spray sixteen 3¼ inch metal *savarin* molds, Mary Ann molds, or miniature tube pans (available in gourmet cookware stores) with a nonstick vegetable spray. Fill each with about 3 tablespoons to ¼ cup of the batter and place on two baking sheets. Bake in a preheated 375°F oven until a cake tester inserted into the centers comes out clean, about 12 to 15 minutes. Loosen the edges with a small knife and turn out the *savarins* onto a rack to cool. Use immediately, filling the centers with sautéed vegetables, creamed seafood, or as unique little bowls for fresh fruit. They can be frozen in plastic freezer bags for up to 1 month and reheated just before serving.

Steamed Pecan Cornbread

Steaming cornbread over a hot water bath results in a beautifully moist texture. For an added dimension of flavor, toast the cornmeal gently on a baking sheet or in a heavy, dry skillet in a 325°F oven for 15 to 20 minutes, stirring occasionally until it turns a pale, golden brown. Transfer immediately to a bowl to stop the cooking process and cool before making the batter. Slice Steamed Pecan Cornbread into fat rounds and serve fresh or toasted with honey and butter.

YIELD: Two 1-pound loaves

1 cup fine-grind yellow cornmeal, preferably stone-ground
2 cups unbleached all-purpose flour
1 cup (4 ounces) pecans, finely chopped
2 teaspoons baking soda
½ teaspoon salt
2 cups cultured buttermilk
½ cup pure maple syrup
2 eggs

1. Generously grease two 1-pound coffee cans and line the bottoms with a circle of parchment paper.

2. In a large bowl, combine the cornmeal, flour, pecans, baking soda, and salt. In a 4-cup measure or bowl, combine the buttermilk, maple syrup, and eggs. Stir with a whisk. Pour into the dry ingredients. Beat well until evenly moistened.

3. Scrape the batter into the prepared molds, filling no more than two-thirds full. Cover each tightly with a lid or with foil and thick rubber bands. Place on a rack in a deep kettle. Add boiling water to a depth of 1 to 2 inches up the sides of the molds. Cover pot and adjust heat to a low simmer. Steam about 2½ hours, or until a cake tester inserted into the center of each loaf comes out clean. Add more boiling water, if necessary, during the steaming if too much has evaporated.

4. Preheat oven to 400°F. When breads are done, remove the lids and place in the oven for no more than 5 minutes to dry slightly. Remove from the cans, peel off parchment paper, and cool loaves on their sides on a rack. Serve warm, sliced into rounds. Store wrapped in plastic wrap at room temperature for up to 3 days.

Note: Steamed breads can also be baked in a conventional 350°F oven for 40 to 50 minutes in two 8-by-4-by-3-inch loaf pans, but the consistency will be a bit drier and there will be a crusty top surface.

~ Coffee Cakes ~

Coffee cakes are an American passion, a homey concoction crossing a muffin and a cake, being at the same time neither too sweet nor too rich. They are never frosted, but may be glazed with jam, dusted with an ethereal layer of powdered sugar, or sport a spice- or nut-enhanced crumb top. They are excellent showcases for seasonal fresh fruit. Often referred to as "morning cakes," they offer a wide range of delightfully versatile interpretations on the simple butter cake and result in cakes that need not be restricted to breakfasting. They satisfy the "I baked it from scratch" urge most cooks get at one time or another. In the world of cake baking, these cakes are by far the easiest to prepare, and they enable even a beginning baker to produce a cake that tastes as wonderful as it looks. These recipes, such as Blueberry Cheese Crumbcake and Fresh-Apple Coffee Cake, reflect pure nostalgic American traditions, with simple batters made in the same manner as they were decades ago, when home baking was a country art, as well as a necessity.

The beginning of the eighteenth century brought coffee, tea, and chocolate drinks to the upper classes of Europe, and baked goods were the natural accompaniment. Coffee- and tea-time became an established small meal for all classes of society, with toasted breads, tea cakes, and scones with jam very popular. High tea in Britain, the Viennese *Kaffeejause,* and the German home *Kaffeetisch* all featured favorite simple-to-elaborate baking-powder cakes, served unadorned or covered with precious spices, sugared crumbs, nuts, chestnuts, orchard fruits, or sweet cheese. German, Swiss, Austrian, and Hungarian home bakers were proud of their hospitality skills and inspired by the high quality and artistic presentation of their tables. From this era we have inherited many of the basic styles and recipes still served today.

Coffee cakes are simple batters leavened with baking powder, baking soda or both, mixed in one bowl, baked in the center of a preheated oven, and often served from the pan as soon as they've cooled enough not to scorch the fingers. Batters may be mixed briskly by hand or with an electric mixer until fluffy and scraped into a well-greased pan with a plastic spatula. Coffee cakes all contain the same basic ingredients: butter or vegetable oil; eggs; sugar or some other sweetening; flour; milk, sour cream, or buttermilk; leavening; and one or more flavorings creamed together to create a moist, rich cake after baking. The proportion of these ingredients varies slightly from recipe to recipe and dictates the finished flavor and texture of each individual cake, so take care to measure the ingredients as directed.

A coffee cake should be baked immediately after mixing. To avoid overbaking, always set the timer for 5 to 10 minutes before the end of the suggested baking time to start testing with a toothpick or metal tester for doneness. If the edges have pulled away from the sides of the pan, it is a good indication the cake is baked. A coffee cake may be quite fragile or very moist coming directly out of the oven, but it then cools on a rack into a delicate or richly dense cake. A wire or wooden cake rack is important here to allow for the air to circulate fully. A properly cooled cake sets and contracts enough to either turn out of the pan to finish cooling or to cut into serving pieces. To unmold a cake, loosen the sides with a knife or spatula, if necessary. Place a wire cake rack over the top rim of the cake pan. Place your outstretched palm against the rack to secure it and gently turn the pan upside down onto the rack. The cake will release onto the rack. Carefully remove the pan and allow the cake to finish cooling. A cake left to cool too long will form a crusty outer layer, so a few hours is the maximum time needed. Each recipe will specify the best handling techniques.

For baking a wide range of coffee cakes, collect a selection of lightweight aluminum, Pyrex, rustic stoneware, imported porcelain, or antique metal baking dishes in a variety of sizes and shapes in addition to the standard round, square, or rectangular pans. This is the place to use those beautifully crafted fluted tube molds, square angel food pans, fluted tin tart pans, scalloped Turk's-head molds, and heavy aluminum bundt pans. Antique stores often turn up the simple, early models of central tunnel-cake pans made of beaten tin, or elaborately embossed ones of fired clay or copper that were used for special-occasion baking. Cakes look extraordinarily stately made in these pans, turned out onto and served from a pedestal cake plate. The center tube may be filled with flowers or whole fresh berries to create a centerpiece.

Most coffee cakes keep well at room temperature for up to 3 days (please refrigerate cakes with cheese toppings), but they also freeze well for 2 to 3 weeks after being completely cooled and tightly wrapped in plastic wrap, then foil, which retains the moist, crumbly texture and full flavor. To defrost, let stand at room temperature fully wrapped but slightly open, to allow for the excess moisture to evaporate. Serve at room temperature or warm in a 350°F oven for 10 to 15 minutes, depending on the size of the cake.

Good not only served for brunch, coffee cakes may also be served as a casual dessert or afternoon repast. They're great picnic fare and make wonderful gifts because they are easy to pack and easy to wrap. And coffee cakes needn't be served just with coffee. Brewed and iced English teas, savory coffee substitutes derived from malt and chicory, an array of herbal teas, or even a glass of cold milk or fresh juice are all worthy partners to these delicious cakes.

Fresh Apple Coffee Cake

Fresh Apple Coffee Cake is luscious and extravagant in flavor. Since it is a large cake, it is important that it be baked in a pan sporting a center tube, such as an angel food cake pan, scalloped bundt pan, or highly decorative fluted *kugelhof* mold. Early fall I make it with homegrown Rome Beauty apples, but any firm tart cooking apple, such as a Granny Smith or Winesap, will do nicely. The cake needs no embellishment, since the fruit adds a fragrant touch to the orange-scented batter.

YIELD: One 10-inch tube cake

*4 cups peeled, cored, and coarsely chopped tart
   cooking apples*
⅓ cup light brown sugar
1½ tablespoons ground cinnamon
3 cups unbleached all-purpose flour
1¾ cups granulated sugar
1 tablespoon baking powder
½ teaspoon salt
Grated zest of 1 orange
4 eggs
1 cup vegetable oil
½ cup fresh or frozen orange juice

1. Preheat the oven to 375°F. Grease and flour a 10-inch plain tube pan, fluted *kugelhof* mold, or bundt pan and set aside. In a small bowl, combine the apples with the brown sugar and the cinnamon. Set aside.

2. In a medium bowl, combine the flour, sugar, baking powder, salt, and orange zest.

3. With an electric mixer, balloon whisk, or blender, beat the eggs and oil until thick and creamy, about 2 minutes at high speed. Add to the dry ingredients with the orange juice and beat just until moistened, but thoroughly blended. Do not overmix, but there should be no lumps or dry spots.

4. Place one third of the batter over the bottom of the prepared tube pan. Cover evenly with half the apple mixture and cover with another one third of the batter. Use a spatula to smooth the batter over the apples to cover completely. Repeat with the remaining apples and batter, ending with a smooth layer of batter.

5. Bake in the center of the preheated oven 60 minutes. Cover loosely with a piece of aluminum foil and bake an additional 15 minutes, or until a cake tester inserted into the center comes out clean. Remove from the oven and cool in the pan on a rack about 1 hour before inverting onto a rack to cool completely before serving. Securely wrapped, this cake freezes well.

Spiced Brown Sugar–Pecan Coffee Cake

~

This is a soft-textured buttermilk cake with a crunchy nut topping that is a must for the quick-bread baker's repertoire. I often substitute macadamias or blanched slivered almonds for the pecans, but the buttery flavor of pecans infuses a taste all its own into the whole cake. Spiced Brown Sugar–Pecan Coffee Cake is known as an old-fashioned "keeping cake," as it is naturally preserved by the cultured buttermilk and can be stored tightly wrapped in plastic wrap and foil at room temperature for up to 5 days before serving.

YIELD: One 8-inch cake

SPICED PECAN CRUMB TOPPING

¼ cup light brown sugar
¼ cup granulated sugar
½ cup unbleached all-purpose flour
½ teaspoon each ground cinnamon, mace, and ginger
6 tablespoons cold unsalted butter, cut into pieces
2 cups (8 ounces) pecans, coarsely chopped

COFFEE CAKE

4 tablespoons unsalted butter
½ cup light brown sugar
½ cup granulated sugar
2 eggs
2 teaspoons pure vanilla extract
2 cups unbleached all-purpose flour
1 teaspoon each baking powder and baking soda
¼ teaspoon salt
1 cup cultured buttermilk

1. Preheat the oven to 350°F. Line the bottom of an 8-inch springform pan, an 8-inch fluted ceramic clafouti baking dish or a 2-inch-deep removable-bottom tart pan with parchment paper and grease the sides.

2. To make the crumb topping: Combine the sugars, flour, and spices in a small bowl or the workbowl of a food processor. Cut in the butter with your fingers or process just until the mixture forms coarse crumbs. Add the pecans and set aside.

3. To make the coffee cake: In a bowl with a wooden spoon, or in the workbowl of a heavy-duty electric mixer, cream the butter and sugars until fluffy. Add the eggs and vanilla extract. Beat until smooth. In another bowl, combine the flour, baking powder, baking soda, and salt. Add to the creamed mixture alternately with the buttermilk. Beat hard until the batter has a creamy consistency, about 1 minute.

4. Scrape half of the batter into the prepared pan. Sprinkle evenly with half of the crumb topping. Spoon over the remaining batter and sprinkle with the remaining crumb topping. Bake in the center of the preheated oven until a cake tester inserted into the center comes out clean, about 40 to 45 minutes. Remove from the oven and cool in the pan on a rack. To serve, remove the sides of the springform pan or serve from the baking dish, as desired.

Blueberry Cheese Crumbcake

~

Blueberry Cheese Crumbcake is one of those little gems of the baking world. It is a sublime combination of elements: fruit, cake, cheese, and ample crumbly topping—a harmony of tastes that is really pleasing to the palate. It is temptingly rich and decadent, with each element lending distinctive flavor and texture. I also like the cake made with fresh tart raspberries, big boysenberries, pitted Bing cherries, or homegrown red currants, when available.

YIELD: One 10-inch cake

CHEESE FILLING

8 ounces natural cream cheese, room temperature
⅓ cup sugar
2 tablespoons fresh lemon juice
1 egg
1 tablespoon unbleached all-purpose flour

CRUMB TOPPING

1¼ cups unbleached all-purpose flour
(can be one half whole-wheat pastry flour,
if desired)
½ cup sugar
½ teaspoon ground cinnamon
6 tablespoons cold unsalted butter, cut into
small pieces

CAKE BATTER

8 tablespoons (1 stick) unsalted butter,
room temperature
⅔ cup sugar
2 eggs
1½ teaspoons pure vanilla extract
1½ cups unbleached all-purpose flour
1½ teaspoons baking powder
¼ teaspoon salt
½ cup milk
1 pint fresh blueberries, rinsed and well
drained

1. Preheat the oven to 350°F. Grease and flour a 10-inch springform pan and set aside.

2. To make the cheese filling: In a bowl, beat the cream cheese with a wooden spoon or electric mixer until creamy. Beat in the sugar, lemon juice, egg, and flour. Beat until smooth, about 1 minute. Set aside.

3. To make the crumb topping: In a small bowl, combine the flour, sugar, and cinnamon. Cut in the butter with a fork or your fingers until coarse crumbs are formed. Set aside.

4. To make the cake batter: In a bowl with a wooden spoon, or in the workbowl of a heavy-duty electric mixer, cream the butter and sugar until fluffy. Add the eggs and vanilla extract and beat well. In a small bowl, combine the flour, baking powder, and salt. Beat the dry ingredients into the creamed mixture in two additions, alternating with the milk. Beat until smooth and fluffy.

5. Spread the batter into the prepared spring-form pan, building the sides up slightly. Sprinkle the surface of the batter with 1 cup of the blueberries and spoon over the cheese filling. Scatter the remaining 1 cup blueberries over the surface. Sprinkle the top evenly with the crumb topping and gently press slightly into the cheese mixture.

6. Bake in the center of the preheated oven for 60 to 70 minutes, or until the top is golden, the cheese filling is set, and the cake separates slightly from the sides of the pan. Cool in the pan on a wire rack 30 minutes before removing the sides to serve.

Fresh Fruit Cobbler

⁓

This fruit cobbler is certainly one of the simplest coffee cakes to make. The cobbler is low in sugar, baking up into an appealing fruit-laden cake that is as flavorful as it is tender. Based on traditional German everyday coffee-time cake recipes known as *kuchens,* the simple cakes are leavened with *backpulver,* the baking powder used in German, Swiss, and Austrian baking.

My favorite fruits for this recipe include pitted, fleshy, sweet Tartarian cherries from my local farmer's market. Peeled and pitted ripe summer peaches in combination with Santa Rosa plums, apricots, or nectarines; field-grown red rhubarb; delicate winter pears; even sliced bananas or big Watsonville raspberries are also nice. For the adult palate, try substituting 2 tablespoons of the milk with a complementary fruit brandy.

The cake batter can be made in two 6-inch springform pans or it doubles perfectly to be baked in a 12-inch round or 9-by-13-inch rectangle. The cobbler can be frozen for up to 2 weeks and reheated, although it is best served the day it is made, either warm or at room temperature, accompanied by a pitcher of cold heavy cream.

YIELD: One 8-inch cake, or two 6-inch cakes

¼ cup unsalted butter, room temperature
½ cup sugar
1 egg
1 cup unbleached all-purpose flour
1 teaspoon baking powder
¼ teaspoon salt
½ cup milk
1½ teaspoons pure vanilla extract
About 3 cups pitted and halved or sliced fresh
fruit, such as plums, peaches, cherries, pears,
or nectarines
Juice of ½ lemon

CINNAMON TOPPING

¼ cup sugar
1 teaspoon ground cinnamon

1. Preheat the oven to 350°F. Grease and flour an 8-inch springform pan, two 6-inch springforms, or an 8-inch square pan and set aside. In a bowl with a wooden spoon, or in the workbowl of a heavy-duty electric mixer, cream the butter and sugar until fluffy. Add the egg and beat well.

2. In another bowl, combine the flour, baking powder, and salt. In a measuring cup, combine the milk and vanilla extract. Beat the dry ingredients into the creamed mixture in two additions, alternating with the milk. Beat until smooth and fluffy.

3. Spread the batter evenly into the prepared pan. Cover with all of the fruit to create a thick layer, and drizzle with the lemon juice. To make the cinnamon topping: In a small bowl, combine the sugar and the cinnamon, and sprinkle evenly over the fruit.

4. Bake in the center of the preheated oven until the fruit is bubbly and a cake tester inserted into the center comes out clean, about 40 to 45 minutes for the 8-inch pans or 25 to 30 minutes for the 6-inch pans. Serve warm or at room temperature, straight from the pan.

Marbled Chestnut–Sour Cream Coffee Cake
~

Vanilla- and chestnut-flavored batters are baked together to form a quintessential coffee cake that is excitingly different, yet exceptionally simple to mix and bake. Be certain to obtain sweetened *crème de marron* purée, often available in the jam or specialty food section of supermarkets, rather than unsweetened chestnut purée. I have served this cake with fresh jumbo strawberries for dessert, as well as for brunch. A fluted pan, known as a *kugelhof* mold, will bake the batter into a handsome cake that is suitable for a pedestal cake stand, but the plain tube pan, also known as an angel-food cake pan, will be just as beautiful.
YIELD: One 10-inch bundt or tube cake, or two 9-by-5-inch loaves

3 cups unbleached all-purpose flour
1½ teaspoons baking powder
1½ teaspoons baking soda
¼ teaspoon salt
½ cup (1 stick) unsalted butter,
  room temperature
1¼ cups sugar
3 eggs
1 tablespoon pure vanilla extract
2 cups sour cream
One 8¾-ounce can imported French sweetened
  chestnut spread (crème de marron), *or 1 cup*
  plus 1 tablespoon homemade chestnut purée
  (page 115)

2 ounces (⅓ cup) semisweet or bittersweet
  chocolate chips
3 tablespoons powdered sugar and 1½ teaspoons
  unsweetened cocoa for dusting

1. Preheat the oven to 325°F. Grease and flour a 10-inch plain or fluted tube pan or bundt pan or two 9-by-5-inch loaf pans and set aside. In a medium bowl, combine the flour, baking powder, baking soda, and salt. Set aside.

2. In a large bowl, cream the butter and sugar with a wooden spoon or electric mixer until light and fluffy. Add the eggs, one at a time, beating thoroughly after each addition. Add the vanilla extract and sour cream, blending just until smooth.

3. Gradually add the dry ingredients to the sour cream mixture and beat well until fluffy and smooth yet thick, about 2 minutes. There should be no lumps or dry spots. Remove 1 cup of the batter and place in a small bowl. Add the chestnut spread and chocolate chips. Stir briskly to evenly combine.

4. With a large spatula, scrape half of the vanilla batter into the prepared tube pan. Gently top with half of the chestnut batter. Layer the remaining vanilla batter over the top and finish with the remaining chestnut batter. Place a butter knife straight down into the batter and gently swirl around the pan once or twice, distributing the chestnut batter.

5. Bake in the center of the preheated oven 60 to 65 minutes for the tube pans and 45 to 50 minutes for the loaves, or until a cake tester comes out clean and the top of the cake is no longer shiny. Let stand in the pan for 15 minutes before removing from the pan by inverting the cake onto a rack right side up to cool completely. Combine the powdered sugar and the cocoa in a small sieve, place the rack over a piece of waxed paper, and dust the mixture over the cake. Transfer the cooled cake to a serving plate. Serve at room temperature, cut into wedges. This cake freezes well for up to 2 months, but dust with the cocoa powdered sugar just before serving.

Italian Lemon and Anise Sweet Bread

~

My favorite Italian flavors—lemons, walnuts, anise, and raisins—are the spirited Mediterranean additions to this barely sweet cake, which you will be proud to serve for a festive occasion. It also toasts nicely after a day or two.
YIELD: One 10-inch tube cake

6 eggs
2 cups sugar
¾ cup vegetable oil
4½ cups unbleached all-purpose flour
2 tablespoons baking powder
Grated zest of 2 lemons
¾ teaspoon salt
1 cup milk

2 teaspoons pure anise extract
1 cup golden raisins
1 cup (4 ounces) walnuts, coarsely chopped
Powdered sugar for dusting

1. Preheat the oven to 350°F. Grease and flour a 10-inch plain or fluted tube pan and set aside. With an electric mixer, blender, or balloon whisk, beat the eggs, sugar, and oil on high speed or briskly by hand until thick and creamy, about 2 minutes.

2. In another bowl, combine the flour, baking powder, lemon zest, and salt. Combine the milk and anise extract in a measuring cup. Add the egg mixture to the dry ingredients alternately with the milk mixture. Beat just until moistened but thoroughly blended. Do not overmix, but there should be no lumps or dry spots. Fold in the raisins and the walnuts until evenly combined.

3. Pour the batter into the prepared tube pan. Bake in the center of the preheated oven until a cake tester inserted into the center comes out clean, 55 to 65 minutes. Remove from the oven and let stand in the pan for 15 minutes. Remove from the pan by inverting the cake onto a rack right side up; cool slightly. Place the powdered sugar in a small sieve, place the rack over a piece of waxed paper, and dust the sugar over the cake while slightly warm. Transfer the cake to a serving plate. Serve slightly warm or at room temperature, cut into wedges. This cake freezes well for up to 2 months, but dust with the powdered sugar just before serving.

Jam Tea Cake

~

I have been baking this coffee cake in one form or another for last-minute breakfast guests for twenty years. It is a good way of using all those jars of exceptional store-bought jams that I tend to accumulate in the back of my refrigerator, but it is also an ideal showcase for the wonderful sweetness and flavor of homemade preserves. The small 6-inch cakes are particularly charming.
YIELD: One 8-inch cake, or two 6-inch cakes

1½ cups unbleached all-purpose flour
⅓ cup sugar
1 teaspoon baking powder
½ teaspoon baking soda
Pinch of salt
4 tablespoons unsalted butter, melted
2 eggs
½ cup sour cream
1½ teaspoons pure almond extract
½ to ⅔ cup good-quality thick fruit jam, preserves, or all-fruit spread
½ cup sliced almonds

1. Preheat the oven to 350°F. Grease and flour an 8-inch springform pan, two 6-inch springforms, or an 8-inch square cake pan and set aside. In a mixing bowl, combine the flour, sugar, baking powder, baking soda, and salt.

2. In another bowl, combine the butter, eggs, sour cream, and almond extract with a whisk. Add to the dry ingredients and beat until smooth and fluffy.

3. Spread the batter evenly into the prepared pan. Cover with spoonfuls of the jam, dotting it over the surface of the batter. Insert a butter knife straight into the batter and gently swirl a few times to distribute the jam slightly through the batter. Sprinkle with the almonds.

4. Bake in the center of the preheated oven until a cake tester inserted into the center comes out clean, about 40 to 45 minutes for the 8-inch pan or 25 to 30 minutes for the 6-inch pans. Let stand 10 minutes before removing the springform sides. Serve warm or at room temperature.

Peach and Almond Torte

~

An adaptation of a recipe for *Pfirsichtorte mit Mandelin* that appeared years ago in the women's section of a newspaper in the Black Forest region of West Germany, this is a baking specialty of my friend Jutta. It has a flavor I find utterly irresistible, with peach halves sunk into a ground almond-laced batter. I was always dropping hints to Jutta to bake it for me, so she finally gave me the original recipe written in grams and centimeters. After adapting the ingredient amounts for my American kitchen, I can now make it for myself. Use blanched fresh peaches or nectarines during the summer, but canned peaches are also fine during the winter. Serve warm for brunch or as a dessert with a scoop of vanilla ice cream.

YIELD: One 9-inch cake

*4 large peaches (about 1¼ pounds) or one
    29-ounce can peach halves in light syrup,
    drained and patted dry with paper towel*
1½ cups unbleached all-purpose flour
1½ cups whole unblanched almonds
1½ teaspoons baking powder
1 teaspoon ground cinnamon
*1 cup (2 sticks) unsalted butter, room
    temperature*
1 cup sugar
4 eggs
½ teaspoon almond extract

1. To prepare the peaches, fill a deep, medium saucepan with water and bring to a boil. Add the peaches and blanch for 10 to 15 seconds. Remove with a slotted spoon and cool under running water. Place on a cutting board, slip off the skins, cut the peaches in half, and pit. Drain on paper towels. If peaches are very tart, sprinkle with some sugar. Set aside at room temperature.

2. Preheat the oven to 350°F. Grease and flour a 9-inch springform pan and set aside. Place the flour and the almonds in the workbowl of a food processor fitted with a metal blade and process until a flour is formed. The almonds will be finely ground. Alternatively grind the almonds separately using a nut grinder or blender, then combine with the flour. In a mixing bowl, combine the almond flour, baking powder, and cinnamon.

3. In another bowl, cream the butter and sugar until light and fluffy. Add the eggs, one at a time, beating thoroughly after each addition. Add the almond extract. Gradually add the flour-nut mixture and beat well until a fluffy, smooth, and quite thick batter is formed. There should be no lumps or dry spots. Spread the batter evenly into the prepared pan. Cover the surface evenly with the peach halves, cut sides down.

4. Bake in the center of the preheated oven until the cake begins to pull away from the sides of the pan, the center springs back when gently touched, and a cake tester inserted into the center comes out clean, about 55 to 60 minutes. Let stand 10 minutes before removing the springform sides. Serve warm or at room temperature, cut into wedges. The cake is best eaten the same day it is made.

～ Muffins ～

A muffin is easily defined: It is a quick bread baked in a pan designed for single servings. Known as a "Little Muff" in centuries past, muffins warmed the hands that held them nestled inside a lady's fur muff on cold days. Corn, blueberry, bran, banana, and apple muffins seem to be among the most favored recipes. But the gently sweet muffin medley just begins with these, as the limitless assortment grows with combinations of your favorite ingredients: apple and oats, bananas and chocolate, maple and cranberry, orange with dates, and cinnamon with nuts. Whatever the ingredients, I've never known a diner to refuse a homemade crumb-top gem.

The basic techniques for making muffins are very simple. The wet ingredients are beaten as long as you like and the dry ingredients are mixed in a separate bowl to evenly distribute the leavenings. Some oil or melted butter is necessary to create the tender, coarse crumb typical of most muffins. Some muffin recipes call for creaming the butter and sugar as for a cake, which results in a finer texture. Acidic liquids, such as buttermilk, yogurt, molasses, and citrus, also make for tenderness and balance flavor with the leaveners. Nutritious grains and brans are often soaked in liquid to soften before being added to the batter.

The liquid and dry mixtures are combined just until the batter holds together, no more than about 15 seconds. Do not worry about lumps and clumps. They are natural. The less a muffin is beaten, the better. An overbeaten muffin is tough and flat, with undesirable tunnels on the inside.

Although muffins are usually round, they can be made into a wide variety of sizes and shapes. I enjoy them made in individual heart shapes or the cast-iron gem pans that look like a variety of fruits. Look for unusual rectangular-shaped muffin pans, popular from the last century, in antique stores, or substitute miniature bread pans. My specialty heart mold sports 5 connected cups that hold the same amount of batter (⅓ cup) as a standard 2½-inch cup. Standard round cups come in pans of 6, 12, and 24 connected cups. The larger pans, easily available from restaurant supply houses, are nice if you have a big family and a big oven. Muffins can also be made in mega 3¼-inch oversized pans or 1 5/8-inch miniature round pans, with the batter making half or double the yield, respectively. Commercial muffin shops make a muffin size that seems to fall in between the oversized and the standard by custom ordering their pans from restaurant suppliers.

For thick batters, fill greased, sprayed, or paper-lined muffin cups level with the tops of the cups with a ¼ cup-capacity ladle, ice cream scoop, or large spoon. For very thin batters, filling the cups three-fourths full works nicely to prevent overflowing. If all the cups are not used, pour some water into the empty cups to keep the muffin tin from buckling and to enlarge the baked muffins with a bit of added oven moisture. Muffin batters made with only baking powder can be mixed and kept in the refrigerator up to 3 days successfully. Much after that the leavening will lose its punch and the flour breaks down, resulting in an unappetizing grayish tinge.

Bake muffins in the center of a preheated, never cold, oven. The lower rack seems to consistently brown the bottoms too much and the top rack cooks the tops faster than the rest of the muffin, so use a middle rack to evenly bake each cup. An oven that is too hot will result in asymmetrical shapes, with the sides of the muffins extending above the cups. Although most muffins bake at about 400°F, temperatures can vary. If a batch of muffins is becoming asymmetrical or browning too quickly, decrease the heat by 25°F. Conversely, muffins will be leaden and will not rise if the temperature is too low.

Muffins are done when the tops are domed and dry to the touch, the sides have slightly pulled away from the pan, and a tester inserted into the center of one muffin comes out with no particles attached. The muffins on the outside of the tin may bake a few minutes faster than those in the center. After removing from the oven, let the muffins set a minute or two to allow them to shrink a bit from the pan sides. Then remove from the cups, loosening with a knife if they do not easily come out, and turn them upside down onto a rack to cool. If they stay in the pan any longer, moisture will become trapped and the bottoms will be wet.

Muffins are best eaten fresh the day they are made, but they freeze perfectly. After they have cooled completely, store in plastic freezer bags in your freezer up to 3 months. Keep a fresh supply on hand, ready for reheating on the spur of the moment. Reheat in a microwave oven for a minute or less, or in a 350°F conventional oven, wrapped in foil, for 10 to 15 minutes.

Everyday Maple Bran Muffins

~

This bran muffin is made with the unsweetened, high-fiber, whole-bran commercial cereals easily found in supermarkets. The cereal works perfectly, giving the muffin a unique double bran flavor that is not too sweet for everyday breakfasts. I usually make double batches to bring to friends or to share with the children who show up at my screen door when the aromas waft out during baking.

YIELD: 10 large muffins

1½ cup cultured buttermilk
2 eggs
¼ cup unsalted butter, melted
¼ cup sunflower seed or other vegetable oil
¼ cup pure maple syrup
1½ cups All-Bran whole-grain cereal
1 cup chopped dried apricots
¼ cup dried cranberries
1 cup unbleached all-purpose flour
½ cup wheat or oat bran flakes
¼ cup light brown sugar
1 teaspoon baking powder
1 teaspoon baking soda
¼ teaspoon salt
½ cup raw sunflower seeds

1. Preheat the oven to 400°F. Grease ten standard 2½-inch-diameter muffin cups. In a large bowl, combine the buttermilk, eggs, melted butter, oil, maple syrup, and cereal. Stir with a whisk until evenly moistened. Add the dried apricots and cranberries. Let stand at room temperature 5 to 10 minutes.

2. In another bowl, combine the flour, wheat or oat bran flakes, sugar, baking powder, baking soda, salt, and sunflower seeds. Add the dry ingredients to the buttermilk mixture and stir with a large spatula or spoon just until evenly moistened, using no more than 15 to 20 strokes.

3. Spoon the batter into each muffin cup until just level with the top of the pan. Bake in the center of the preheated oven until browned, the tops feel dry and springy, and a cake tester inserted into the center of a muffin comes out clean, 20 to 25 minutes. Do not overbake. Let the muffins rest in the pan 5 minutes before turning out onto a rack to cool.

BLUEBERRY BRAN MUFFINS

Add 3 tablespoons orange juice concentrate to the wet ingredients in Step 1. Substitute 1½ cups fresh or unthawed frozen blueberries for the dried apricots, sunflower seeds, and cranberries. Continue to mix and bake as for Everyday Maple Bran Muffins.

Sour Cream-Apple Muffins

~

Exciting and sublime, cakelike apple muffins with a crisp sugar crust, tart chunks of fruit, and the soulful dimension of spicy cinnamon are an ever-popular combination. The all-American homespun apple is certainly the commonest of fresh seasonal fruits, perfect for baking. From the crisp lime-green Granny Smith and Pippin to the blushing red, honey-sweet MacIntosh, the fruit is comforting and satisfying. Apples are harvested throughout the summer months in the world's temperate zones, but cold-storage methods enable us to have firm, fresh fruit year-round. Make certain to fill the batter to the tops of the cups, so that the baked muffins sport a queen-sized dome.
YIELD: 12 large muffins

STREUSEL TOPPING

½ cup light brown sugar
⅓ cup unbleached all-purpose flour
4 tablespoons unsalted butter, chilled

BATTER
2 cups unbleached all-purpose flour
¾ cup sugar
1 tablespoon baking powder
¾ teaspoon baking soda
1 teaspoon ground cinnamon

¼ teaspoon each ground nutmeg, allspice,
  and cloves
¼ teaspoon salt
½ cup walnuts, chopped
2 tablespoons dried currants
2 eggs
4 tablespoons unsalted butter, melted
1½ cups sour cream
2 cups (2 large) chopped tart green apples

1. Prepare the streusel: In a small bowl with a pastry blender or fork, or in a food processor, combine the sugar and flour. Add the butter in chunks and cut in until coarse crumbs are formed. Set aside. Preheat the oven to 375°F. Grease twelve standard 2½-inch-diameter muffin cups.

2. In a large bowl, combine the flour, sugar, baking powder, baking soda, spices, salt, walnuts, and currants. In another bowl, combine the eggs, melted butter, and sour cream with a whisk until well blended. Add the chopped apples and sour cream mixture to the dry ingredients and stir just until evenly moistened, no more than 15 to 20 strokes.

3. Spoon the batter into each mufffin cup until no more than two-thirds full. Bake in the center of the preheated oven until browned, the tops feel dry and springy, and a cake tester inserted into the center of a muffin comes out clean, 20 to 25 minutes. Do not overbake. Let the muffins rest in the pan 5 minutes before turning out onto a rack to cool.

Cherry-Almond Muffins

~

Cherries and almonds are natural flavor mates, as this muffin beautifully illustrates. Cherries need to be pitted carefully, as the juice splatters relentlessly. Use fresh cherries during the early summer, and, for later use, freeze pitted whole cherries for up to 12 months in freezer bags. One pound of stemmed, unpitted cherries equals about 3 cups. If you use a sour fresh cherry, such as an English Morello or Montmorency, increase the sugar to ½ cup.
YIELD: 10 large muffins

6 tablespoons unsalted butter, room temperature
¼ cup sugar
3 eggs
2 teaspoons pure almond extract
2 cups unbleached all-purpose flour
2 teaspoons baking powder
1 teaspoon baking soda
¼ teaspoon salt
½ cup milk
1½ cups (about ½ pound) pitted fresh
  sweet cherries, such as red Bings, Black
  Tartarians, or yellow Royal Anns

1. Preheat the oven to 375°F. Grease ten standard 2½-inch-diameter muffin cups. In a large bowl, combine the butter and sugar. Cream with a spoon or an electric mixer 1 minute, or until light colored. Add the eggs one at a time and beat another minute, until thick and light colored. Add the almond extract.

2. In another bowl, combine the flour, baking powder, baking soda, and salt. With a large spatula or an electric mixer, add the dry ingredients to the creamed mixture alternately with the milk just until evenly moistened, using no more than 15 to 20 strokes. Fold in the cherries.

3. Spoon the batter into each mufffin cup until just level with the top of the pan. Bake in the center of the preheated oven until browned, the tops feel dry and springy, and a cake tester inserted into the center of a muffin comes out clean, 20 to 25 minutes. Do not overbake. Let the muffins rest in the pan 5 minutes before turning out onto a rack to cool.

Raspberry Cornmeal Muffins
~

I consider this muffin the merging of earthy with a touch of glitter. Cornmeal and raspberries: simple and flawless. If your raspberries are very tart, sprinkle them with some of the sugar and macerate 15 minutes to sweeten them up before folding into the batter.

YIELD: 9 large muffins

1¼ cups unbleached all-purpose flour
¾ cup fine-grind yellow cornmeal, preferably
   stone-ground
⅔ cup sugar
2 teaspoons baking powder
½ teaspoon baking soda
¼ teaspoon salt
Grated zest of 1 lemon
1 cup milk
2 eggs
⅓ cup corn oil
1½ cups fresh red or golden raspberries

1. Preheat the oven to 400°F. Grease nine standard 2½-inch-diameter muffin cups. In a large bowl, combine the flour, cornmeal, sugar, baking powder, baking soda, salt, and zest.

2. In another bowl, beat the milk, eggs, and corn oil with a whisk or an electric mixer for 1 minute. Pour into the flour mixture and stir with a large spatula just until moistened, using no more than 15 to 20 strokes. Gently fold in the raspberries, taking care not to break them up. The batter will be lumpy.

3. Spoon the batter into each mufffin cup until just level with the top of the pan. Bake in the center of the preheated oven until browned, the tops feel dry and springy, and a cake tester inserted into the center of a muffin comes out clean, 20 to 25 minutes. Do not overbake. Let the muffins rest in the pan 5 minutes before turning out onto a rack to cool.

CORNMEAL MUFFINS WITH CRANBERRIES & GOLDEN RAISINS

Substitute 1 cup chopped fresh cranberries and ½ cup golden raisins for the fresh raspberries in Step 2. Continue to mix and bake as for Raspberry Cornmeal Muffins.

Buckwheat and Hazelnut Muffins
~

Buckwheat is really an acquired taste, but I find these muffins an easy and delicious way to prepare the hardy ethnic grain. Because buckwheat is so sturdy, it is a commercial crop that is grown without chemical pesticides, making a flour that is very pure. It is incredibly nutritious, with twice the amount of B vitamins as whole-wheat flour, and it is low in calories. If you can find it, use dark buckwheat honey in place of the maple syrup. Serve these muffins with fresh fruit and hot tea.

YIELD: 9 large muffins

1½ cups unbleached all-purpose flour
⅓ cup buckwheat flour
¼ cup rolled oats
¼ cup chopped toasted hazelnuts
2 teaspoons baking powder
½ teaspoon baking soda
¼ teaspoon salt
1 cup cultured buttermilk
4 tablespoons unsalted butter, melted
¼ cup pure maple syrup
2 eggs

1. Preheat the oven to 400°F. Grease nine standard 2½-inch-diameter muffin cups. In a large bowl, combine the unbleached flour, buckwheat flour, rolled oats, nuts, baking powder, baking soda, and salt.

2. In another bowl, beat the buttermilk, butter, maple syrup, and eggs with a whisk or an electric mixer for 1 minute. Pour into the flour mixture and stir with a large spatula just until moistened, using no more than 15 to 20 strokes. The batter will be lumpy.

3. Spoon the batter into each muffin cup until just level with the top of the pan. Bake in the center of the preheated oven until browned, the tops feel dry and springy, and a cake tester inserted into the center of a muffin comes out clean, 20 to 25 minutes. Do not overbake. Let the muffins rest in the pan 5 minutes before turning out onto a rack to cool.

Blueberry-Blue Corn Muffins

~

Popular in the Southwest for centuries as part of religious ceremonies and as a beloved culinary ingredient, blue cornmeal is now available nationwide. Along with yellow, red, and white corn, blue corn has its own unique flavor. Blue corn is naturally very hardy and it is not necessary for it to be sprayed with pesticides of any kind. When you buy blue corn flour, also known as *harinilla,* you are supporting small New Mexican farmers, the primary growers of blue corn. Although blue is an unusual color in food, take a chance here if this ingredient is new to you. Its flavor and aroma are very sweet.

YIELD: 10 large muffins

1 cup fresh blueberries
2 to 4 tablespoons granulated sugar
1 cup blue corn flour
1 cup unbleached all-purpose flour
¼ cup fine-grind yellow cornmeal, preferably
  stone-ground
¼ cup light brown sugar
1 tablespoon baking powder
¼ teaspoon salt
1 cup milk
½ cup sour cream
2 eggs
4 tablespoons unsalted butter, melted

CINNAMON SUGAR
¼ cup granulated sugar mixed with
1 teaspoon ground cinnamon

1. In a small bowl, sprinkle the blueberries with granulated sugar to taste and let macerate for 15 minutes.

2. Preheat the oven to 375°F. Grease ten standard 2½-inch-diameter muffin cups. In a large bowl, combine the flours, cornmeal, brown sugar, baking powder, and salt

3. In another bowl, beat the milk, sour cream, eggs, and melted butter with a whisk or an electric mixer for 1 minute. Pour into the dry ingredients and stir with a large spatula just until moistened, using no more than 15 to 20 strokes. The batter will be lumpy.

4. Spoon the batter into each muffin cup until half full. Sprinkle each with a thick layer of berries. Cover the berries with the remaining batter until just level with the top of the pan. Sprinkle with cinnamon sugar. Bake in the center of the preheated oven until browned, the tops feel dry and springy, and a cake tester inserted into the center of a muffin comes out clean, 20 to 25 minutes. Do not overbake. Let the muffins rest in the pan 5 minutes before turning out onto a rack to cool.

Rye Muffins with Orange and Fennel
~

I like to include some savory muffins in my repertoire of recipes. Uniquely flavored rye breads and crackers shaped rather like tortillas are featured extensively in Scandinavian folk recipes. Adapted from a recipe by East Coast food writer Leslie Land, the following muffin reflects the flavoring of *Vørtlimpor,* a Swedish holiday bread often flavored with beer or ale as the liquid ingredient. Serve with Honey-Almond Cheese (following) for breakfast, or with butter and a hearty soup for dinner.

YIELD: 9 large muffins

1¼ cups unbleached all-purpose flour
¾ cup medium or light rye flour
¼ cup light brown sugar
1 tablespoon baking powder
½ teaspoon fennel seeds, crushed
½ teaspoon whole aniseed
¼ teaspoon salt
Grated zest of 1 orange
1 cup milk
2 eggs
4 tablespoons unsalted butter, melted
3 tablespoons light molasses
Honey-Almond Cheese, following

1. Preheat the oven to 375°F. Grease nine standard 2½-inch-diameter muffin cups. In a large bowl, combine the flours, brown sugar, baking powder, spices, salt, and zest.

2. In another bowl, beat the milk, eggs, butter, and molasses with a whisk or an electric mixer for 1 minute. Pour into the flour mixture and stir with a large spatula just until moistened, using no more than 15 to 20 strokes. The batter will be lumpy.

3. Spoon the batter into each mufffin cup until just level with the top of the pan. Bake in the center of the preheated oven until browned, the tops feel dry and springy, and a cake tester inserted into the center of a muffin comes out clean, 20 to 25 minutes. Do not overbake. Let the muffins rest in the pan 5 minutes before turning out onto a rack to cool. Serve with Honey-Almond Cheese.

HONEY-ALMOND CHEESE

YIELD: About 1¼ cups

¼ cup whole toasted almonds
4 ounces fresh cream cheese, room temperature
1 cup plain kefir cheese or cottage cheese
3 tablespoons honey, preferably local

Grind the almonds in a food processor. Add the cheeses and honey, processing just until evenly combined. Store, covered, in the refrigerator for up to 1 week.

Black Olive and Goat Cheese Muffins
~

This muffin is a rustic dinner gem with Italian flavors, my contribution to *cucina povera.* Use an imported or domestic pitted olive as your taste dictates. The recipe also makes eighteen 1⅜-inch miniature muffins that are good for serving with cocktails. Pair with smoked turkey and fresh fruit for picnics.

YIELD: 9 large muffins

2¼ cups unbleached all-purpose flour
2 tablespoons fine-grind yellow cornmeal, preferably stone-ground
2 teaspoons baking powder
Pinch salt
1 cup milk
¼ cup olive oil
2 eggs
½ cup coarsely chopped, pitted black olives
¼ cup drained oil-packed sun-dried tomatoes, chopped
6-ounce round plain, herb, or chive chèvre goat cheese, cut into 9 wedges and rolled into balls
9 walnut halves

1. Preheat the oven to 375°F. Grease nine standard 2½-inch-diameter muffin cups. In a large bowl, combine the flour, cornmeal, baking powder, and salt.

2. In another bowl, beat the milk, olive oil, and eggs with a whisk or an electric mixer for 1 minute. Pour into the flour mixture and stir with a large spatula just until moistened, using no more than 15 to 20 strokes. Gently fold in the olives and tomatoes. The batter will be lumpy.

3. Spoon the batter into each mufffin cup until half full. Press a ball of goat cheese on top of the batter in each cup. Spoon the remaining olive batter over the cheese until mounded just level with the top of the pan. Place a walnut half on top of each muffin. Bake in the center of the preheated oven until browned, the tops feel dry and springy, and a cake tester inserted into the center of a muffin comes out clean, 20 to 25 minutes. Do not overbake. Let the muffins rest in the pan 5 minutes before turning out onto a rack to cool.

Zucchini-Basil Baby Cakes

Basil is an herb from the mint family and is considered an omen of happiness in Mediterranean cuisines, as well as a popular flavoring. All of my gardening friends have surplus squash and basil to share at the end of the summer, to my delight. Homegrown zucchini is very sweet and an excellent ingredient for added moisture in quick breads. These savory muffins are best served to happy diners the day they are made. Serve alongside egg dishes, hot and cold soups, or salads.

YIELD: Six 3 ¼-inch baby cakes

2½ cups unbleached all-purpose flour
1 tablespoon sugar
1 teaspoon each baking powder and baking
    soda
¼ teaspoon salt
Grated zest of 1 lemon
¾ cup cultured buttermilk
2 eggs
3 tablespoons olive oil
2 tablespoon Pernod liqueur
1¼ cups (2 medium) coarsely grated, unpeeled
    zucchini, drained on paper towels
¼ cup chopped fresh basil leaves
⅓ cup grated Parmesan cheese

1. Preheat the oven to 375°F. Grease six oversized 3¼-inch-diameter muffin cups. In a large bowl, combine the flour, sugar, baking powder, baking soda, salt, and zest.

2. In another bowl, beat the buttermilk, eggs, olive oil, and liqueur with a whisk or an electric mixer for 1 minute. Pour into the flour mixture and stir with a large spatula just until moistened, using no more than 15 to 20 strokes. Gently fold in the grated zucchini and basil until evenly distributed. The batter will be lumpy.

3. Spoon the batter into each muffin cup until just level with the top of the pan. Sprinkle each with a tablespoon of the Parmesan cheese. Bake in the center of the preheated oven until browned, the tops feel dry and springy, and a cake tester inserted into the center of a muffin comes out clean, 20 to 25 minutes. Do not overbake. Let the muffins rest in the pan 5 minutes before turning out onto a rack to cool.

~ Sweet and Savory Pancakes ~

Americans call them flapjacks, hotcakes, flannel cakes, johnnycakes, but the Europeans have the strong tradition of pancakes that parented them all. The popular fluffy American breakfast pancakes are direct descendants of the Dutch *pannekoen* brought to New Amsterdam hundreds of years ago. The pancake's European origins go back even further; they were originally a symbol of the Christian Eucharist wafer.

Almost every culture has its own unique pancake variation. The French have immortalized the oversized wheat *crêpe;* in Gaelic Brittany savory griddlecakes, *krampouz,* are often made with a splash of brandy and lemon juice or with thick farm-style dairy cottage cheese. Scots still make a "girdle" oatcake, and the Welsh, a large barley-meal pancake. Rich Shrovetide pancakes have been eaten before Lent from England to Russia since the Middle Ages. Russians make wheat as well as buckwheat *blini,* a miniature *crêpe* perfect for entertaining; the Germans created *pfankuchen* and puffy oven "Dutch Babies;" the Austrians love the soufflelike *nockerln;* and Swedes serve a traditional Thursday night supper of pea soup and thin *pannkakor* rolled with tart lingonberry jam inside. Upper-class Viennese created the women-run *mehlspeisköchins* kitchens, specializing in a pancake dessert course made of flour, eggs, butter, and milk. Hanukkah is celebrated with grated potato *latkes* topped with applesauce and sour cream. The Italians have chestnut flour pancakes, *castagnaccio,* often served in place of potatoes, or as a Tuscan-style dessert with olive oil, pine nuts, walnuts, orange peel, rosemary, and raisins in the batter, served hot from the griddle with scoops of fresh ricotta cheese. Hungarians make the popular *palacsintas,* and even the Chinese make a crêpe-like scallion pancake. American lumber camps made hearty flannel cakes, also known as a "string of flats," household words. All describe the familiar pancake, a thin, thinner, or thinnest batter that is baked on a lightly greased hot griddle until bubbles break the surface, turned once, and served immediately.

Related to all breads that are risen without yeast and baked over an open fire, flat breads were without a doubt the first breads to be made. Ancient Egyptian bakers pounded whole grains to a meal, added water, and baked the mixture on a hot stone, much like the Native American *piki* is still made today. The Romans carried flat breads back to Europe and they have been gracing tables ever since. Early Christian symbolism gave the simple ingredients spiritual qualities: flour the gift of sustenance from Mother Earth, eggs for fertility, milk for innocence, and salt for wholesomeness.

The first colonial settlers were taught by local Native Americans to make their staple johnnycake griddlecakes from Rhode Island Narragansett maize. The origin of the word "jonnycake" is still disputed today. Some say it is from "Shawnee cake," after the native northeastern tribes who taught traveling French and English trappers how to make the daily hoecakelike bread. Pancakes prevailed as the household bread in homes with no ovens, only an open hearth. They utilized gluten-free flours and meals, such as oats, barley, buckwheat, and corn, that did not stretch and rise high like ones made with wheat. Each household owned a slate bakestone, or English "bak-stun," under which a fire could be built and onto which batters would be ladled. Even today, New Englanders enjoy their corn johnnycakes and "lace cakes," a thin johnnycake batter that crinkles around the edges as it cooks, made from finely ground Rhode Island stone-ground cornmeal in much the same manner as their ancestors did.

From such a rich history, pancakes somehow evolved to be

exclusively Sunday morning or overnight-guest breakfast fare. Since they are easy to make and there are so many different ways to prepare them, it is a favorite hearty food to cook for a crowd. But today, frugal epicureans use the versatile griddlecake for any meal, as a vehicle for mashed and grated vegetables, nutty-flavored whole grains, tangy cheeses, or fresh fruits and nuts. They may be thick, thin, small, large, rolled, cut into pie-shaped wedges, embellished with vegetables, or sweetened for dessert. Although the long-favored topping for a griddlecake is maple syrup and sweet pats of butter, it is easy to be creative with other favorite flavors, such as warm honey, fruit-flavored butters, hot applesauce, buttered syrups, stewed fruit, liqueur-flavored sauces, thick cream, melted cheese, shaved maple sugar, and a variety of luscious savory sauces. Homemade fruit syrups (page 124) are quickly made and easily stored in the refrigerator, with less-than-perfect and over-ripe fruits used during the summer months for a less sweet, full-flavored alternative to commercial toppings.

Pancake batters do well when made a few hours in advance and refrigerated until baking. Gently and quickly assemble the batter, paying no attention to a few lumps. All-purpose flour is a standard ingredient, but many bakers also use cake flour for an extra lighter-than-air texture. If the batter is leavened only with baking powder, not baking soda, it can be made the night before, refrigerated, and ladled cold onto the greased, hot griddle. If a batter looks and

feels too thick, thin it with a tablespoon or two of liquid; if too thin, whisk in an extra tablespoon or so of flour until the consistency looks right to you. For the extra-busy baker, following is a recipe for a Homemade Buttermilk Griddle Mix. This mixture allows you to premix the dry ingredients similar to commercial pancake mixes such as Aunt Jemima's, but gives you control over the amounts of fiber, fat, sodium, and sugar. Having this mixture on hand allows you to quickly mix Sunday pancakes (page 59) or waffles (page 72) with a minimum amount of fuss.

Unless otherwise specified in the recipes, for even cooking use a large, heavy aluminum sauté pan with a nonstick surface or an electric, cast-iron, or soapstone griddle to make your pancakes. The soapstone griddle has a copper-rimmed blue-green surface that retains heat and needs no additional greasing. It is a very special lifetime investment for the pancake buff.

Before cooking the pancakes, the baking surface is preheated over medium-high to high heat. The age-old system for testing whether a griddle surface is hot enough is by drizzling it with a few drops of cold water. When sufficiently hot, the water will dance over the surface. If the water evaporates immediately, the surface is too hot, and if it sits and boils, it is definitely too cool. When hot, the surface is lightly greased once for the first batch. One of the best ways to grease the griddle is to lightly rub the end of a firm stick of butter or margarine once

across the hot surface, but you can also brush with vegetable oil or lightly coat with a vegetable cooking spray while still cold.

Next, pour the required amount of batter onto the hot griddle and let it bake about 2 minutes, unless otherwise specified in the recipe. Using the amount of batter specified in each recipe to form each cake is important for even, thorough cooking. When bubbles appear across the pancake surface and the edges are slightly dry, check the underside for an even browning, and turn once. The second side takes only half the amount of time as the first to cook. Serve immediately or keep warm in a 200°F oven, covered loosely with foil to prevent drying, until all cakes are baked and ready to serve. It is important that pancakes be warmed in a single layer or, if stacked, separated by a tea towel or paper towels to prevent sogginess. Pancakes also can be cooled, wrapped in plastic freezer bags, and frozen for impromptu reheating in a toaster or microwave.

Homemade Buttermilk Griddle Mix

~

YIELD: About 6 cups

3 cups unbleached all-purpose flour
1 cup whole-wheat pastry flour
1 cup dried buttermilk or goatmilk powder
½ cup wheat bran flakes, oat bran, or
    wheat germ
½ cup fine-grind yellow or blue cornmeal,
    preferably stone-ground
¼ cup sugar (optional)
1 tablespoon baking powder
1 tablespoon baking soda
1 teaspoon salt

In a plastic container with an airtight lid, combine all the ingredients and stir with a whisk until evenly mixed. Store in a cool, dry place up to 3 months.

MAKING PANCAKES FROM HOMEMADE BUTTERMILK GRIDDLE MIX

YIELD: Twelve 4-inch pancakes

2 eggs
3 tablespoons unsalted butter or margarine,
    melted, or vegetable oil
¾ cup water
1½ cups Homemade Buttermilk Griddle Mix

1. In a bowl, whisk the eggs, butter or margarine, and water. Add the griddle mix and stir until just blended. Do not overmix; the batter will have small lumps. Gently fold in any optional additions, such as berries, grated zucchini, or chopped nuts, at this time.

2. Heat a griddle or heavy skillet over medium heat until a drop of water skates over the surface, and lightly grease. Using a ¼-cup measure for each pancake, pour the batter onto the griddle. Cook until bubbles form on the surface, the edges are dry, and the bottoms are golden brown, about 2 minutes. Turn once, cooking the opposite sides until golden brown, about 1 minute. The second side will take half the amount of time to cook as the first side. Serve immediately or keep warm in a 200°F oven until ready to serve.

Old-Fashioned Buttermilk Pancakes

~

Here lies the perfect American hotcake, flapjack, or pancake in all its glory. When you walk into your kitchen to prepare them, first put on some hot water for a pot of tea and some favorite music to match your mood while assembling the ingredients. Use a sweet-tasting cultured buttermilk, as its flavor is very important. Set a skillet on the stove and sauté some corncob-smoked bacon or fresh turkey sausage patties. Cut some cool fruit of any sort, such as melon or berries, or perhaps pour a small glass of juice. Set the table with a pitcher of syrup and a mound of sweet butter. As the sun rises higher in the sky, heat up the old soapstone griddle and ladle on the batter. Then summon your breakfasters, who will assemble gladly at the table, forks in hand, to await the fresh, hot pancakes. The following variations are sensational, so try them also.

YIELD: Twelve 4-inch pancakes

2 cups unbleached all-purpose flour
1 teaspoon baking soda
Large pinch of salt
2 ¼ cups cultured buttermilk
3 eggs
4 tablespoons unsalted butter, melted, or
    vegetable oil

1. Combine the flour, baking soda, and salt in a mixing bowl. In another bowl, whisk together the buttermilk, eggs, and melted butter. Add the buttermilk mixture to the dry ingredients, stirring just until combined. Do not overmix; the batter will have small lumps. Gently fold in any additional ingredients at this time.

2. Heat a griddle or heavy skillet over medium heat until a drop of water skates over the surface, and lightly grease. Using a ¼-cup measure for each pancake, pour the batter onto the griddle. Cook until bubbles form on the surface, the edges are dry, and the bottoms are golden brown, about 2 minutes. Turn once, cooking the opposite sides until golden, about 1 minute. The second side will take half the amount of time to cook as the first side. Serve immediately or keep warm in a 200°F oven until ready to serve.

MULTI-GRAIN BUTTERMILK PANCAKES

Substitute 1 heaping tablespoon *each* stone-ground cornmeal, toasted wheat germ, rolled oats, rolled barley flakes, and oat bran for ¼ cup of the unbleached all-purpose flour in Step 1.

RICE BUTTERMILK PANCAKES

Stir ⅔ cup cooked, cooled white or brown rice into the batter in Step 1.

STRAWBERRY BUTTERMILK PANCAKES

Fold 1½ cups sliced fresh strawberries into the batter in Step 1.

BANANA BUTTERMILK PANCAKES

Distribute 1 cup sliced fresh banana over the tops of the batter after the pancakes have been ladled onto the griddle.

VANILLA-MILLET BUTTERMILK PANCAKES

Add ⅓ cup raw whole millet and 1½ teaspoons pure vanilla extract to the batter in Step 1.

Vineyard Pancakes

These pancakes could be aptly named Jim's Make-Them-From-Scratch-Quick Pancakes. They are the specialty of Jim Spaulding, the husband of my literary agent, Martha. She often requests them for breakfast in their Calistoga home before heading out to work in their grape vineyards. Martha heats the pure maple syrup, ordered by mail from New York State, in the microwave for a minute while Jim mixes the mild-flavored batter and heats the griddle. Please note that the batter stands 3 minutes to give the baking powder time to start bubbling and that it should not be stirred down before ladling onto the hot griddle.

YIELD: Twelve 4-inch pancakes

1 cup unbleached all-purpose flour
⅓ cup whole-wheat flour
2 tablespoons buckwheat flour or fine-grind
   yellow cornmeal
1 cup nonfat milk
1 egg
2 tablespoons vegetable oil, such as canola,
   safflower, peanut, or corn
1½ teaspoons baking powder

1. Combine half of the unbleached flour, the whole-wheat flour, buckwheat or cornmeal, and milk in a mixing bowl. Stir in the egg and oil. Add the remaining ½ cup unbleached flour and baking powder, stirring gently just until combined. Do not overmix; the batter will have small lumps. Let stand 3 minutes at room temperature.

2. Heat a griddle or heavy skillet over medium heat until a drop of water skates over the surface, and lightly grease. Using a ¼-cup measure or large spoon for each pancake, pour the batter onto the griddle. Cook until bubbles form on the surface, the edges are dry, and the bottoms are golden brown, about 2 minutes. Turn once, cooking the opposite sides until golden, about 1 minute. The second side will take half the amount of time to cook as the first side. Serve immediately or keep warm in a 200°F oven until ready to serve.

Cornmeal-Yogurt Pancakes

A stack of gently crunchy cornmeal pancakes is simple and delicious. Serve alongside chicken-apple sausages, a wedge of chilled melon, fresh sweet butter, and maple syrup for a memorable breakfast. A very special touch is smooth and tangy Homemade Fruit Syrup (page 124), which can be made with over-ripe as well as fresh-picked fruit.

YIELD: Twelve 4-inch pancakes

2 cups plain yogurt
2 eggs
¼ cup milk
¼ cup corn oil
1¼ cups medium-grind yellow cornmeal,
   preferably stone-ground
¾ cup unbleached all-purpose flour
2 tablespoons sugar
2 teaspoons baking soda
¼ teaspoon salt

1. Combine the yogurt, eggs, milk, and corn oil in a mixing bowl with a whisk. In another bowl, combine the cornmeal, flour, sugar, baking soda, and salt. Add the yogurt mixture to the dry ingredients, stirring just until combined. Do not overmix; the batter will have small lumps.

2. Heat a griddle or heavy skillet over medium heat until a drop of water skates over the surface, and lightly grease. Using a ¼-cup measure for each pancake, pour the batter onto the griddle. Cook until bubbles form on the surface, the edges are dry, and the bottoms are golden brown, about 2 minutes. Turn once, cooking the opposite sides until golden, about 1 minute. The second side will take half the amount of time to cook as the first side. Serve immediately or keep warm in a 200°F oven until ready to serve.

Whole-Wheat Blueberry Buttermilk Pancakes
~

People tend to gather together more often for dinner than for breakfast, but when they do, whole-wheat pancakes are perfect for satisfying early-morning appetites, especially if you plan a day at the beach or a hike in the woods before lunch. Whole-wheat pancakes have a nutty, heartier nature than cakes made just with unbleached flour. The blueberries are an important ingredient, giving a counterpoint of taste and texture. Freeze your own during

the summer season, unrinsed, in airtight plastic bags. Serve these pancakes with maple syrup and butter or, for special occasions, Yogurt Chantilly (following) and more fresh berries.

YIELD: Sixteen 4-inch pancakes

1 cup unbleached all-purpose flour
¾ cup whole-wheat flour
1 tablespoon light brown sugar
1 teaspoon baking powder
1 teaspoon baking soda
½ teaspoon ground cinnamon
¼ teaspoon salt
2 cups cultured buttermilk
2 eggs
¼ cup vegetable oil
¼ teaspoon pure vanilla extract
1½ cups fresh or drained canned blueberries, or one 12-ounce package unsweetened, unthawed frozen blueberries
Yogurt Chantilly, following (optional)

1. Combine the flours, brown sugar, baking powder, baking soda, cinnamon, and salt in a mixing bowl. In another bowl, whisk together the buttermilk, eggs, oil, and vanilla. Add the buttermilk mixture to the dry ingredients, stirring just until combined. Do not overmix; the batter will have small lumps. Let the batter stand at room temperature 15 minutes. Gently fold in the blueberries, taking care not to break them.

2. Heat a griddle or heavy skillet over medium heat until a drop of water skates over the surface, and lightly grease. Using a

¼-cup measure for each pancake, pour the batter onto the griddle. Cook until bubbles form on the surface, the edges are dry, and the bottoms are golden brown, about 2 minutes. Turn once, cooking the opposite sides until golden, about 1 minute. The second side will take half the amount of time to cook as the first side. Serve immediately or keep warm in a 200°F oven until ready to serve. Accompany with Yogurt Chantilly, if desired.

YOGURT CHANTILLY

YIELD: About 3 cups

1 cup unsweetened heavy cream, whipped to soft peaks
1 cup vanilla yogurt

Using a balloon whisk or large spatula, gently combine the whipped cream and yogurt in a bowl. Chill up to 8 hours, covered, until serving.

Four-Grain Sour Cream Pancakes
~

Sour cream adds a luxurious texture to this healthy morning pancake made with a combination of wheat, corn, oats, and barley flakes. Barley flakes are toasted and rolled pearl barley, resulting in a cereal grain that can be used exactly like rolled oats. Serve Four-Grain Sour Cream Pancakes with warm Whole-Blueberry Syrup (following), a very special topping made with Asti Spumante, the fruity Italian dessert wine.

YIELD: Eighteen 4-inch pancakes

2 cups cultured buttermilk
½ cup sour cream
2 teaspoons baking soda
2 tablespoons corn oil
2 eggs
1 cup unbleached all-purpose flour
½ cup rolled oats
¼ cup corn flour
¼ cup barley flakes
1 teaspoon ground cardamom
½ teaspoon baking powder
¼ teaspoon salt
Whole-Blueberry Syrup following (optional)

1. Combine the buttermilk, sour cream, and baking soda in a mixing bowl with a whisk. Stir until foaming stops. Add the oil and eggs. In another bowl, combine the unbleached flour, oats, corn flour, barley flakes, cardamom, baking powder, and salt. Add the buttermilk mixture to the dry ingredients, stirring just until combined. Do not overmix; the batter will have small lumps. Gently fold in any optional additions, such as a cup of blueberries or a chopped banana, at this time, if desired.

2. Heat a griddle or heavy skillet over medium heat until a drop of water skates over the surface, and lightly grease. Using a ¼-cup measure for each pancake, pour the batter onto the griddle. Cook until bubbles form on the surface, the edges are dry, and the bottoms are golden brown, about 2 minutes. Turn once, cooking the opposite sides until golden, about 1 minute. The second side will take half the amount of time to cook as the first side. Serve immediately or keep warm in a 200°F oven until ready to serve. Accompany with Whole-Blueberry Syrup, if desired.

WHOLE-BLUEBERRY SYRUP

YIELD: 2 cups

½ cup Asti Spumante sparkling wine, or water
5 tablespoons sugar
Zest and juice of 1 orange
1 tablespoon cornstarch
2 teaspoons water
2 cups fresh blueberries or one 12-ounce package
  unsweetened frozen blueberries

Place the wine, sugar, orange zest, and juice in a medium saucepan. Bring to a boil, then reduce heat to medium. In a small bowl, beat together the cornstarch and the water until smooth. Add to the hot wine mixture and stir constantly with a whisk until the mixture has thickened slightly and become clear. Immediately add the blueberries and cook until the blueberries are heated through. Serve immediately. The sauce can be stored in a covered container in the refrigerator for up to 3 weeks.

Hopi Blue Corn Hotcakes with Fruit Salsa

~

This is a traditional recipe for blue cornmeal pancakes that a friend brought to me from Second Mesa on the Hopi Indian Reservation in northeast Arizona. The Hopi are part of the tribes of Western Pueblo that also include the Zuni and Acoma, which all grow their sacred corn amidst an arid landscape. Please note that blue corn flour, also known commercially as *harinella,* is called for in this recipe rather than coarser-grind cornmeal. There is a big difference in texture between the two, as well as in the finished product. Substitute ⅔ cup fine-grind blue cornmeal and ⅓ cup unbleached all-purpose flour for the 1 cup blue corn flour, if you are unable to find it in your local natural foods store. Serve with tangy, fresh Fruit Salsa to wake up your taste buds.

YIELD: Twelve 3-inch hotcakes

1 cup blue corn flour
1 tablespoon sugar
1 tablespoon baking powder
¼ teaspoon salt
1 cup milk
2 eggs
3 tablespoons corn oil
Fruit Salsa, following

1. Combine the blue corn flour, sugar, baking powder, and salt in a mixing bowl. In another bowl, whisk together the milk, egg, and corn oil. Add the milk mixture to the dry ingredients, stirring just until combined. Do not overmix; the batter will have small lumps. Let the batter stand 10 minutes at room temperature. Gently fold in any optional additions at this time, such as berries or pine nuts.

2. Heat a griddle or heavy skillet over medium heat until a drop of water skates over the surface, and lightly grease. Using a 2-tablespoon measure for each pancake, pour the batter onto the griddle. Cook until bubbles form on the surface, the edges are dry, and the bottoms are golden brown, about 2 minutes. Turn once, cooking the opposite sides until golden, about 1 minute. The second side will take half the amount of time to cook as the first side. Serve immediately or keep warm in a 200°F oven until ready to serve. Accompany with Fruit Salsa.

FRUIT SALSA

YIELD: About 2½ cups

2 medium fresh or canned peaches, peeled, stoned, and chopped, or 1 pint fresh or thawed frozen raspberries or strawberries, coarsely mashed

2 medium fresh ripe pears, such as Bartlett or Comice, cored and chopped

½ cup dark or light raisins, currants, dried cherries, dried cranberries, or dried blueberries

2 tablespoons fresh or frozen orange juice

2 tablespoons honey, preferably local, or to taste

2 tablespoons raspberry vinegar

Combine all the ingredients and their juices in a small bowl and pour into a springtop jar or plastic storage container. Cover and store up to 1 day in the refrigerator. Serve chilled.

Buckwheat Pancakes with Maple-Nut Syrup

~

This is a light-textured buckwheat flour pancake that will have a wide appeal at breakfast. Serve with warm Maple-Nut Syrup and cold cranberry juice, or for a lavish brunch during the holidays, serve with imported chestnuts in syrup. For dinner, transform them into a sophisticated stack of pancakes with sour cream or *crème fraîche* topped with cold caviar, smoked salmon, or smoked trout, all washed down with cold champagne. The secret to the excellent flavor of the pancakes is a small proportion of musky buckwheat flour. For even lighter pancakes, separate the eggs and fold in the stiffly beaten egg whites last.

YIELD: Sixteen 4-inch pancakes

1¾ cups unbleached all-purpose flour

¼ cup dark buckwheat flour

2 tablespoons rolled oats

1 teaspoon baking powder

1 teaspoon baking soda

Grated zest of 1 orange

¼ teaspoon salt

1½ cups cultured buttermilk

4 eggs

3 tablespoon unsalted butter, melted

Maple-Nut Syrup, following (optional)

1. Combine the flours, rolled oats, baking powder, baking soda, zest, and salt in a mixing bowl. In another bowl, whisk together the buttermilk, eggs, and melted butter. Add the buttermilk mixture to the dry ingredients, stirring just until combined. Do not overmix; the batter will have small lumps. Let the batter rest at room temperature 15 minutes.

2. Heat a griddle or heavy skillet over medium heat until a drop of water skates over the surface, and lightly grease. Using a ¼-cup measure or large spoon for each pancake, pour the batter onto the griddle. Cook until bubbles form on the surface, the edges are dry, and the bottoms are golden brown, about 2 minutes. Turn once, cooking the opposite sides until golden, about 1 minute. The second side will take half the amount of time to cook as the first side. Serve immediately or keep warm in a 200°F oven until ready to serve. Accompany with warm Maple-Nut Syrup, if desired.

Banana Buckwheat Pancakes
with Maple-Nut Syrup

BLUEBERRY BUCKWHEAT PANCAKES

Add 2 cups fresh or frozen unthawed blueberries into the batter in Step 1.

BANANA BUCKWHEAT PANCAKES

Add 1 cup chopped or mashed fresh banana to the batter in Step 1.

MAPLE-NUT SYRUP

YIELD: About 1 cup syrup

¾ cup pure maple syrup
½ cup pecans, toasted lightly and chopped
2 tablespoons unsalted butter
Splash of pure vanilla extract

In a small saucepan or microwave-proof bowl, combine all the ingredients. Heat over low heat or warm on full power in the microwave until the butter is melted and the nuts are warmed. Serve immediately.

Apple Oatcakes
~

Apples are a year-round fruit in California because cold-storage is so efficient, but for a treat, use apples that have been fresh-picked, in July and August. Use an all-purpose, firm-fleshed cooking apple, such as Granny Smith, Rome Beauty, Golden Delicious, or Pippin, for these low-fat breakfast cakes. The batter is essentially prepared the night before serving, leaving only the leavenings to be added just before baking.

YIELD: Twelve 4-inch pancakes

1½ cups water
½ cup (1 stick) unsalted butter
1 teaspoon ground cinnamon
½ teaspoon fresh ground nutmeg
½ teaspoon salt
1 teaspoon pure vanilla extract
¾ cup brown sugar
1 cup rolled oats
⅓ cup toasted wheat germ
2 eggs
1 medium apple, peeled, cored, and
   coarsely grated
1 cup unbleached all-purpose flour
1 teaspoon baking powder
1 teaspoon baking soda

1. In a small saucepan, bring the water to a boil. Add the butter, spices, salt, vanilla, and brown sugar. Whisk in the oats and wheat germ. Cover, remove from heat, and let cool for 20 to 30 minutes.

2. With a spatula, scrape the mixture into a bowl and beat with an electric mixer or by hand with a whisk. Add the eggs, apple, and flour. Beat until well mixed. Cover and refrigerate overnight.

3. Just before baking, stir in the baking powder and baking soda. Thin the batter with extra water if it has become too thick overnight. Heat a griddle or heavy skillet over medium heat until a drop of water skates over the surface, and lightly grease. Using a ¼-cup measure for each pancake, pour the batter onto the griddle. Cook until bubbles form on the surface, the edges are dry, and the bottoms are golden brown, about 2 minutes. Turn once, cooking the opposite sides 1 minute. When done, the pancakes will look more moist than regular hotcakes and will have a lacy edge. They will take half the amount of time to cook on the second side. Serve immediately or keep warm in a 200°F oven until ready to serve.

Chili Corn Cakes

~

Chili Corn Cakes are a good accompaniment to grilled and roasted meats. They have a pronounced corn flavor that comes from the large proportion of cornmeal and fresh corn kernels in the batter. The Homemade Chili Powder (following) gives a unique hint of spiciness, but you may use a good commercial brand, if you wish. Serve with a tablespoon of sour cream or plain yogurt and a drizzle of a sweet pepper jelly. For hors d'oeuvres, I often make the pancakes the size of a silver dollar and serve with a thin slice of Red Pepper Butter (following). To transform this recipe into breakfast fare, substitute vanilla extract for the chili powder and serve with maple syrup.

YIELD: Sixteen 4-inch pancakes

¾ cups fine-grind yellow cornmeal, preferably
   stone-ground
1¼ cup unbleached all-purpose flour
1 teaspoon Homemade Chili Powder
   (following)
2 teaspoons baking powder
2 teaspoons sugar
¼ teaspoon salt
2 cups milk
3 eggs
¼ cup corn oil
¼ cup unsalted butter, melted
2 cups fresh or frozen, yellow or white
   corn kernels

1. Combine the cornmeal, flour, chili powder, baking powder, sugar, and salt in a mixing bowl. Make a well in the center of the mixture and add the milk and eggs to the dry ingredients, stirring just until combined. Drizzle with the oil and melted butter and gently mix. Fold in the corn with a spatula. Do not overmix; the batter will have small lumps.

2. Heat a griddle or heavy skillet over medium heat until a drop of water skates over the surface, and lightly grease. Using a ¼-cup measure or large spoon for each pancake, pour the batter onto the griddle. Cook until bubbles form on the surface, the edges are dry, and the bottoms are golden brown, about 2 minutes. Turn once, cooking the opposite sides until golden, about 1 minute. The second side will take half the amount of time to cook as the first side. Serve immediately or keep warm in a 200°F oven until ready to serve.

HOMEMADE CHILI POWDER

To make this very delicious spice mixture, use a pure chile powder to suit your taste, such as those ground from New Mexico, California, pasilla negro, ancho, or mulatto dried chiles, available in the ethnic section of supermarkets or acquired on your last trip to the Southwest. Or, use several kinds of chili powders and blend them together for your own unique mixture. If you grind your own from whole dried chiles, rinse off the dust and place the chiles on a baking sheet. Bake at 300°F for about 5 minutes, or until puffy. Break open, shake out the seeds, and pull out the vein. Grind to a powder in a blender or electric coffee grinder reserved just for chiles.

YIELD: About ⅓ cup

¼ cup ground dried chile powder (mild,
   medium, or hot, or a mixture to taste)
1 tablespoon ground cumin
1 teaspoon each garlic powder and dried
   Greek oregano
½ teaspoon each ground cloves, allspice, and
   Hungarian paprika

1. Place ground red chile powder and cumin on a baking sheet. Toast lightly in a preheated 325°F oven for 3 to 4 minutes. Remove from the oven and let cool.

2. Combine chile-cumin mixture and all other herbs and spices in a small bowl. Mix until all ingredients are evenly combined. Store indefinitely in a tightly covered container, away from heat and light.

Red Pepper Butter

YIELD: About 2 cups

1 cup (2 sticks) unsalted butter,
    room temperature
One 7½-ounce jar roasted red peppers,
    drained and patted dry
1 tablespoon fresh lemon juice
2 tablespoons chopped fresh flat-leaf parsley

Purée all the ingredients in a blender or food processor until fluffy and smooth. Form into 2 narrow log shapes using plastic wrap to protect your hands. Wrap in clean plastic and twist the ends. Store, covered, in the refrigerator up to 5 days or freeze up to 6 months. Cut off slices as needed.

Savory Wild Rice Pancakes

Delicate and elegant is the best description of these silver dollar-sized gems. They nestle nicely next to sautéed vegetables and a roasted meat for a very special main-course accompaniment. If you have friends who claim they don't like wild rice, this is the recipe to serve, as the pancakes have an appealing flavor and texture that are hard to resist. Serve plain or topped with *crème fraîche*. Frugal epicureans will rave.
YIELD: Twenty 3-inch pancakes

4 tablespoons unsalted butter
1 medium shallot, minced
1 cup unbleached all-purpose flour
1 tablespoon baking powder
½ teaspoon salt
3 eggs
1 cup milk
1½ cups cooked and cooled wild rice
    (page 125)

1. Melt the butter in a medium skillet, add the shallot, and sauté until tender. Set aside.

2. Combine the flour, baking powder, and salt in a bowl, with a whisk, or in a food processor. Add the shallots and butter, eggs, and milk. Beat or process just until smooth. The batter will be thin, yet thicker than crêpe batter. Stir in the wild rice.

3. Heat a griddle or heavy skillet over medium heat until a drop of water skates over the surface, and lightly grease. Using a 2-tablespoon measure for each pancake, pour the batter onto the griddle. Cook until bubbles form on the surface, the edges are dry, and the bottoms are golden brown, about 2 minutes. Turn once, cooking the opposite sides until golden, about 1 minute. The second side will take half the amount of time to cook as the first side. Serve immediately or keep warm in a 200°F oven until ready to serve.

Spinach Dinner Cakes

Luckily, the pancake is not relegated only to breakfast fare. These spinach pancakes are just as appealing as a first course, garnished with some sour cream and smoked fish or sautéed mushrooms, as they are for lunch, alongside grilled sausages.
YIELD: Twenty 3-inch pancakes

1¼ cups milk
1 cup unbleached all-purpose flour
1 teaspoon baking powder
½ teaspoon salt
½ teaspoon fresh ground nutmeg
4 tablespoons unsalted butter, melted
2 eggs
½ pound fresh spinach, washed, stemmed, and
    steamed, or one 9-ounce package frozen
    chopped spinach, thawed, and drained
3 tablespoons chopped fresh Italian parsley

1. Combine all the ingredients except the spinach and parsley in a blender or food processor and blend just until smooth. Transfer the batter to a bowl. Squeeze out the excess liquid from the spinach. In the scraped-clean blender or workbowl, process the spinach and parsley until finely chopped. Add to the batter and stir until evenly blended. Let the batter rest 1 hour at room temperature.

2. Heat a griddle or heavy skillet over medium heat until a drop of water skates over the surface, and lightly grease. Using a 2-tablespoon measure for each pancake, pour the batter onto the griddle, spreading with the back of the spoon into even circles. Cook until bubbles form on the surface, the edges are dry, and the bottoms are golden brown, about 2 minutes. Turn once, cooking the opposite sides until golden, about 1 minute. The second side will take half the amount of time to cook as the first side. Serve immediately or keep warm in a 200°F oven until ready to serve.

Zucchini Pancakes

There is always room for one more recipe using abundant homegrown summer squashes. I sometimes vary this recipe by combining delicious oblong yellow, pale green, and dark green Italian *zuchettas* along with scalloped pattypan and yellow crookneck squashes, which gives the pancakes a slightly varigated color. This simple dinner pancake is a delicious complement to grilled meats, hot whole mushrooms with garlic, roasts, and even omelettes.

YIELD: Sixteen 2-inch pancakes

2 cups unpeeled shredded zucchini or other
*   summer squash, drained on paper towels*
*   10 minutes*
2 tablespoons chopped fresh Italian parsley
Salt and fresh-ground pepper to taste

1 egg
½ cup unbleached all-purpose flour
1 teaspoon baking powder
Olive or other vegetable oil for frying
½ cup finely shredded imported or domestic
*   Parmesan cheese for sprinkling*

1. In a medium bowl, combine the zucchini, parsley, salt, pepper, and egg. Combine the flour and baking powder and add to the zucchini mixture; stir until combined. Let stand at room temperature 30 minutes.

2. In a small, heavy skillet, heat ½ inch of oil until hot, but not smoking. Drop the batter by tablespoonfuls into the oil. Cook until bubbles form on the surface, the edges are dry, and the bottoms are golden brown, about 2 minutes. Turn once, cooking the opposite sides until golden, about 1 minute. The second side will take half the amount of time to cook as the first side. Drain briefly on paper towels. Serve immediately or keep warm in a 200°F oven until ready to serve, sprinkled liberally with the Parmesan cheese.

Potato-Spinach Pancakes with Goat Cheese

I have always had a fondness for crispy homemade potato pancakes, but these are the ultimate in elegant country food. The humble russet potato was the invention of Luther Burbank earlier this century, and it has become the most widely grown variety of potato in the country. The russet's high starch content makes a pancake that cooks up crisp and does not fall apart. Serve these pancakes topped with cold unsweetened applesauce and leafy greens for a light meal or as a complement to simple roast chicken for a satisfying dinner.

YIELD: Eight 4-inch pancakes

4 tablespoons unsalted butter
1 large shallot, minced
6 large spinach or Swiss chard leaves, ribs
*   removed and chopped*
Salt and fresh-ground black pepper to taste
3 large (2½ to 3 pounds) russet potatoes
2 eggs, lightly beaten
3 tablespoons unbleached all-purpose flour
¼ cup vegetable oil
4 ounces goat cheese, such as domestic chabi or
*   French Montrachet, sliced into 8 pieces*

1. In a large skillet, melt 2 tablespoons of the butter. Add the shallot and cook 1 minute over medium heat to soften. Add the spinach or Swiss chard leaves, stirring until wilted, and carefully drain off any excess liquid, if necessary. Season with salt and pepper to taste.

2. Peel and coarsely grate the potatoes; you should have about 2½ cups total. Place in a tea towel and wring out excess moisture. Place in a mixing bowl and add the eggs, flour, and spinach mixture. Stir to evenly combine.

3. Wipe out the skillet with a paper towel and place over medium-high heat. Add the remaining butter and the oil. When melted, drop in the batter by ¼-cup measures to make 8 patties and flatten slightly with the back of a spoon. Sauté until crisp and golden brown on both sides, about 5 minutes total. While the second side is cooking, place a slice of the goat cheese over each pancake to melt slightly. Drain on paper towel, if necessary, and serve very hot with cold unsweetened applesauce.

Roasted Red Pepper Pancakes with Hot Chèvre Sauce

Roasted Red Pepper Pancakes taste extravagant napped with silky Hot Chèvre Sauce. For a less rich alternative, they may also be topped with chopped garden-fresh chives with their colorful blossoms or cold California golden caviar and sour cream for a celebration lunch. Serve as a first course or alongside fresh corn on the cob and roasted meats or fish.

YIELD: Ten 3-inch pancakes

1½ cups unbleached all-purpose flour
2½ teaspoons baking powder
½ teaspoon salt
3 eggs, separated
1 cup milk

1 large red bell pepper, roasted, peeled, and minced (see page 123)
3 to 4 tablespoons unsalted butter for sautéeing
Hot Chèvre Sauce, following

1. In a bowl, combine the flour, baking powder, and salt. In a small bowl, whisk together the egg yolks and milk. Add the milk mixture to the dry ingredients and beat well until evenly blended.

2. In a clean bowl, beat the egg whites with an electric mixer or a balloon whisk until stiff peaks form. Fold the whites gently into the batter until no white streaks are visible. Fold in the minced roasted red pepper until evenly distributed.

3. Heat a griddle or heavy skillet over medium heat until a drop of water skates over the surface. Using a tablespoon at a time for each batch, melt the butter in an even layer over the surface to grease. Using a 2-tablespoon measure for each pancake, drop the batter onto the griddle, making pancakes no more than 3 inches in diameter. Cook until bubbles form on the surface, the edges are dry, and the bottoms are golden brown, about 2 minutes. Turn once, cooking the opposite sides until golden, about 1 minute. The second sides will take half the amount of time to cook as the first sides and the pancakes will be quite light in texture. Serve immediately with Hot Chèvre Sauce.

HOT CHÈVRE SAUCE

YIELD: 1¾ cups

½ cup dry white wine
1 clove garlic
1 cup heavy cream
5 ounces creamy fresh goat cheese
Pinch of white pepper

Combine the wine and garlic in a small saucepan. Bring to a boil, lower the heat to a simmer, and reduce the liquid to ¼ cup. Add the cream, cheese, and white pepper. Stir with a whisk until smooth. Use immediately or keep warm by setting in a hot water bath for up to 2 hours.

~ Waffles ~

Bringing out the honeycombed waffle iron is a sure sign that a meal is going to be a special occasion. A homey comfort food that has gone in and out of style, waffles have withstood the tests of time and fashion. The classic waffle, with its decorative grid pattern, is ready-made to hold dark amber pools of maple syrup and melted butter. Although waffles are certainly not categorized as fancy food, they dress up well. With the addition of a number of savory ingredients, a morning waffle is ready for supper. With a dusting of powdered sugar, sweet topping or spirit-spiked sauce, ice cream or flavored whipped cream, they make an unusual dessert.

Waffles have a rich and illustrious history. The original European waffle irons, with handles attached for baking over an open fire, date back to the twelfth century, when they were used to shape and bake religious sacramental wafers. Chaucer wrote of English "wafers," and crisp French *gaufres* have been enjoyed as a dessert for centuries. La Varrene's culinary bible, *La Cuisinier Français,* published in 1651, featured waffle recipes. In the seventeenth century, German *waffelen* were cooked between hinged cast-iron disks, which created a waffle with intricately embossed landscapes and patterns worthy of the Dutch masters. In the late 1700s, Thomas Jefferson brought a long-handled French open-fire waffle iron home to Virginia from one of his forays to Europe and created the first *gaufres* party supper for his friends. The traditional Dutch wedding gift in early New Amstersdam was a waffle iron carved with the bride's initials, and the butter-rich recipe for *wafels,* like the pancake, is credited with most influencing the modern American waffle. Belgian waffle makers, with their exaggerated deep grids, were introduced at the New York World Fair in 1964 and are still popular in many homes.

Waffle batters are similar to those for muffins and pancakes, with the wet and dry ingredients first mixed separately, then, just before baking, combined with a minimum of strokes to form a soft, thick, pourable batter. Cake flour makes a more tender waffle than all-purpose flour, but it is an optional variation depending on your preference. To provide the crispness characteristic of waffles, there is usually a bit more fat in the recipes as compared to pancake batters. Many recipes suggest beating egg whites until fluffy and then folding them into the batter for a lighter waffle, rather than adding the whole egg into the wet ingredients, but this step is quite optional. One exception to this is for batters that are very low in fat, when the additional leavening power of the stiffly beaten egg whites is essential. As with all quick breads, beat the batter just until blended (there will be a few lumps), because overmixing produces a tough, dense waffle.

Bake waffles on a lightly greased and heated iron, whether it be a preheated countertop electric iron with reversible grids; a hinged, stove-top model, which is heated on both sides and flipped once during baking; the delicate "Five of Hearts" circular-shaped models; a curly-edged waffle iron embossed with carousel figures; a thick Belgian waffler; or even an exotic European model picked up while traveling. Unless you have a nonstick model, a waffle iron needs to be seasoned before its first use (see Notes from the Kitchen (page 132) for specific instructions). For the best results, always follow the manufacturer's instructions for your model. Spray-on vegetable oil is the most efficient way to grease all the little corners, even on a nonstick surface (*always* spray onto a cold surface).

Heat the waffle iron until the indicator light says the surface is hot. Depending on the recipe, ladle in about one-half to a full cup of batter, covering the surface one-half to two-thirds full, depending on the size of the iron, and gently close the top. The batter will spread out when the iron is closed, making a full-sized waffle. After a try or two, you will know exactly how much batter to pour onto your iron.

Timing is crucial to a waffle's color and texture. As with all culinary techniques, it is a skill best learned by experience. The general rule is about 4 to 5 minutes cooking time in a standard electric model, or until the steam stops. A high temperature tends to make a crisp waffle, while a lower temperature bakes a waffle that is more moist and tender. When the lid is lifted, the waffle should not stick. If it does, close the iron and wait another minute. Remove the waffle with a fork and touch only the handles to prevent burns.

When cleaning, waffle irons should never be submerged in water; instead wipe with a damp cloth or scrub gently with a kitchen brush (a clean toothbrush also works well), protecting the electrical element. The manufacturer's instructions will provide the best method of cleaning your specific model, whether electric or stove-top.

As with all griddlecakes, waffles are best eaten as soon as they are baked. Leftover batter can be stored in the refrigerator for a day. To refresh the batter, combine ½ teaspoon of baking powder with 2 tablespoons of milk per 2 cups of flour in the batter, and stir into the batter before baking. Fully baked waffles can be frozen up to two months. To freeze, cool waffles completely before wrapping each waffle separately in plastic wrap or freezer bags. To serve, reheat frozen waffles on a clean baking sheet in a 350°F oven for 10 to 15 minutes, or pop the frozen waffle into the toaster, where it will emerge as hot and crisp as freshly made, for an impromptu meal or snack.

MAKING WAFFLES FROM THE HOMEMADE BUTTERMILK GRIDDLE MIX

As an alternative to commercial mixes, Homemade Buttermilk Griddle Mix (page 59) is a nutritious mixture of dry ingredients that are combined ahead of time and stored in an airtight container. This allows the busy baker to quickly mix in the eggs, butter, and milk or water to create a batter that makes crisp and tasty waffles with a minimal amount of time and effort in the kitchen. YIELD: 6 to 8 large waffles, depending on iron size

3 eggs, separated
6 tablespoons unsalted butter or margarine, melted
1½ cups water or milk
2 ¼ cups Homemade Buttermilk Griddle Mix

1. Heat the waffle iron to medium-high or according to manufacturer's instructions. In a clean bowl, beat the egg whites to stiff, but not dry, peaks. In another bowl, whisk the egg yolks, butter or margarine, and water or milk until foamy.

2. Place the griddle mix in a large bowl, add the wet ingredients, and combine with a few strokes. Fold in the beaten whites until there are no white streaks visible. The batter will be just evenly moistened. Do not overmix.

3. Brush the waffle iron grids with oil or melted butter. For each waffle, pour about 1 cup of the batter onto the grid. Close the lid and bake until the waffle is crisp and well browned, about 4 to 5 minutes. Remove from the iron with a fork to protect your fingers. Serve immediately, or cool completely on racks, store in plastic bags, and freeze for up to 2 months.

Buttermilk Waffles

Today, recipes for waffles are remarkably similar to their early ancestors, and they have nourished a steadfast group of waffle-eaters over the centuries. Waffles are at home with sweet breakfast toppings as well as savory dinner accompaniments throughout the seasons. These waffles only get better when a handful of toasted pecans or chopped fresh herbs from the garden are added to create an array of sweet or savory crisp honeycombs. If you love waffles, do not miss the variations listed here, each one creating a very different flavor. Serve with sweet butter and pure maple syrup or delightful Fresh-Strawberry Spumante Sauce (following) for special summer brunches.

YIELD: 6 to 8 large waffles, depending on iron size

2 cups unbleached all-purpose flour
1 teaspoon baking soda
½ teaspoon baking powder
¼ teaspoon salt
4 eggs, separated
¼ cup vegetable oil
2 cups cultured buttermilk
Fresh-Strawberry Spumante Sauce, following
(optional)

1. Heat the waffle iron to medium-high or according to manufacturer's instructions. In a large bowl, combine the flour, baking soda, baking powder, and salt. In another bowl, beat the egg yolks, oil, and buttermilk with a whisk until foamy.

2. With an electric mixer, beat the egg whites in a separate bowl until soft peaks form. Pour the buttermilk mixture into the dry ingredients, stirring just until moistened. Fold in the whites until no streaks are visible.

3. Brush the waffle iron grids with oil or melted butter. For each waffle, pour about 1 cup of the batter onto the grid. Close the lid and bake until the waffle is crisp and well browned, about 4 to 5 minutes. Remove from the iron with a fork to protect your fingers. Serve immediately with Fresh-Strawberry Spumante Sauce, if desired, or cool completely on racks, store in plastic bags, and freeze for up to 2 months.

SUPER WHOLE-GRAIN BUTTERMILK WAFFLES

Substitute ¾ cup whole-wheat flour, 3 tablespoons each oat bran and wheat germ, 2 tablespoons cornmeal or buckwheat flour, and 1 tablespoon brown sugar in place of 1 cup unbleached all-purpose flour and add to the dry ingredients in Step 1. Continue to mix and bake as for Buttermilk Waffles.

LEMON BUTTERMILK WAFFLES

Substitute the zest and juice of 2 large lemons and 2 tablespoons sugar for ¼ cup buttermilk, and 5 tablespoons melted unsalted butter for the oil when combining the liquid ingredients in Step 1. Continue to mix and bake as for Buttermilk Waffles.

RICE BUTTERMILK WAFFLES

Add ¾ cup cold, cooked short- or long-grain white or brown rice (try imported white basmati or domestic brown basmati for a real treat) when combining the liquid ingredients in Step 1. Continue to mix and bake as for Buttermilk Waffles.

SOUR CREAM BUTTERMILK WAFFLES

Add ⅔ cup sour cream and 2 tablespoons melted unsalted butter when combining the liquid ingredients in Step 1. Continue to mix and bake as for Buttermilk Waffles.

SEVEN-GRAIN BUTTERMILK WAFFLES

Substitute ½ cup seven-grain cereal (a flavorful combination of cracked wheat, oats, bran, rye, cornmeal, millet, and flaxseed) for an equal amount of flour. Combine the seven-grain cereal and 1 cup of the buttermilk in a bowl, cover, and refrigerate 2 hours to overnight to soften the grains. Add the soaked grains and 2 tablespoons maple syrup to the liquid ingredients in Step 1. Continue to mix and bake as for Buttermilk Waffles.

FRESH-STRAWBERRY SPUMANTE SAUCE

YIELD: About 3 cups

2 pint baskets fresh strawberries, rinsed
and hulled
½ cup Asti Spumante sparkling wine
3 tablespoons superfine sugar

In a blender or food processor, combine all the ingredients and process until smooth. Cover and chill for several hours to overnight. Pour or ladle onto any of the hot Buttermilk Waffles.

Banana Waffles

Waffles are a great way to start the day because they can provide a quarter of the day's calories and a boost of complex carbohydrates in one meal. Add a few tablespoons of honey-crunch wheat germ to these banana-enriched waffles for more fiber. Serve with spicy turkey sausage and fresh juice, and top with vanilla yogurt and sliced fresh bananas or maple syrup.

YIELD: 6 to 8 large waffles, depending on iron size

1¼ cups unbleached all-purpose flour
1 teaspoon baking powder
1 teaspoon baking soda
Pinch of salt and ground cinnamon
2 eggs, separated
5 tablespoons melted unsalted butter or nut oil
2 large bananas, mashed (about 1 cup)
¾ cup milk, coconut milk (page 116), papaya
    or passion fruit juice

1. Preheat the waffle iron to medium-high heat or according to manufacturer's instructions. In a large bowl, combine the flour, baking powder, baking soda, salt, and cinnamon. In another bowl, beat the egg yolks, butter or oil, mashed banana, and milk with a whisk until foamy.

2. With an electric mixer, beat the egg whites in a separate bowl until soft peaks form. Pour the banana mixture into the dry ingredients and combine with a few strokes. Fold in the beaten whites until no streaks are visible. The batter will be just evenly moistened. Do not overmix.

3. Brush the waffle iron grids with oil or melted butter. For each waffle, pour about 1 cup of the batter onto the grid. Close the lid and bake until the waffle is crisp and well browned, about 4 to 5 minutes. Remove from the iron with a fork to protect your fingers. Serve immediately, or cool completely on racks, store in plastic bags, and freeze for up to 2 months.

Whole-Wheat Waffles with Cherry Sauce

~

I was first served these waffles in a rustic restaurant below Bucks Lake in the California Sierras, north of Lake Tahoe. They were hot and crunchy, served with cut-glass pitchers of pure maple syrup, and I couldn't stop eating them. When I returned home, I successfully re-created the recipe. For variety, sprinkle the batter with sesame or sunflower seeds just before closing the lid to bake. If you decide to try making these with buttermilk, be sure to substitute ½ teaspoon baking soda for an equal amount of baking powder to achieve the best leavening action. The Cherry Sauce may be used on any breakfast waffle in place of maple syrup.

YIELD: 6 to 8 large waffles, depending on iron size

1 cup unbleached all-purpose flour
1 cup whole-wheat flour
2½ teaspoons baking powder
¼ teaspoon salt

3 eggs, separated
⅓ cup vegetable oil, or 6 tablespoons unsalted
    butter, melted
1¼ cups milk
Cherry Sauce, following

1. Preheat the waffle iron to medium-high heat or according to manufacturer's instructions. In a large bowl, combine the flours, baking powder, and salt. In another bowl, beat the egg yolks, oil or butter, and milk with a whisk until foamy.

2. With an electric mixer, beat the egg whites in a separate bowl until soft peaks form. Pour the milk mixture into the dry ingredients, stirring just until moistened. Fold in the whites until no streaks are visible.

3. Brush the waffle iron grids with oil or melted butter. For each waffle, pour about 1 cup of the batter onto the grid. Close the lid and bake until the waffle is crisp and well browned, about 4 to 5 minutes. Remove from the iron with a fork to protect your fingers. Serve immediately topped with Cherry Sauce, or cool completely on racks, store in plastic bags, and freeze for up to 2 months.

WHOLE-WHEAT HAZELNUT WAFFLES

Add ½ cup ground toasted hazelnuts to the dry ingredients in Step 1. Continue to mix and bake as for Whole-Wheat Waffles.

CHERRY SAUCE

YIELD: About 2 cups

2 tablespoons cornstarch
2 tablespoons fresh orange or lemon juice
2 tablespoons sugar
1 cup unsweetened apple juice or water
One 12-ounce package frozen unsweetened
    dark sweet cherries

In a saucepan, combine the cornstarch, orange or lemon juice, sugar, and apple juice with a whisk. Bring to a boil, then reduce the heat to a simmer. Cook until slightly thickened, stirring occasionally, about 2 minutes. Add the cherries and cook until hot. Serve warm. Store, covered, in the refrigerator for up to 1 week. Reheat to warm before serving.

Oat-Cornmeal Waffles with Dried Fruit Syrup
~

This is an old-fashioned, hearty, whole-grain waffle with a crunchy texture. Cornmeal, oats, and wheat are a particularly harmonious combination of grains that adds a robust flavor. Serve with warm, homemade Dried Fruit Syrup and sweet butter or equal amounts of whipped *crème fraîche* and plain yogurt folded together to make an ethereal topping, with lots of sliced fresh fruit on the side.
YIELD: 6 to 8 large waffles depending on iron size

1¼ cups unbleached all-purpose flour
1 cup fine-grind yellow cornmeal, preferably
    stone-ground
⅓ cup rolled oats
3 tablespoons light brown sugar
1 teaspoon baking powder
1 teaspoon baking soda
¼ teaspoon salt
2 eggs
2½ cups cultured buttermilk
6 tablespoons unsalted butter, melted
Dried Fruit Syrup, following

1. Preheat the waffle iron to medium-high or according to manufacturer's instructions. In a large bowl, combine the flour, cornmeal, oats, brown sugar, baking powder, baking soda, and salt. In another bowl, beat the eggs and the buttermilk with a whisk until foamy.

2. Pour the buttermilk mixture into the dry ingredients and combine with a few strokes. Drizzle the surface with the melted butter and fold in. The batter will be just evenly moistened. Do not overmix.

3. Brush the waffle iron grids with oil or melted butter. For each waffle, pour about 1 cup of the batter onto the grid. Close the lid and bake until the waffle is crisp and well browned, about 4 to 5 minutes. Remove from the iron with a fork to protect your fingers. Serve immediately with Dried Fruit Syrup, or cool completely on racks, store in plastic bags, and freeze for up to 2 months.

DRIED FRUIT SYRUP

YIELD: About 1 cup

½ cup pure maple syrup
¼ cup dried cranberries
¼ cup finely chopped dried apricots or figs

Combine the ingredients in a small saucepan. Over low heat, simmer a few minutes until the mixture is warmed and the dried fruit is plumped. Transfer to a pitcher and serve warm.

Wild Rice Buttermilk Waffles
~

Wild rice is often referred to as the "gourmet grain," and some brands are still harvested by hand in the Great Lakes region by Native Americans. Wild rice has a husky flavor that mellows considerably when added to a batter. These waffles will become a staple in your repertoire, so keep extra cooked rice on hand in the freezer. For an exceptional flavor combination, substitute ½ cup of chopped toasted pecans for an equal amount of the wild rice. Serve with pure maple syrup or Apple Cider Syrup (following) for breakfast. For a substantial supper, a topping of creamed mushrooms or poultry is excellent along with a leafy green salad.
YIELD: 6 to 8 large waffles, depending on iron size

2 cups unbleached all-purpose flour
2 teaspoons baking powder
½ teaspoon baking soda
¼ teaspoon salt
1½ cups cultured buttermilk
4 eggs, separated
⅓ cup hazelnut or other flavorful nut oil
1½ cups cooked wild rice (page 125)
Apple Cider Syrup, following (optional)

1. Preheat the waffle iron to medium-high heat or according to manufacturer's instructions. In a bowl, combine the flour, baking powder, baking soda, and salt. In another bowl, whisk together the buttermilk, egg yolks, nut oil, and wild rice.

2. With an electric mixer, beat the egg whites in a separate bowl until soft peaks form. Pour the wild rice mixture into the dry ingredients, stirring just until moistened. Fold in the whites until no streaks are visible.

3. Brush the waffle iron grids with oil or melted butter. For each waffle, pour about 1 cup of the batter onto the grid. Close the lid and bake until the waffle is crisp and well browned, about 4 to 5 minutes. Remove from the iron with a fork to protect your fingers. Serve immediately, drizzled with Apple Cider Syrup, if desired, or cool completely on racks, store in plastic bags, and freeze for up to 2 months.

APPLE CIDER SYRUP

YIELD: About 1¼ cups

1 cup fresh unfiltered apple cider or apple juice
2 tablespoons light brown sugar
2 tablespoons light corn syrup
Juice of ½ lemon
2 cinnamon sticks
3 tablespoons unsalted butter

Combine the cider or juice, brown sugar, corn syrup, lemon juice, and cinnamon sticks in a small, heavy saucepan. Bring to a boil and reduce the liquid by one third, about 10 minutes. Remove from the heat, discard cinnamon sticks, add the butter, and swirl to melt. Serve the syrup warm. Keeps for one week, covered, in the refrigerator. Rewarm before serving.

Spiced Gingerbread Waffles with Pan-Glazed Apples

~

These waffles are delightfully spiced and molasses laced and very popular with waffle lovers. Serve for brunch with yogurt or for a Mardi Gras dessert, with ice cream and the warm, spicy Pan-Glazed Apples.
YIELD: 6 to 8 large waffles, depending on iron size

2 cups unbleached all-purpose flour
½ cup whole-wheat flour
¼ cup light or dark brown sugar
4 teaspoons baking powder
1 teaspoon baking soda

1 tablespoon each *instant espresso powder and ground ginger*
1 teaspoon each *ground cinnamon and allspice*
¼ teaspoon salt
2 eggs
1½ cups cultured buttermilk
½ cup light molasses, slightly warmed for easy mixing
6 tablespoons unsalted butter, melted
¾ cup golden raisins
Pan-Glazed Apples, following

1. Preheat the waffle iron to medium-high or according to manufacturer's instructions. In a large bowl, combine the flours, brown sugar, baking powder, baking soda, espresso powder, spices, and salt. In another bowl, beat the eggs, buttermilk, and molasses with a whisk until foamy.

2. Pour the buttermilk-molasses mixture into the dry ingredients and combine with a few strokes. Drizzle the surface with the melted butter and fold in along with the golden raisins. The batter will be just evenly moistened. Do not overmix.

3. Brush the waffle iron grids with oil or melted butter. For each waffle, pour about 1 cup of the batter onto the grid. Close the lid and bake until the waffle is crisp and well browned, about 4 to 5 minutes. Remove from the iron with a fork to protect your fingers. Serve immediately topped with warm Pan-Glazed Apples, or cool completely on racks, store in plastic bags, and freeze for up to 2 months.

PAN-GLAZED APPLES

YIELD: Enough for one batch of Gingerbread Waffles

4 tablespoons unsalted butter
3 large tart apples, peeled, cored, and cut into ¼-inch-thick slices
3 tablespoons sugar or to taste
1 teaspoon ground cinnamon or to taste

Melt the butter in a 12-inch sauté pan over medium heat and add the apples. Sprinkle with sugar and cinnamon to taste and cook until tender, stirring occasionally, about 8 to 10 minutes. Serve immediately.

Vanilla Belgian Waffles

Belgian waffles have a larger, more exaggerated honeycombed grid than standard waffles, which makes for a dramatic pooling of sweet syrups or sauces. Although any waffle recipe can be made in a Belgian waffle maker, this is a quick recipe to begin your experimentation. This batter is wonderful with a cup of fresh blueberries or pitted cherries gently folded in just before baking, and served with pure Vermont maple syrup. You may also substitute whole-wheat pastry flour for the unbleached flour. I've included a chocolate version to be served with a warm Brandied Orange Syrup (following) that is really special for after-theater or after-movie dessert gatherings. Belgian waffles are also spectacular topped with a thin wedge of Brie or Bel Paese soft cheese, then heated in a 350°F oven for about 4 minutes just to melt the cheese. Serve hot, ladled with defrosted frozen strawberries or raspberries in syrup—perfect on a rainy night in the dead of winter.

YIELD: 6 to 8 large waffles, depending on iron size

2 cups unbleached all-purpose flour
1 tablespoon baking powder
1 tablespoon sugar
Pinch of salt
3 eggs
½ cup (1 stick) unsalted butter, melted
1¼ cups milk
1 tablespoon pure vanilla extract

1. Preheat the Belgian waffle iron to medium-high or according to manufacturer's instructions. In a bowl, combine the flour, baking powder, sugar, and salt.

2. In another bowl, beat the eggs with a whisk or electric mixer until thick and foamy, about 2 minutes. Add the butter, milk, and vanilla extract. Add the dry ingredients and beat until smooth. Do not overmix.

3. Brush the waffle iron grids with oil or melted butter. For each waffle, pour about ⅔ to 1 cup of the batter onto the grid, depending on the size of your iron. Close the lid and bake until the waffle is crisp and well browned, about 4 to 5 minutes. Remove from the iron with a fork to protect your fingers. Serve immediately, or cool completely on racks, store in plastic bags, and freeze for up to 2 months.

CHOCOLATE BELGIAN WAFFLES

Add ½ cup unsweetened Dutch cocoa powder and 5 additional tablespoons sugar to the dry ingredients in Step 1. Mix and bake as for Vanilla Belgian Waffles. These are good served with Brandied Orange Syrup (following), or with Raspberry Purée (page 131).

BELGIAN WAFFLES WITH NUTS

Add ½ cup ground pecans, hazelnuts, walnuts, or almonds and 1 additional tablespoon sugar to the dry ingredients in Step 1. Mix and bake as for Vanilla Belgian Waffles. Serve with 1 cup of homemade Yogurt Cheese, mascarpone (page 118), or unsweetened whipped cream mixed with 3 tablespoons of hazelnut or other nut liqueur and fresh fruit.

BRANDIED ORANGE SYRUP

YIELD: About 2 cups

1 cup granulated sugar
½ cup orange juice concentrate
¼ cup water
¼ cup good-quality brandy or cognac
½ cup (1 stick) unsalted butter

In a medium saucepan, combine all the ingredients and bring to a boil, stirring with a whisk. Reduce for 1 to 2 minutes, or until thickened. (This can also be made in the microwave oven.) Remove from heat. Serve warm or chilled. For a more pronounced brandy flavor, stir in an extra tablespoon before serving.

~ Popovers and Oven Pancakes ~

From crusty deep golden to ruddy brown, puffed and airy popovers, also known as puffovers and mahogany cakes, are the miracles of the quick-bread world. Aerated solely by the power of beaten eggs and high baking temperatures, the thin crêpe-like batter with a high proportion of liquid must be *cold* and then baked at a high temperature for the outer surface of the popover to set properly. The moisture in the batter creates enough steam in its short time in the oven for a dramatic doming and almost hollow interior. Despite legions of recipes calling for preheated hot pans and preset oven temperatures as high as for baking pizza, popovers can also be baked just as successfully by placing in a cold oven before setting the temperature to medium-high, which gives the baker an easy alternative to juggling scalding equipment.

Making popovers is as simple as making oatmeal, but to ensure success it is essential that all instructions be followed precisely. The batter must have the correct proportions of liquid to flour to fat, although the recipes can be doubled or tripled with no problem. Popovers with added ingredients such as vegetables, herbs, or whole-grain flours will not rise quite as high as plain ones, so there is a limit to variations.

Ingredients are mixed with a whisk, rotary, or electric beater and refrigerated from one hour to overnight, if possible. Individual cups should be placed on a baking sheet for easiest handling and must be well greased with butter, oil, or a nonstick cooking spray such as Pam. Timing is quite crucial for a crisp crust and moist interior. Bake the popovers on the center rack of a cold oven set at 375°F. Overbaked popovers are very rigid, underbaked ones tend to collapse, and if the pan is not greased enough, they will stick mercilessly. To test for doneness, take one popover out of its pan. It should feel feather-light, be dry to the touch, and look golden brown.

There are many popover pans available, but I favor the heavy-duty black steel 4-inch Yorkshire pudding pans, with 6 deep oval cups suspended by a wire frame, available in gourmet cookware shops. These pans are also available in a commercial tinned steel family-size popover frame with 20 cups, made by Chicago Metallic, available in restaurant supply stores. All these frames make the classically shaped popover. If you use the black steel pans, reduce the oven temperature by 25°F during baking to prevent over-baking. The other excellent alternative for small popovers are heavy-gauge aluminum baba molds. They are tapered and measure approximately 3 by 2 inches. Other pans that can be used for popovers are individual 3½-by-2-inch heat-proof porcelain soufflé dishes, cast-iron gem pans, standard 2½-inch muffin tins, or individual 6-ounce Pyrex cups. Do not use thin aluminum equipment. Whatever receptacles are used, the cups should be deeper than wider for that traditional popover shape, hold about ⅓ cup batter each, and be filled no more than two-thirds full. Although wider popovers will not dome as high as smaller popovers made in deep cups (as in the baba molds), they are just as delicious. Miniature popovers, which are great for cocktails, can be made in 1¾-inch miniature or tartlet muffin pans. Oversized popovers can be made in 4½-inch fluted porcelain quiche dishes or 10-ounce Pyrex custard cups. Adjust the amount of batter, greasing, and baking time for small or oversized popovers. Some bakers make one large popover using a ceramic gratin dish or an 8-by-8-inch square Pyrex baking dish, filling it with all of the batter. After baking, it is served cut into wedges at the table.

Serve popovers instead of bread at any meal. They are as at

home alongside roasted meats for dinner as with eggs and jam for breakfast, but whatever the meal, they must be made fresh and eaten immediately. Consider using a sweet popover as you would a cream-puff pastry: remove the top dome, fill with ice cream, and serve with a hot fudge sauce. Fill split savory popovers with creamed poultry, seafood, or vegetables for brunch. And of course, the most famous of all popovers is a stalwart holiday addition: Yorkshire pudding, in which roasted meat fat is usually substituted in place of melted butter.

The recipes for oven pancakes use batters that are basically similar to popovers or crêpes, but are a lot less fussy. The baked pancake is the popular *pfankuchen* of German ancestry and rightly claims to be one of the easiest, yet most delicate of breakfast foods. The ingredients are pantry staples and the assembly time is very minimal. They make a spectacular savory light meal for a group, along with a salad and fruit; a mildly sweet brunch entrée; or a European-style dessert served with a sweet wine.

Mile-High Popovers

My girlfriend Julie loves dining in the casually elegant ambiance of the Thunderbird Bookstore & Cafe in Carmel Valley, where entrées are served in front of a cozy fireplace, accompanied by fresh-baked, hot popovers as the bread offering. Here is my attempt to re-create a recipe worthy of her description. I've included lots of variations, which will change the flavor significantly depending on the addition of whole grains, cheese, vegetables, herbs, or sweet spices. For a version with less fat, substitute 8 egg whites for the 6 whole eggs. If you want extra protection against sticking, line the bottom of the popover cups with parchment.

YIELD: 1 dozen popovers

6 large eggs
2 cups whole milk
2 cups unbleached all-purpose flour
4 tablespoons melted unsalted butter or
*   vegetable oil*
¼ teaspoon salt

1. In a 1-quart measuring cup with a pouring spout, using a whisk or hand rotary beater, or in an electric blender, beat the eggs until foamy. Add the milk, flour, melted butter or oil, and salt. Beat just until smooth. Do not overmix. Cover and refrigerate 1 hour to overnight.

2. Generously grease 12 popover or muffin cups, individual Pyrex or soufflé dishes, or baba molds with nonstick vegetable cooking spray, butter, or oil. Place the individual dishes so they are not touching on a baking sheet. Pour the batter into each cup until two-thirds full.

3. Place the pans in a cold oven and immediately set the temperature to 375°F. Bake 30 minutes *without opening the oven door.*

Bake 10 to 15 minutes more, until the popovers are firm and golden brown, piercing the side of each popover to allow steam to escape during this last phase of baking. Let cool briefly, again pricking each to allow the steam to escape. Remove from the molds by running a knife around the rim and inverting. Serve *immediately* while hot and puffy.

Note: Popovers can be made a day ahead and reheated. After baking, cool completely on a rack and place in an airtight plastic storage bag at room temperature up to 24 hours. To heat and recrisp, spread popovers spaced apart on a flat baking sheet and bake in a preheated 375°F oven until warm, about 5 to 7 minutes.

BRAN POPOVERS

Add ¼ cup miller's wheat, oat, or rice bran with the flour in Step 1. Proceed to mix and bake as for Mile-High Popovers.

CORNMEAL POPOVERS

Substitute ½ cup cornmeal or *masa harina* (tortilla flour) for an equal amount of unbleached flour and add with the flour in Step 1. Proceed to mix and bake as for Mile-High Popovers.

BUCKWHEAT POPOVERS

Substitute ⅓ cup light or dark buckwheat flour for an equal amount of unbleached flour and add with the flour in Step 1. Proceed to mix and bake as for Mile-High Popovers.

SPINACH POPOVERS

Stir ½ cup fresh chopped spinach leaves and ¼ teaspoon fresh-ground nutmeg into the batter in Step 1. Proceed to mix and bake as for Mile-High Popovers.

SUN-DRIED TOMATO AND BACON POPOVERS

Stir in ⅓ cup crumbled cooked bacon and 3 tablespoons minced sun-dried tomatoes into the batter in Step 1. Proceed to mix and bake as for Mile-High Popovers.

ROASTED GARLIC AND CHEDDAR POPOVERS

Substitute olive oil for the butter in Step 1. Stir in ½ cup shredded Cheddar cheese and about 6 large cloves roasted garlic (page 123) into the batter in Step 1. Proceed to mix and bake as for Mile-High Popovers. These work best if the pans are lined with parchment to prevent sticking.

PARMESAN-HERB POPOVERS

Stir in ½ cup shredded or grated Parmesan cheese and 2 tablespoons chopped fresh basil, dill, tarragon, or thyme into the batter in Step 1. Proceed to mix and bake as for Mile-High Popovers.

YORKSHIRE PUDDING WITH WILD RICE

Stir 1 cup cooled, cooked wild rice (page 125) into the popover batter in Step 1. Place 6 tablespoons unsalted butter (may be all or part roasted meat drippings, if available) in a 9-by-13-inch casserole or oval gratin dish and place in a preheated 425°F oven until melted and hot. Remove from the oven when sizzling and pour in the wild rice batter. Return to bake in the center of the oven until golden and puffed, about 25 to 30 minutes. Serve immediately, cut into squares.

SWEET CINNAMON POPOVERS

Add 2½ teaspoons ground cinnamon and 2 tablespoons brown sugar to the flour in Step 1. Proceed to mix and bake as for Mile-High Popovers.

ORANGE-NUT POPOVERS

Add 2 tablespoons ground walnuts, hazelnuts, pecans, or almonds, 2 tablespoons sugar, and the grated zest of 1 orange to the flour in Step 1. Proceed to mix and bake as for Mile-High Popovers.

Baked Pancake with Cucumber Salsa

~

A baked pancake is one big, puffy round, baked in the oven rather than on top of the stove. Also known as a "Dutch Baby," it looks and tastes like a delicate, oversized popover. This savory version is very popular because it is easy and fast to assemble and ready to serve in 20 minutes, giving the cook time to brew the coffee and set the table. Make the vegetable-laden Cucumber Salsa the night before to develop its flavor.

YIELD: Serves 4

4 tablespoons unsalted butter
3 eggs
¾ cup milk
⅔ cup unbleached all-purpose flour
3 tablespoons whole-wheat flour
½ cup grated Monterey Jack or crumbled goat cheese, such as French Montrachet or domestic chabi
Cucumber Salsa, following

1. Place the butter in 1 large or 4 individual gratin dishes, or in a 10-inch cast-iron skillet or deep pie plate. Place on the center rack of a preheated 400°F oven to melt the butter.

2. Meanwhile, in a small bowl, using a whisk, or in a blender or food processor, beat the eggs until foamy, about 1 minute. Add the milk and flours. Beat hard just until smooth.

3. Remove the hot pan from the oven and carefully pour in the batter. The pan will be less than half full. Bake 15 minutes, until puffy and golden. Sprinkle with the cheese and bake 5 minutes longer to melt the cheese. Serve immediately, cut into wedges and topped with spoonfuls of Cucumber Salsa.

CUCUMBER SALSA

YIELD: About 1½ cups

1 English cucumber, seeded and chopped
1 slightly underripe medium tomato, seeded,
  peeled, and chopped
1 fresh mild poblano, New Mexico, or
  Anaheim green chile, roasted, peeled,
  and minced (see page 123)
3 tablespoons finely chopped fresh cilantro
2 tablespoons good-quality olive oil
1 tablespoon red wine or apple cider vinegar
¼ teaspoon crushed hot pepper flakes, or to taste
1 small clove garlic, minced

Mix all ingredients together in a small bowl. Refrigerate, covered, 2 hours to overnight to meld flavors.

Mushroom Oven Pancake

~

This oven pancake is a heavenly brunch or light supper dish, and considering that medieval cooks believed that mushrooms sprang from bolts of lightning that hit the earth, it is heavenly in more than one sense. Sautéed cultivated or wild mushrooms are covered with a thin batter, baked until brown and puffy in the oven, and served with chilled Chive Sauce (following). This recipe is inspired by a recipe of Elizabeth Schneider, one of my favorite food writers and an earthy gourmand.

YIELD: Serves 4

6 tablespoons unsalted butter
1 pound fresh domestic or wild mushrooms, such
  as morel, shiitake, or oyster, stems removed
  and tops sliced
2 shallots, minced
Salt and fresh-ground pepper to taste
4 eggs
1¼ cups milk
1 cup unbleached all-purpose flour
Chive Sauce, following

1. Preheat oven to 400°F. In a heavy skillet over high heat, melt 4 tablespoons of the butter. When sizzling, add the sliced mushrooms and the shallots. Sauté until the mushrooms are just cooked and slightly browned and the liquid has evaporated, about 3 minutes. Season with salt and pepper. Remove from heat and set aside.

2. Place the remaining butter in 1 large or 4 individual gratin dishes, or in a 10-inch cast-iron skillet or deep pie plate. Place on the center rack of the preheated oven to melt butter.

3. Meanwhile, in a small bowl, using a whisk, or in a blender or food processor, beat the eggs until foamy, about 30 seconds. Add the milk and flour. Beat hard just until smooth.

4. Remove the hot pan from the oven and spread mushrooms over the bottom. Carefully pour the batter over the mushrooms. The pan will be about half full. Bake 20 to 25 minutes, until puffy and golden. Serve immediately, cut into wedges, with spoonfuls of Chive Sauce on the side.

CHIVE SAUCE

YIELD: About ¾ cup

⅓ cup plain yogurt
⅓ cup sour cream or crème fraîche
2 tablespoons minced fresh chives
1 tablespoon olive oil
1 tablespoon Dijon mustard

In a small bowl, combine the yogurt, sour cream or *crème fraîche*, chives, olive oil, and mustard with a whisk until blended. Decorate the top with a few chive blossoms, cover, and refrigerate until serving.

Baked Apple and Pear Oven Pancake

~

Serve this sweet *pfankuchen* hot from the oven sprinkled with a mist of powdered sugar and with lemon wedges. Or go for the gold by napping it with an elegant Berry Coulis (following).

YIELD: Serves 6

6 tablespoons unsalted butter
2 medium tart apples, such as Granny Smith, peeled, cored, and sliced
2 medium firm pears, such as Red Bartlett or Comice, peeled, cored, and sliced
⅓ cup light brown sugar
1½ teaspoons ground cinnamon
Juice of 1 lemon
6 eggs
1½ cups milk
1½ cups unbleached all-purpose flour
1 teaspoon vanilla extract
¼ teaspoon salt
Berry Coulis, following (optional)

1. Preheat oven to 425°F. Melt the butter in a skillet and sauté the apple and pear slices over medium-high heat just until tender, but still firm. Sprinkle with the brown sugar, cinnamon, and lemon juice. Stir to combine. Place a 12-inch round or 9-by-13-inch rectangular glass baking dish in the oven to heat for 2 minutes. Remove the baking dish with oven mitts and scrape the sautéed fruit into it. If the skillet is ovenproof, the fruit may be distributed evenly over the bottom.

2. In a bowl, using a whisk, or in a blender or food processor, mix together the eggs, milk, flour, vanilla extract, and salt until well blended and smooth. Pour the batter over the hot fruit. Immediately place the pancake in the oven and bake for about 20 minutes, until puffed and brown. Let stand 5 minutes before cutting into wedges. Serve immediately with Berry Coulis, if desired.

BERRY COULIS

YIELD: About 1½ cups

One 16-ounce package unsweetened frozen raspberries, strawberries, or boysenberries
1 to 2 tablespoons sugar
1/8 cup Chambord or orange liqueur

In a small bowl, place the berries and sprinkle with the sugar to taste. Let stand 30 minutes, or until defrosted. Add the liqueur and stir to combine. Cover and refrigerate 4 hours to overnight. Serve chilled over the hot Baked Apple and Pear Oven Pancake.

Quick Dough Breads

~ Scones and Soda Breads ~

Most recipes for scones and soda breads are the direct descendants of the nourishing whole-grain griddle breads prepared daily in rural Celtic and Scottish highland country kitchens. By nature they are coarse, crumbly, and chewy flat grain cakes. These were usually home fare, baked over peat fires, since they are best when mixed, baked, and eaten within a few hours. More and more, however, I am finding these marvelous quick dough breads have found a wider audience and have become the darlings of coffee houses and cafés.

With a few tips, scones are an easily made and satisfying addition to breakfast, tea, and hors d'oeuvres and the base for unusual sandwiches. They are at once tender, rich, flaky, and versatile. They are excellent plain or can be easily embellished with nuts, herbs, or even chocolate chips for flavor variations. They can be cut into endless shapes: wedges, squares, stars, hearts, or half-moons. Even better, they are fast to make. Entire preparation time for assembling, mixing, forming, and baking is about 45 minutes.

Use fresh ingredients such as aluminum-free baking powder, sweet butter, eggs, all-purpose and pastry flours for the best flavor. All types of flours, such as barley, oats, corn, rye, and bran, make beautiful scones. Liquids commonly used for moistening the dry ingredients include buttermilk, milk, yogurt, or cream.

Use the following techniques for perfect results: Quickly mix the dry ingredients with the cold fat to make big coarse crumbs, and when stirring in the cold liquid, a quick hand is again needed so the air is not forced out of the dough. This is especially important when the scones do not contain eggs to help with the leavening. Measure the liquids carefully to make a soft, pliable dough that is gently kneaded just until the dough holds together. Too much liquid makes a heavy scone that is hard to shape.

Knead briefly, just enough for the dough to come together, since overhandling will make a very tough and chewy scone. The kneading is not a vigorous technique as called for in yeast-bread making to activate the gluten, but a very gentle working just to form a cohesive ball.

When rolling out the scone, keep it thicker than ½ inch to achieve the best shape. For even browning, bake only one sheet at a time in the center of a preheated oven. They will rise double their raw size in the oven. Pay close attention to baking times. Always remember that after they are out of the oven, quick breads continue to cook during the cooling process, and overbaking makes them dry, a disaster for the texture of the scone.

After baking and cooling, scones and soda breads can be frozen in heavy-duty plastic freezer bags for up to a month and reheated in a warm oven for 5 to 8 minutes. The shaped raw dough can also be frozen on a parchment-lined baking sheet and placed in freezer bags when frozen. To bake, remove the frozen scones from the freezer, place on a parchment-lined baking sheet, and immediately bake in a preheated oven about 5 minutes longer than specified in the recipe.

Serve sweet scones with sweet butter, jams and preserves, fruit curds, honeys, yogurt cheese, homemade herb butters, or clotted and Devonshire creams. Savory scones are good served with such diverse foods as seafood salads with avocado mayonnaise, sliced meats with cornichons and honey mustard, and hard cheeses spread with chutney.

Also in this quick dough family are soda breads, the legendary homemade Celtic country hearth loaves popular for centuries in the bastions of Celtic culture since Roman times: Ireland, Wales, Cornwall, the Scottish Highlands, and Brittany. They are still very much alive, made today throughout the British Isles utilizing the same techniques as for scones. They have a thick, rather chunky crisp crust that when bitten into reveals a moist-textured interior. They are made with a variety of flours, but the very best are made with a proportion of Irish wheat, which is renowned for its wholesome flavor. In the United States, use a good-quality, very fresh, stone-ground whole-wheat flour as a substitute.

Traditionally, soda breads were baked over banked peat fires in a suspended cast-iron pot, on a bakestone or griddle, or in clay ovens. Now baked in modern conventional ovens, soda breads are still a beloved staple. If you own a baking stone, soda breads bake nicely on them.

Recipes for authentic loaves made in centuries past contained no baking powder or yeast; the sole leavening was bicarbonate of potash, or saleratus, an early form of modern baking soda, which gave the breads a unique tangy flavor. Baking soda and small amounts of baking powder are the leavenings used exclusively today. These breads are low in sugar and fat, yet high in fiber, so the flavors of the whole grains and fresh buttermilk speak for themselves. When making these ancient Celtic breads, I suggest beating the doughs in a "sunwise" (clockwise) direction, as per Druidic recipe instructions from the Middle Ages, to come as close to the authentic results as possible.

Maple Tea Scones with Homemade Devonshire Cream

Essentially a plain scone, its delicate undercurrent of maple flavor is subtle and barely sweet. I like these cut with a heart-shaped cutter and served barely cool, piled on a flat basket lined with giant fresh fig leaves for a dramatic presentation. They are an undisputed star on a brunch table, but you'll probably make them often as they also satisfy cravings for a "something special" little bread. The cool, creamy Homemade Devonshire Cream spread complements the hot scones with a bit of tang.

YIELD: 12 scones

3 cups unbleached all-purpose flour
1 tablespoon baking powder
½ teaspoon baking soda
¼ teaspoon salt
¾ cup (1½ sticks) cold unsalted butter,
  cut into pieces
½ cup milk
½ cup pure maple syrup
1½ teaspoons pure vanilla extract
Homemade Devonshire Cream, following

1. Preheat the oven to 375°F. In a medium bowl, combine the flour, baking powder, baking soda, and salt. Cut in the butter with a fork or a heavy-duty electric mixer until the mixture resembles coarse crumbs. In a 1-cup measure, combine the milk, maple syrup,

and vanilla extract. Add to the dry mixture and stir until a sticky dough is formed, adding a few more tablespoons milk if the dough is too stiff.

2. Turn out the shaggy dough onto a lightly floured work surface and knead gently just until the dough holds together, about 6 times. Divide into 3 equal portions and pat each into a 1-inch-thick round about 6 inches in diameter. With a knife or straight edge, cut each round into quarters, making 4 wedges. The scones can also be formed by cutting out with a 3-inch biscuit cutter.

3. Place the scones about 1 inch apart on a greased or parchment-lined baking sheet. Bake in the preheated oven until crusty and golden brown, 16 to 20 minutes. Serve immediately with jam and Homemade Devonshire Cream.

HOMEMADE DEVONSHIRE CREAM

YIELD: 1½ cups

½ cup heavy whipping cream
1 tablespoon powdered sugar
¾ cup cultured sour cream

In a clean mixing bowl, whip the heavy whipping cream with the powdered sugar until soft peaks form. Add the sour cream and beat until just fluffy and well combined. Scrape into a covered container and refrigerate until serving.

Old-Fashioned Lemon Cream Scones

~

One bite of this warm, homemade scone and you'll be transformed into a lover of these exquisitely simple tea breads. The crust should be a thin, slightly crunchy exterior band over a dense, yet moist and fluffy interior. The cream is important in producing the crumb, but substitute milk if you must. This basic recipe is the springboard for many variations, but I always come back to the plain scones. Served with butter and homemade Fresh Strawberry or Peach Jam (following), they cannot be beat. If you desire scones made with fresh summer berries, rather than mixing them into the dough, incorporate by gently sandwiching between two rounds of the dough and pinching the outer edges before cutting into wedges. This technique keeps the berries from being squashed, losing their shape, and bleeding heavily into the dough.

YIELD: 8 scones

2 cups unbleached all-purpose flour, unsifted

2 tablespoons sugar

1 tablespoon baking powder

Grated zest of 2 lemons

¼ teaspoon salt

4 tablespoons cold unsalted butter, cut into pieces

2 eggs

½ cup heavy cream

½ teaspoon ground cinnamon mixed with 2 tablespoons sugar for sprinkling (optional)

1. Preheat the oven to 400°F. In a medium bowl, combine the flour, sugar, baking powder, lemon zest, and salt. Cut in the butter with a fork or a heavy-duty electric mixer until the mixture resembles coarse crumbs. In a small bowl or 1-cup measure, whisk together the eggs and cream. Add to the dry mixture and stir until a sticky dough is formed.

2. Turn out the shaggy dough onto a lightly floured work surface and knead gently just until the dough holds together, about 6 times. Divide into 3 equal portions and pat each into a 1-inch-thick round about 6 inches in diameter. With a knife or straight edge, cut each round into quarters, making 4 wedges. The scones can also be formed by cutting out with a 3-inch biscuit cutter to make 10 to 12 smaller scones.

3. Place the scones about 1 inch apart on a greased or parchment-lined baking sheet. Sprinkle the tops with the cinnamon sugar, if desired. Bake in the preheated oven until crusty and golden brown, 15 to 20 minutes. Serve immediately with butter and homemade jam.

CURRANT LEMON CREAM SCONES

Add ⅔ cup dried currants to the dry ingredients in Step 1 of the Old-Fashioned Lemon Cream Scones. Mix, shape, and bake as directed. Dried blueberries, cranberries, or cherries may also be substituted.

FRESH ROSEMARY LEMON CREAM SCONES

Add 1 tablespoon fresh chopped rosemary to the dry ingredients in Step 1 of the Old-Fashioned Lemon Cream Scones. Mix, shape, and bake as directed.

CORNMEAL LEMON CREAM SCONES

Substitute ¾ cup fine-grind yellow, white, or blue cornmeal for an equal amount of flour in Step 1 of the Old-Fashioned Lemon Cream Scones. Mix, shape, and bake as directed.

DARK AND WHITE CHOCOLATE LEMON CREAM SCONES

Add ¼ cup each bittersweet and white chocolate chips to the dry ingredients in Step 1 of the Old-Fashioned Lemon Cream Scones. Mix, shape, and bake as directed.

HONEY LEMON CREAM SCONES

Substitute an equal amount of honey, preferably local, for the sugar and reduce the cream by 1 tablespoon in Step 1 of the Old-Fashioned Lemon Cream Scones. Mix, shape, and bake as directed. Brush the hot scones with additional warmed honey before serving.

FRESH STRAWBERRY JAM

Exceptional, chunky, fresh-fruit jams are easily made within half an hour. Homemade jams are less sweet than commercial jams and much more exciting in both flavor and color.

Using this recipe, you may substitute raspberries, blackberries, ollalaberries, or blueberries for the strawberries, but definitely taste while adding the sugar to adjust for differing tartness. For sophisticated palates, add ¼ cup good-quality cognac, port, or orange liqueur as the jam finishes cooking in Step 3. Use over- as well as under-ripe berries. Because they absorb water quickly, never float berries in water to clean, just rinse under running water.

The microwave is excellent for jam making because the sugar will not easily scorch, as it tends to do on the stovetop, although recipe instructions are included for both methods. The following recipes are geared to a 700-watt oven, so adjust the times accordingly if you have a different oven power. Pectin is important for thickening microwaved jams, as the liquid does not evaporate during cooking, resulting in a greater yield per batch than the stove-top method. If you decide to make the jam on the stove-top, expect less yield and more stirring. Store your homemade jams in a covered container in the refrigerator up to 2 months; freeze in plastic containers; or, more traditionally, process, pack, and seal in sterilized jars.

YIELD: About 8 cups (eight ½-pint jars)

2 quarts (8 cups) fresh strawberries, washed, drained, and hulled
One 1¾- or 2-ounce box powdered pectin
5 cups granulated sugar, or to taste

1. Coarsely crush the berries by hand or in the food processor, leaving a few whole berries or chunks, as desired, to make about 4 cups. Place in a deep stainless steel or enamel saucepan or deep straight-sided microwave-proof glass or porcelain casserole about three times the volume of the fruit, preferably with a pouring spout. Sprinkle with the pectin. Let stand 10 minutes.

2. Over medium-high heat on the stove-top, or on high power in the microwave, bring to a rolling boil that cannot be stirred down. Boil for about 8 minutes, uncovered. Add the sugar and stir well.

3. Bring the mixture back to a rolling boil over medium-high heat, or on high power for about 10 minutes in the microwave, stirring twice. Boil for exactly 1 minute. Remove from the heat and skim off the white foam with a large metal spoon. Stir occasionally for 10 minutes before ladling into storage jars such as French *confiture* glass jars with plastic lids, quilted jelly jars, or glass-topped jars with wire closures. Let stand until cool. Store, covered, in the refrigerator for up to 2 months.

FRESH PEACH JAM

Stone fruits, and all overripe fruits, are low in natural pectin and acid, so both powdered pectin and lemon juice need to be added to create a jam with substance and proper flavor balance. Please note that this recipe may vary in cooking time and may yield a different amount of jam each time you make it, depending on the juiciness and seasonal variations of the fruit.

YIELD: About 6 cups (six ½-pint jars)

4 cups peeled, pitted, and finely chopped fresh peaches
2 tablespoons fresh lemon juice
One 1¾- or 2-ounce box powdered pectin
3 to 3½ cups granulated sugar, or to taste

Follow directions for Fresh Strawberry Jam, preceding, adding the lemon juice to the fruit in Step 1. This recipe can also be used for unpeeled apricots, plums, and nectarines.

Crème Fraîche Scones

These are especially tender, unique scones with no extra added fat or eggs, apart from the *crème fraîche*. This recipe is adapted from the *Crème Fraîche Cookbook* by Sadie Kendall (Ridgeview Press, Box 686, Atascadero, CA 93423; © 1989). Sadie serves them with Homemade Mascarpone (page 118) and a Seville orange marmalade or a sublime rose-hip jelly. I like them coated with slivered blanched almonds before baking. They are especially good with a tablespoon of freshly grated nutmeg or pure vanilla extract added to the *crème fraîche* the night before mixing the dough.

YIELD: 8 scones

2 cups white cake flour or whole-wheat
    pastry flour
1 tablespoon sugar
2¼ teaspoons baking powder
¼ teaspoon salt
1¼ cups crème fraîche

1. Preheat the oven to 425°F. In a medium
bowl, combine the flour, sugar, baking powder, and salt. Cut in the *crème fraîche* with a
fork or a heavy-duty electric mixer until the
mixture makes a sticky, yet cohesive dough.

2. Turn the dough out onto a lightly floured
work surface and knead gently just until the
dough holds together, about 6 times. Divide
into 2 equal portions and pat each into a 1-
inch-thick round about 6 inches in diameter.
With a knife or straight edge, cut each round
into quarters, making 4 wedges. The scones
can also be formed by cutting out with a 2-
inch biscuit cutter to make 12 to 14 smaller
scones.

3. Place the scones about 1 inch apart on
a greased or parchment-lined baking sheet.
Bake in the preheated oven until crusty
and golden brown, about 15 to 18 minutes.
Serve immediately.

Oat Scones with Apple-Pear Butter

Oat scones are a crumbly and tender relative
of Scottish scones. They can be dressed up for
a special breakfast or tea by adding ½ cup
chopped moist, pitted dates to the batter and
serving them spread with Apple-Pear Butter.
Substitute an equal amount of barley flour for
the rolled oats to create another traditionally
flavored scone. Since the time my friend
Zelda left a pot of cinnamon basil on my
porch for a gift, I have become quite taken
with the intensely scented basils, including
the anise, lemon, and opal varieties. For a
subtle summer scone, bring the cream to a
boil with half a dozen fresh scented basil
leaves and chill overnight before removing
the leaves and using the infusion in the
following recipe.

YIELD: 12 scones

1 cup unbleached all-purpose flour or whole-
    wheat pastry flour
1 cup rolled oats
3 tablespoons light brown sugar
2 teaspoons baking powder
¼ teaspoon salt
6 tablespoons cold unsalted butter, cut
    into pieces
1 egg
½ cup half-and-half light cream
Apple-Pear Butter, following

1. Preheat the oven to 375°F. Combine the
flour and oats in the workbowl of a food processor and process until the oats are ground. In
a medium bowl, combine the flour-oat mixture, brown sugar, baking powder, and salt.
Cut in the butter with a fork or a heavy-duty
electric mixer until the mixture resembles
coarse crumbs. In a small bowl or 1-cup measure, whisk together the egg and half-and-
half. Add to the dry mixture and stir until a
sticky dough is formed.

2. Turn the dough out onto a lightly floured
work surface and knead gently just until
the dough holds together, about 6 times. Pat
the dough into a ¾-inch-thick round about
8 inches in diameter. Cut out the scones with
a 2-inch biscuit cutter to make 12 to 14
smaller scones.

3. Place the scones about 1 inch apart on a
greased or parchment-lined baking sheet.
Bake in the preheated oven until crusty and
golden brown, about 15 to 18 minutes. Serve
immediately, split in half and spread with
Apple-Pear Butter.

APPLE-PEAR BUTTER

YIELD: About 2 cups

¼ pound (2 cups) dried unsulphered
   sliced apples
2 ounces (1 cup) dried pears
2 cups unsweetened apple or pear juice
2 teaspoons ground cinnamon
1 teaspoon ground allspice
½ teaspoon ground cloves
2 tablespoons unsalted butter

Combine all the ingredients in a heavy
saucepan and bring to a boil. Reduce heat to
a simmer and cook, uncovered, for 30 minutes, stirring occasionally. Remove from the
heat, stir in the butter, and cool. Purée the
apple-pear butter in a blender or food processor until smooth. Scrape into a springtop
glass jar and refrigerate until needed. Keeps
for about 2 months.

Oat Bran Scones with Dried Apricots

Oat bran is milder in flavor than wheat bran
and seems to have found a permanent home
in the whole-grain stable for bakers. It has a
natural sweet flavor that is inherent to the oat
family, and it combines with dried fruits and
other grains to create baked goods with a
unique hearty texture. Tuck these alongside a
plate of scrambled brown eggs for breakfast,
spread with luscious Apricot-Orange Curd.
YIELD: 12 small scones

⅔ cup chopped dried apricots
1½ cups unbleached all-purpose flour
½ cup oat bran, ground in a blender or
   food processor for a finer texture
2 tablespoons light brown sugar
1 tablespoon baking powder
¼ teaspoon salt
5 tablespoons cold unsalted butter, cut
   into pieces
¾ cup cold cultured buttermilk
⅓ cup rolled oats for sprinkling
Apricot-Orange Curd, following (optional)

1. In a small bowl, cover the dried apricots
with boiling water and let stand 10 minutes.

2. Preheat the oven to 400°F. In a medium
bowl, combine the flour, oat bran, brown
sugar, baking powder, and salt. Cut in the
butter with a fork or a heavy-duty electric
mixer until the mixture resembles coarse
crumbs. Drain the plumped dried apricots
and add to the dry mixture along with
the buttermilk. Stir until a sticky dough
is formed.

3. Turn the dough out onto a lightly floured
work surface and knead gently just until the
dough holds together, about 6 times. Divide
into 3 equal portions and pat each into a 1-
inch-thick round about 4 inches in diameter.
With a knife or straight edge, cut each round
into quarters, making 4 wedges. The scones
can also be formed by cutting out with a 2-
inch biscuit cutter to make 12 to 14 smaller
scones.

4. Place the scones about 1 inch apart on a
greased or parchment-lined baking sheet that
has been sprinkled with the rolled oats. Bake
in the preheated oven until crusty and golden
brown, about 15 to 18 minutes. Serve immediately with Apricot-Orange Curd, if desired.

WHEAT BRAN SCONES WITH DRIED CRANBERRIES

Substitute an equal amount of dried cranberries for the dried apricots in Step 1. Substitute an equal amount of All-Bran commercial
whole-grain cereal for the oat bran in Step 2.
Continue to mix, shape, and bake as for Oat
Bran Scones with Dried Apricots.

APRICOT-ORANGE CURD

An age-old spread for toasted English muffins, waffles, and fresh scones is this thick jam
made with eggs and citrus. Heat the whole
lime in the microwave for 30 seconds to yield
more juice when squeezing.
YIELD: About 2 cups

½ cup (1 stick) unsalted butter
6 dried apricot halves, soaked in boiling water
   for 20 minutes and drained
⅔ cup thawed frozen orange juice concentrate
Grated zest of 2 oranges
Juice of 1 lime
⅔ cup sugar
4 eggs
2 egg yolks

Melt the butter in the top section of a double boiler. In a blender or food processor, purée the apricots with the orange juice concentrate. Add the remaining ingredients and blend until well combined. With the water at a simmer, slowly add the apricot-egg mixture to the butter, stirring constantly with a whisk. Cook over medium heat, stirring constantly, until thickened, a full 10 minutes. Pour into a jar and let cool slightly before storing in the refrigerator, covered, for up to 3 weeks.

Fig-Walnut Scones

California is the home of beautiful black, amber, and violet figs: the Mission (or Franciscana), the Kadota (or Italian Dottato), and the Calimyrna (or Smyrna). Figs survived the Ice Age along with the olive, and I certainly am glad they did. A lover of temperate weather, the fig is a prolific and succulent summer fruit with deeply lobed green leaves that I often use as decoration. The dried fruit is intensely sweet and naturally deeply nourishing. If you love buttermilk scones, as I do, this combination of nuts and fruit will give you a good reason to make them more often.
YIELD: 12 scones

3 cups unbleached all-purpose flour
⅓ cup sugar
1 tablespoon baking powder
½ teaspoon baking soda
½ teaspoon salt
Grated zest of 1 orange
¾ cup (1½ sticks) cold unsalted butter, cut into small pieces
¾ cup coarsely chopped dried figs
½ cup chopped walnuts
1 cup cold cultured buttermilk
2 tablespoons sugar mixed with ¼ teaspoon each ground cinnamon, allspice, and mace, for sprinkling

1. Preheat the oven to 400°F. In a medium bowl, combine the flour, sugar, baking powder, baking soda, salt, and zest. Cut in the butter with a fork or a heavy-duty electric mixer until the mixture resembles coarse crumbs. Stir in the figs and walnuts. Add the buttermilk to the dry mixture and stir until a sticky dough is formed.

2. Turn out the shaggy dough onto a lightly floured work surface and knead gently just until the dough holds together, about 6 times. Divide into 3 equal portions and pat each into a 1-inch-thick round about 6 inches in diameter. With a knife or straight edge, cut each round into quarters, making 4 wedges. The scones can also be formed by cutting out with a 2-inch biscuit cutter to make 12 to 14 smaller scones. Sprinkle the tops lightly with the spiced-sugar mixture.

3. Place the scones about 1 inch apart on a greased or parchment-lined baking sheet. Bake in the preheated oven until crusty and golden brown, 15 to 20 minutes. Serve immediately.

FRESH CRANBERRY–WALNUT SCONES

Substitute 1½ cups whole fresh or frozen unthawed cranberries or 1 cup dried cranberries for the dried figs in Step 1 of the Fig-Walnut Scones. Mix, shape, and bake as directed.

Graham Scones with Pine Nuts and Golden Raisins

These days we all know the virtues of whole-grain flour: the fiber, the carbohydrates, the vitamins and minerals—good nutrition in every bite. But beyond these virtues is the gloriously nutty flavor that is totally unique to graham flour, a special grind of whole wheat. Although fresh whole-wheat flour is perfectly acceptable, please search out coarse-textured graham flour for these scones, and savor the taste. For more information on whole-grain flours, please refer to Notes from the Kitchen (page 120).
YIELD: 8 scones

2¼ cups graham or finely ground
    whole-wheat flour
3 tablespoons light brown sugar
2 teaspoons baking powder
½ teaspoon baking soda
¼ teaspoon salt
½ cup (1 stick) cold unsalted butter,
    cut into pieces
½ cup pine nuts
½ cup golden raisins
2 eggs
⅔ cup cultured buttermilk

1. Preheat the oven to 400°F. In a medium
bowl, combine the flour, brown sugar, baking
powder, baking soda, and salt. Cut in the
butter with a fork or a heavy-duty electric
mixer until the mixture resembles coarse
crumbs. Add the pine nuts and the golden
raisins. Toss to combine. In a small bowl
or 1-cup measure, whisk together the eggs
and buttermilk. Add to the dry mixture
and stir until a sticky dough is formed.

2. Turn out the shaggy dough onto a lightly
floured work surface and knead gently just
until the dough holds together, about 6
times. Divide into 3 equal portions and pat
each into a 1-inch-thick round about 6 inches
in diameter. With a knife or straight edge,
cut each round into quarters, making 4
wedges. The scones can also be formed by
cutting out with a 2-inch biscuit cutter to
make 12 to 14 smaller scones.

3. Place the scones about 1 inch apart on a
greased or parchment-lined baking sheet.
Bake in the preheated oven until crusty and
golden brown, 15 to 20 minutes. Serve
immediately.

Santa Fe Scones

The flavors of the Southwest have leapt
into middle America's kitchens with a passion. Creamy mild Monterey Jack cheese,
pungent red chili powder, sweet cornmeal,
and crunchy fresh red bell peppers make
a savory scone good served with egg dishes
for brunch or alongside supper entrées.
YIELD: 8 scones

2 cups unbleached all-purpose flour
½ cup fine-grind yellow, white, or blue
    cornmeal, preferably stone-ground
1 tablespoon baking powder
1 teaspoon commercial or homemade chili
    powder, page 66
¼ teaspoon each cumin and salt
½ cup (1 stick) cold unsalted butter,
    cut into pieces
2 ounces (½ cup) Monterey Jack cheese,
    cut into small cubes
½ cup minced raw red bell pepper, drained
    on a paper towel
2 eggs
¾ cup cold cultured buttermilk

1. Preheat the oven to 400°F. In a medium
bowl, combine the flour, cornmeal, baking
powder, chili powder, cumin, and salt. Cut in
the butter with a fork or a heavy-duty electric mixer until the mixture resembles coarse
crumbs. Add the cheese and red pepper. Toss
to combine. In a small bowl or 1-cup measure, whisk together the eggs and buttermilk. Add to the dry mixture and stir until
a sticky dough is formed.

2. Turn out the shaggy dough onto a lightly
floured work surface and knead gently just
until the dough holds together, about 6
times. Divide into 2 equal portions and pat
each into a 1-inch-thick round about 6 inches
in diameter. With a knife or straight edge,
cut each round into quarters, making 4
wedges. The scones can also be formed by
cutting out with a 2-inch biscuit cutter
to make 12 to 14 smaller scones.

3. Place the scones on a greased or parchment-lined baking sheet about 1 inch apart.
Bake in the preheated oven until crusty
and golden brown, about 15 to 18 minutes.
Serve immediately.

Soda Bread with Caraway and Drambuie

~

Soda breads are Celtic country hearth breads made throughout the British Isles and originally baked in the wood-fired clay ovens built into home chimneys. It is a bread easily mixed and baked, ready to serve to hungry diners in less than an hour. Drambuie is a romantic, Gaelic liqueur made of good Scotch malt whiskey, heather honey, and a secret collection of spices. Soda breads beg to be eaten crusty and warm, spread with butter or served with cheeses.

YIELD: 2 medium free-form round loaves

1½ cups golden raisins
6 tablespoons Drambuie liqueur
2 cups unbleached all-purpose flour
2 cups whole-wheat flour, preferably
    stone-ground
¼ cup light brown sugar
2 teaspoons baking powder
1 teaspoon baking soda
1 teaspoon salt
1 tablespoon caraway seeds
1½ cups cultured buttermilk
2 eggs
2 tablespoons unsalted butter, melted

1. Combine the raisins and liqueur in a small bowl. Let stand at room temperature to macerate 30 minutes.

2. Preheat oven to 375°F. In a large bowl, combine the flours, sugar, baking powder, baking soda, salt, and caraway seeds. In another bowl, combine the buttermilk, eggs, and butter and beat slightly with a whisk. Add the macerated raisins.

3. Make a well in the dry ingredients and pour in the buttermilk-raisin mixture. Stir with a wooden spoon just to moisten. The dough will not be as stiff as yeast bread dough. Turn out onto a lightly floured work surface and knead gently until the dough comes together, about 5 times. Form into 2 free-form round loaves by hand and place on a greased or parchment-lined baking sheet or into two 8-inch cake pans. With a serrated knife, make a cross no more than ¼ inch deep on each top to allow for expansion and even baking.

4. Bake in the center of the preheated oven until breads sound hollow when tapped and are brown and crusty, about 40 to 50 minutes. Remove from pans to cool on a rack. Serve warm or at room temperature the same day it is made.

Whole-Wheat Yogurt Bread with Dried Cherries

~

Whole-Wheat Yogurt Bread is low in fat, because there is no butter or eggs in the recipe, in the manner of a traditional soda bread. I have been making this versatile loaf in one form or another for twenty years, serving it for lunch alongside a fresh green salad and a piece of good cheese. This loaf is especially good toasted and spread with homemade Yogurt Cheese (page 118). Mixed dried fruit, dark or golden raisins may be substituted for the dried cherries, if necessary. Please do not forget to slash the X on top to keep the loaf from cracking open during baking and to annoy the devil.

YIELD: 2 small free-form round loaves

2 cups whole-wheat flour,
    preferably stone-ground
¾ cup unbleached all purpose flour
¼ cup wheat bran flakes
2 teaspoons baking soda
½ teaspoon salt
2 cups plain yogurt
⅓ cup light molasses
1 cup dried cherries, soaked in hot water
    10 minutes and drained

1. Preheat oven to 350°F. In a medium mixing bowl, combine the flours, bran, baking soda, and salt. In another bowl, combine the yogurt, molasses, and dried cherries and beat slightly with a whisk.

2. Make a well in the dry ingredients and pour in the wet ingredients. Stir just until moistened. The dough will be very soft, even slightly sticky, and just be able to hold its own shape. Divide into 2 free-form round loaves by hand and turn out onto a greased or parchment-lined baking sheet or into two 8-inch cake pans. The loaves will be rough and cracked looking with some flour on the surface.

3. Bake in the center of the preheated oven until breads sound hollow when tapped and are brown and crusty, about 55 to 60 minutes. Remove from pans to cool on a rack. Serve warm or at room temperature the same day it is made.

Wild Rice Whole-Wheat Soda Bread with Goat Cheese Butter

~

This is a connoisseur's soda bread—pure American ingredients in a traditional setting. Wholesome and sweet, whole-wheat soda breads are certainly not unusual, but the wild rice in this version gives a moist and complex earthy character I find inspiring. I can almost believe a soul lies within each grain, as

the Chinese say. With this I serve my favorite mellow goat cheese spread, its flavor tempered with a mild cream cheese.

YIELD: 2 small free-form round loaves

2 cups whole-wheat flour,
    preferably stone-ground
1 cup unbleached all-purpose flour
½ cup rolled oats
2 tablespoons light brown sugar
1 teaspoon baking soda
½ teaspoon salt
½ cup cooked wild rice (page xx)
1¼ cups cultured buttermilk
2 tablespoons unsalted butter, melted
1 egg
Goat Cheese Butter, following (optional)

1. Preheat oven to 350°F. In a medium bowl, combine the flours, oats, brown sugar, baking soda, and salt. In another bowl, combine the wild rice, buttermilk, melted butter, and egg and beat slightly with a whisk.

2. Make a well in the dry ingredients and pour in the wet ingredients. Stir just until moistened. Turn out onto a lightly floured work surface and knead gently until dough comes together, about 5 times. Form into 2 free-form round loaves by hand and place on a greased or parchment-lined baking sheet or into two 8-inch cake pans. With a serrated knife, make a cross no more than ¼ inch deep on each top to allow for expansion and even baking.

3. Bake in the center of the preheated oven until breads sound hollow when tapped and are brown and crusty, about 40 to 50 minutes. Remove from pans to cool on a rack. Serve warm or at room temperature the same day it is made, with Goat Cheese Butter, if desired.

GOAT CHEESE BUTTER

YIELD: About 1½ cups

4 ounces fresh cream cheese, room temperature
4 ounces fresh goat cheese, such as French
    Montrachet or domestic chabi
½ cup (1 stick) unsalted butter,
    room temperature
Grated zest of ½ orange, optional

By hand in a bowl, or in a food processor, combine the cream cheese, goat cheese, and butter and beat just until smooth, fluffy, and evenly combined. Transfer to a small serving dish or decorative mold and sprinkle the top with the zest. Chill, covered, 1 hour to overnight. Let stand at room temperature 30 minutes before serving.

~ Biscuits and Shortcakes ~

In some households, biscuits are still *the* bread. Whether served for breakfast with jam, hot with cool salads, cold as a small sandwich, or even as a shortcake for dessert, biscuits can grace the most sophisticated dinner table with pride. The most memorable shortcakes I have ever eaten were served to me at the grand opening of Fetzer Vineyards' Valley Oaks Food and Wine Center in Hopland, California. Under a beautiful outdoor arbor, Chef Ralph Tingle served traditional strawberry shortcakes in charming individual bite-sized portions. I will never take a berry shortcake for granted again.

Historically known as "saleratus biscuits" because of the type of leavening used in making them, the satisfying little breads had a quick-to-make and quick-to-bake reputation. Whether baked in old northeast and Appalachian cookstoves, southern plantations, outdoor Dutch ovens, or New York tea rooms, the biscuit quickly became a daily staple. They were firmly adopted by the male-centered cuisine of cowboys, lumberjacks, sea cooks, and Alaskan fishing camps. The simple bread could be made without expensive eggs, unreliable yeasts, and long baking times.

Southern cooks claim the honor of being the best biscuit makers. To achieve their superior results they use smoky-tasting homemade lard (*not* the same as super-processed commercial brands), the softest wheat pastry flour, and a good, strong 30-minute beating to tenderize the dough. But perfect biscuits are available to any baker who sets his or her mind to searching out a good recipe and fresh ingredients, and to following instructions carefully. A warm biscuit fresh from the oven is worth the time invested, even if you live above the Mason-Dixon line and don't own a biscuit brake for folding the beaten biscuit dough.

Many biscuit bakers swear by sifting the flour. If your goal is the most tender biscuits ever, then do it, but you can use your own judgement. The South boasts pure flours milled to a delicate lightness specifically for biscuits, such as White Lily, but all-purpose flour is also used. The War Eagle Grist Mill in Arkansas packages their own whole-grain biscuit mix, as do many small local mills. Another secret is *fresh* baking powder; less than 4 months old is best. Aside from the basic ingredients, biscuits can be further enhanced with the addition of whole grains, chopped fruits, nuts, and citrus rinds for truly endless variations. For shortcakes, sugar is added.

The techniques for making biscuits and shortcakes are very simple. Some type of ice-cold vegetable shortening, salted or unsalted butter, margarine, lard, even bear fat (yes, they are all interchangeable; it is the flavor that will vary) is cut into a mixture of flour, baking powder, and salt. Generally, 2 to 3 tablespoons of fat per cup of flour is the ratio to look for. The swift motion of the fingers, a pastry blender, fork, or two knives may be used to break up the fat to form coarse crumbs. (An electric mixer or food processor makes good biscuits, but taking care not to overmix is important.) It is this step that gives biscuits their unique flaky texture and makes them different than other types of quick breads. The moisture that evaporates from the cold fat in contact with the hot temperature during the baking creates a fine-grained layering effect similar to French puff pastry.

Cold liquid, usually heavy cream, buttermilk, or milk, is added all at once and stirred to create a soft dough that just holds together. Any other wet ingredients, such as pure extracts, juices, or eggs, are added at this time. Always reserve about 2 tablespoons of liquid to add after mixing if the dough is too dry. To form drop biscuits, add at least ¼ cup more liquid. They are not as delicate as their rolled cousins, but very good indeed. The secret to delicate biscuits is to handle the dough gently and to use just enough flour to make the dough manageable. Use a light touch to knead the very soft dough a few times with the heel of the hand and distribute the moisture gently by a soft folding and rolling action. This step is necessary for tender biscuits, but too much kneading makes them tough. Flour is used very sparingly for dusting, just to keep the delicate dough from sticking to the work surface, your hands, and the biscuit cutters. Keep a collection of cutters in a range of sizes and shapes, from the practical fluted round to the whimsical half-moon, for the greatest variety in shaping biscuits.

Roll or pat the dough to a thickness half the size you want the finished biscuit to be. A sharp cutter is pressed straight down into the dough with one push. No twisting or the biscuit will bake unevenly. Biscuits cut from the first rolling are more tender than those cut from subsequent rollings. Square biscuits are cut into a grid with a chef's knife. After they are cut, for even greater height, you can invert the dough onto the pre-pared baking sheet. To reroll, press the scraps together rather than kneading again, keeping the top surface as level as possible for an even biscuit.

Crisp-sided biscuits are made by placing the raw dough ½ inch to 2 inches apart to allow for expansion, on an ungreased or parchment-lined baking sheet. For soft sides, let the raw shapes slightly touch. The tops can be brushed with milk or melted butter for shiny, soft crusts. A superhot oven is imperative, so watch cooking times care-fully. Smaller sizes will bake to a golden brown faster than larger shapes. Although biscuits can be eaten hot from the oven, it is best to allow them to rest a few minutes after baking to allow excess moisture to evaporate. Every so often there is a stray leftover, so wrap the day-olds in foil and reheat at 325°F for 10 to 12 minutes. Biscuits can also be frozen in plastic freezer bags up to 2 months.

To Make Biscuits and Shortcakes in a Food Processor:

Place the dry ingredients in the workbowl fitted with the steel blade. Process a few sec-onds just to aerate and mix. Place the butter in pieces on top of the flour mixture and replace the top. Process by pulsing *just* until the butter is the size of small peas. Do not completely incorporate the butter with the flour or the biscuits will be tough. Add the cold liquid through the feed tube and pulse *just* until a wet mass is formed. Remove the dough from the workbowl and continue to form and bake as per the specific recipe.

Classic Buttermilk Biscuits

~

This classic buttermilk biscuit has a propor-tion of three parts dry ingredients to one part tangy liquid to create a dough that will bake high and crisp-crusted. They sit as easily, fresh and hot, at a regal dinner as they do rewarmed and slightly chewy, spread with jam the next morning. A springboard to in-finite flavor possibilities, the variations on the original recipe range from Pecan to Jalapeño to Blueberry, all superb. Please try them.

YIELD: About 1 dozen 2-inch dinner bis-cuits, or 2 dozen 1¼-inch cocktail biscuits

2 cups unbleached all-purpose flour
2 teaspoons baking powder
¼ teaspoon baking soda
¼ teaspoon salt
6 tablespoons cold unsalted butter, margarine,
*   or solid vegetable shortening, cut into pieces*
1 egg
¾ cup cold cultured buttermilk
2 tablespoons each flour and cornmeal
*   for sprinkling*

1. Preheat the oven to 425°F. In a bowl, combine the flour, baking powder, baking soda, and salt.

2. Cut the butter into the dry ingredients with a pastry blender or 2 knives. The mix-ture will resemble coarse crumbs, with no large chunks of butter. If the butter gets very soft at this point, refrigerate the mixture for 20 minutes to rechill. Add the egg and buttermilk, stirring just to moisten all the ingredients. The dough will be moist, then stiffen while stirring. It should be slightly shaggy, but not sticky.

3. Turn the dough out onto a lightly floured work surface and knead gently about 10 times, or just until the dough holds together. Roll or pat out the dough into a rectangle to a thickness of ¾ inch. Take care not to add too much flour at this point or the biscuits will be tough. Cut with a floured 2½-inch biscuit cutter, pushing straight down without twisting. Cut as close together as possible for a minimum of scraps. Pack together and reroll the scraps to cut out additional biscuits.

4. Place ½ inch apart on a greased or parchment-lined baking sheet that has been sprinkled with 2 tablespoons each flour and cornmeal. Bake immediately in the preheated oven 15 to 18 minutes, or until golden brown. Let rest a few minutes and serve hot.

PECAN BISCUITS

Add ⅓ cup coarsely chopped toasted or raw pecans to the dry ingredients in Step 1. Proceed to mix, form, and bake as for Classic Buttermilk Biscuits. For tea biscuits, add 3 tablespoons of sugar.

WILD RICE BISCUITS

Add ⅔ cup cooled, cooked wild rice (page 125) to the dry ingredients in Step 1. Proceed to mix, form, and bake as for Classic Buttermilk Biscuits.

JALAPEÑO BISCUITS

Add ¼ cup coarsely chopped fresh or canned jalapeños to the liquid ingredients in Step 2. Proceed to mix, form, and bake as for Classic Buttermilk Biscuits.

BLUEBERRY BISCUITS

Add ¼ cup sugar to the dry ingredients in Step 1. Add ½ cup fresh or frozen, unthawed blueberries and the grated zest of 1 orange to the liquid ingredients in Step 2. Proceed to mix, form, and bake as for Classic Buttermilk Biscuits.

WHOLE-WHEAT BISCUITS

Substitute ¾ cup whole-wheat flour or 2 cups whole-wheat pastry flour for an equal amount of unbleached flour and add to the dry ingredients in Step 1. Proceed to mix, form, and bake as for Classic Buttermilk Biscuits.

Old-Fashioned Cream Biscuits

~

Cream Biscuits are as special as they are simple. They are made with heavy cream, which provides both the liquid and fat, to create a creamy-colored, moist-textured little bread. If you love biscuits, these old-fashioned gems are the apex of the genre.
YIELD: About 14 biscuits

1¾ cups unbleached all-purpose flour
¼ cup whole-wheat pastry flour
1 tablespoon baking powder
½ teaspoon salt
1 to 1¼ cups cold heavy cream

1. In a mixing bowl, combine the flours, baking powder, and salt. Stir in 1 cup of heavy cream, then add additional cream, 1 tablespoon at a time, until a soft dough is formed.

2. Turn the dough out onto a lightly floured work surface and knead gently about 10 times, or just until the dough holds together. Roll or pat out the dough into a rectangle to a thickness of ¾ inch. Take care not to add too much flour at this point or the biscuits will be tough. Cut with a sharp knife or pastry wheel to form 14 squares. Alternatively, cut out with a floured 2½-inch biscuit cutter (I like the half-moon shape for these), pushing straight down without twisting, and rerolling the scraps to cut out additional biscuits.

3. Preheat the oven to 425°F. Place ½ inch apart on a greased or parchment-lined baking sheet. Let stand 20 minutes at room temperature. Bake in the preheated oven 15 to 18 minutes, or until golden brown. Let rest a few minutes and serve hot.

SUMMER CREAM BISCUITS

Add ¼ cup total coarsely chopped combination of fresh watercress leaves, Italian parsley, and basil to the dry ingredients in Step 1. Proceed to mix, form, and bake as for Old-Fashioned Cream Biscuits.

BREAKFAST ORANGE CREAM BISCUITS

Substitute ½ cup fresh or frozen orange juice and the grated zest of 1 large orange for an equal amount of the heavy cream in Step 1. Proceed to mix, form, and bake as for Old-Fashioned Cream Biscuits.

Cornmeal-Orange Biscuits

Enjoy Cornmeal-Orange Biscuits made with the juice of fresh oranges, picked from your backyard tree, if possible. Otherwise, search out juicy California or Florida orbs. The nubby texture of cornmeal mingling with the orange undertones makes a mouth-watering dinner or brunch biscuit that will find its way into your cache of best recipes.

YIELD: 16 square biscuits

3 cups unbleached all-purpose flour
1 cup fine-grind yellow cornmeal, preferably
* stone-ground*
2 tablespoons each baking powder and sugar
1 teaspoon cream of tartar
½ teaspoon salt
Grated zest of 1 large orange
¾ cup (1½ sticks) cold unsalted butter,
* cut into pieces*
1 cup cold cultured buttermilk
½ cup fresh orange juice
2 tablespoons each flour and cornmeal
* for sprinkling*

1. Preheat the oven to 425°F. In a bowl, combine the flour, cornmeal, baking powder, sugar, cream of tartar, salt, and zest.

2. Cut the butter into the dry ingredients with a pastry blender or 2 knives. The mixture will resemble coarse crumbs, with no large chunks of butter. Add the buttermilk and orange juice and stir just to moisten all the ingredients. The dough will be moist, then stiffen while stirring. It should be slightly shaggy, but not sticky.

3. Turn the dough out onto a lightly floured work surface and knead gently about 10 times, or just until the dough holds together. Roll or pat out the dough into a ¾-inch-thick rectangle. Take care not to add too much flour at this point or the biscuits will be tough. Cut with a sharp knife or pastry wheel to form 16 small squares.

4. Place ½ inch apart on a greased or parchment-lined baking sheet that has been sprinkled with 2 tablespoons each flour and cornmeal. Bake immediately in the preheated oven 15 to 18 minutes, or until golden brown. Let rest a few minutes and serve hot.

Sweet-Potato Biscuits

I have been making these biscuits every fall for years and I still adore them. The sweet potato makes them dense, sweet, and moist. They are as excellent served with roasted and grilled meats as they are with butter and honey. Sweet-Potato Biscuits are a must for winter holiday tables and for a filling hors d'oeuvre, sandwiching slices of smoked turkey.

YIELD: About 1 dozen biscuits

1 large sweet potato or yam (about 10 ounces),
* baked and peeled*
1 ⅔ cups unbleached all-purpose flour
1 tablespoon light brown sugar
2½ teaspoons baking powder
½ teaspoon salt
6 tablespoons cold unsalted butter,
* cut into pieces*
¼ cup cold milk or cream

1. Mash or purée the sweet potato pulp by hand, in a blender, or in a food processor until smooth to make ¾ cup total. Preheat the oven to 425°F. In a bowl, combine the flour, sugar, baking powder, and salt.

2. Cut the butter into the dry ingredients with a pastry blender or 2 knives. The mixture will resemble coarse crumbs, with no large chunks of butter. Add the sweet potato pulp and milk or cream and stir just to moisten all the ingredients. The dough will be moist, then stiffen while stirring. It should be slightly shaggy, but not sticky.

3. Turn the dough out onto a lightly floured work surface and knead gently about 10 times, or just until the dough holds together. Roll or pat out the dough into a ¾-inch-thick rectangle. Take care not to add too much flour at this point or the biscuits will

be tough. Cut with a floured 2-inch biscuit cutter, pushing straight down without twisting. Reroll the scraps to cut out additional biscuits.

4. Place ½ inch apart on a greased or parchment-lined baking sheet. Bake immediately in the preheated oven 15 to 18 minutes, or until golden brown. Let rest a few minutes and serve hot.

Poppy Seed-Cheese Biscuits
~

Here is a dinner biscuit with a crisp crust, tender texture, golden color, and lofty sides that give a tempting glimpse into a multitude of flaky layers. The cheese is so good with the poppy seed topping, you'll be glad to have made a big batch. Poppy Seed–Cheese Biscuits put to shame the premade commercial types that come from pop-open cans. For before-dinner snacks, cut the biscuits into smaller squares to make about 40 to 48 hot appetizers.
YIELD: About 24 biscuits

3 cups unbleached all-purpose flour
½ cup nonfat dry milk powder
⅓ cup grated mozzarella cheese
⅓ cup grated sharp New York cheddar cheese
¼ cup toasted wheat germ
4 teaspoons baking powder
¾ teaspoon cream of tartar
½ teaspoon salt

¾ cup (1½ sticks) cold unsalted butter, cut into pieces
1 egg
1¼ cups cold water
2 tablespoons each flour and wheat germ for sprinkling
1 egg beaten with 1 teaspoon water for glaze
3 tablespoons poppy seeds for sprinkling tops

1. Preheat the oven to 375°F. In a bowl, combine the flour, milk powder, cheeses, wheat germ, baking powder, cream of tartar, and salt.

2. Cut the butter into the dry ingredients with a pastry blender or 2 knives. The mixture will resemble coarse crumbs, with no large chunks of butter. Add the egg and cold water and stir just to moisten all the ingredients. The dough will be moist, then stiffen while stirring. It should be slightly shaggy, but not sticky.

3. Turn the dough out onto a lightly floured work surface and knead gently about 10 times, or just until the dough holds together. Roll or pat out the dough into a 1-inch-thick rectangle. Take care not to add too much flour at this point or the biscuits will be tough. Cut with a sharp knife or pastry wheel to form 24 squares.

4. Place ½ inch apart on a greased or parchment-lined baking sheet that has been sprinkled with 2 tablespoons each flour and wheat germ. Beat the egg glaze in a small bowl until foamy and brush over the tops of the biscuits to glaze. Sprinkle each with poppy seeds. Bake immediately in the preheated oven 15 to 20 minutes, or until golden brown. Let rest a few minutes and serve hot.

Banana Whole-Wheat Biscuits
~

Bananas are the original forbidden fruit to the Hindus, and for centuries the "Tree of Paradise" was cultivated only in Southeast Asian monasteries to provide shade and sustenance for the holy wise men. Luckily, we mortals can now easily enjoy the nurturing quality and tropical flavor of the banana. These unusual biscuits are luscious for brunch with sweet butter and jam and perfect for a children's snack. For serving with cocktails, use the biscuits to sandwich thin slices of Black Forest ham and honey mustard.
YIELD: About 18 biscuits

1½ cups whole-wheat pastry flour
¾ cup unbleached all-purpose flour
1 tablespoon baking powder
¼ teaspoon baking soda
½ teaspoon salt
6 tablespoons cold unsalted butter, cut into pieces
½ cup sour cream
1 medium ripe banana, mashed
¼ cup cold milk or fresh coconut milk, page 116

1. Preheat the oven to 425°F. In a bowl, combine the flours, baking powder, baking soda, and salt.

2. Cut the butter into the dry ingredients with a pastry blender or 2 knives. The mixture will resemble coarse crumbs, with no large chunks of butter. Add the sour cream, mashed banana, and milk and stir just to moisten all the ingredients. The dough will be moist, then stiffen while stirring. It should be slightly shaggy, but not sticky.

3. Turn the dough out onto a lightly floured work surface and knead gently about 10 times, or just until the dough holds together. Roll or pat out the dough into a ¾-inch-thick rectangle. Take care not to add too much flour at this point or the biscuits will be tough. Cut with a floured 2-inch biscuit cutter, pushing straight down without twisting. Reroll the scraps to cut out additional biscuits.

4. Place ½ inch apart on a greased or parchment-lined baking sheet. Bake immediately in the preheated oven 15 to 18 minutes, or until golden brown. Let rest a few minutes and serve hot.

Old-Fashioned Shortcake Biscuits

~

Genuine fruit shortcakes are an American summer passion. It is the balance of sweet, juicy fruit, fluffy whipped creams, and crumby, rich biscuits that make them irresistible. This version serves them up with Grand Marnier Strawberries and Crème Chantilly (following), the brainchild of my baker-friend, Janet Gentes. Start with ripe berries, then whip the cream with just a dash of sugar and a splash of liqueur for a hint of flavoring. If whipped cream is not part of your diet, substitute *crème fraîche,* plain yogurt, or frozen yogurt. The biscuit must be impeccably fresh, crisp on the outside and soft on the inside.

YIELD: 8 shortcakes

2 cups unbleached all-purpose flour
2 tablespoons sugar
1 tablespoon baking powder
½ teaspoon salt
½ cup (1 stick) cold unsalted butter,
   cut into pieces
1 egg
⅓ cup cold milk, cultured buttermilk, or
   heavy cream
Grand Marnier Strawberries and Crème
   Chantilly, following

1. Preheat the oven to 400°F. In a mixing bowl, combine the flour, sugar, baking powder, and salt. Cut the butter pieces into the dry ingredients with a pastry blender or 2 knives until the mixture resembles coarse cornmeal laced with small chunks of butter. Combine the egg and milk, buttermilk, or cream in a measuring cup. Add to the dry ingredients and stir just until moistened, adding additional milk, buttermilk, or cream 1 tablespoon at a time if the mixture seems too dry.

2. Turn the dough out onto a clean work surface and gently knead a few times just until the dough comes together. The dough will not be totally smooth. Roll out to a thickness of 1 inch and cut into 4-inch circles, squares, or hearts. Individual shortcakes can be made as small as 1½ inches (the dough can also be formed into 1 large biscuit that can be filled and cut into wedges to serve). Place the individual shortcakes about 1 inch apart on an ungreased or parchment-lined baking sheet.

3. Bake in the center of the preheated oven until the tops are brown and firm to the touch, about 15 to 18 minutes. Cool on racks.

4. To serve, cut the warm or room temperature biscuits in half horizontally with a serrated knife. Place the lower portion of each biscuit on an individual serving plate and top with the prepared Grand Marnier Strawberries and chilled Crème Chantilly. Cover with the biscuit tops. Serve immediately.

Cinnamon and Caramelized
Walnut Shortcakes with
Raspberries and Crème Chantilly

POPPY SEED SHORTCAKES

Add 2 tablespoons fresh poppy seeds to the dry ingredients in Step 1. Continue to mix, shape, and bake as for the Old-Fashioned Shortcake Biscuits. These shortcakes are good with fresh plum slices.

LAVENDER SUGAR SHORTCAKES

Substitute 2 tablespoons Homemade Lavender Sugar (recipe follows) for the plain sugar in the dry ingredients in Step 1. Continue to mix and shape as for the Old-Fashioned Shortcake Biscuits. Sprinkle the tops with an additional 2 tablespoons of the Lavender Sugar before baking. These short-cakes are good with fresh nectarine slices.

HOMEMADE LAVENDER SUGAR

YIELD: ½ cup

½ cup granulated sugar
1 heaping tablespoon dried, unsprayed
lavender flowers

In a food processor, combine the sugar and lavender flowers. Process until well combined. Store in an airtight canister.

ORANGE SHORTCAKES

Substitute 3 tablespoons thawed frozen orange juice concentrate in place of an equal amount of milk, buttermilk, or cream in the liquid ingredients in Step 1. Continue to mix and shape as for the Old-Fashioned Shortcake Biscuits. Sprinkle the tops with 2 table-spoons of sugar mixed with the grated zest of 1 orange and bake. These shortcakes are good with fresh peach slices.

CINNAMON AND CARAMELIZED WALNUT SHORTCAKES

Add ⅓ cup chopped caramelized walnuts (recipe follows) and 1 teaspoon ground cin-namon to the dry ingredients in Step 1. Continue to mix, shape, and bake as for the Old-Fashioned Shortcake Biscuits. These shortcakes are good with fresh raspberries.

CARAMELIZED WALNUTS

15 walnut halves
15 bamboo skewers
½ cup granulated sugar
¼ cup water

Skewer each walnut onto the end of a bam-boo pick. In a small saucepan, combine the sugar and water over medium heat. Cover and cook about 3 to 4 minutes without stirring until the syrup is a golden amber. Remove from the heat and dip each walnut halfway into the syrup to completely coat the nut. Set the dipped nuts up against the rim of a plate to cool and harden. Remove

each nut from its skewer and store in a cov-ered container until needed, up to 1 week.

GRAND MARNIER STRAWBERRIES AND CRÈME CHANTILLY

If you would like a shortcake without liqueur, substitute 2 to 3 teaspoons of good imported balsamic vinegar to taste on the berries (it is a remarkable combination) and use a teaspoon of vanilla extract to flavor the whipped cream.

3 to 4 pint baskets of ripe strawberries,
washed, dried, and hulled
3 tablespoons orange liqueur, such as Grand
Marnier
5 tablespoons superfine sugar, or to taste
2 cups cold heavy cream

1. In a large bowl, crush 1 pint of the straw-berries. Mix in a tablespoon of the orange liqueur and 3 tablespoons of sugar. Slice or halve the remaining berries and add to the crushed berries. Set aside.

2. To make the Crème Chantilly: In a chilled bowl with an electric mixer, whip the heavy cream with the remaining 2 tablespoons of sugar and 1 to 2 tablespoons of the orange liqueur until soft peaks form. Cover and chill until serving.

Chocolate Shortcakes with Stewed Rhubarb

~

This unusual shortcake is a memorable pairing of chocolate and ruby-colored rhubarb. A neglected summer fruit, rhubarb is often grown in old-fashioned backyard vegetable gardens. When stewed, it combines well with fresh strawberries or raspberries, so if you wish to, stir some in. Remember to use only the stalks, as the leaves contain a high concentration of oxalic acid, which is poisonous.

YIELD: 12 drop shortcakes

2 cups unbleached all-purpose flour
½ cup unsweetened cocoa powder
½ cup sugar
2 teaspoons baking powder
1 teaspoon baking soda
¼ teaspoon salt
6 tablespoons cold unsalted butter,
  cut into pieces
⅔ cup milk, buttermilk, or heavy cream
Stewed Rhubarb, following
Sweetened whipped cream for topping

1. Preheat the oven to 425°F. In a mixing bowl, combine the flour, cocoa, sugar, baking powder, baking soda, and salt. Cut the butter pieces into the dry ingredients with a pastry blender or 2 knives until the mixture resembles coarse cornmeal laced with small chunks of butter. Add the milk, buttermilk, or cream to the dry ingredients and stir just until moistened and a sticky dough is formed, adding additional milk, buttermilk, or heavy cream 1 tablespoon at a time if the mixture seems too dry.

2. Drop the dough by rounded big tablespoons-full onto an ungreased or parchment-lined baking sheet about 2 inches apart. It is important to mound the dough as the biscuits spread during baking. Place another baking sheet of the same dimensions underneath (known as double-panning) to prevent burning.

3. Bake in the center of the preheated oven until the tops are brown and spring back when touched, about 15 to 17 minutes. Cool on racks. The biscuits will crisp slightly as they cool.

4. To serve, cut the warm or room temperature biscuits in half horizontally with a serrated knife. Place the lower portion of each biscuit on an individual serving plate and top with Stewed Rhubarb and chilled sweetened whipped cream. Cover with the biscuit tops. Serve immediately.

STEWED RHUBARB

YIELD: About 3½ cups

4 cups ½-inch-thick slices fresh rhubarb
  (3 to 4 stalks), or two 12-ounce packages
  frozen rhubarb, thawed
¾ cup orange dessert wine, such as Essencia
1½ cups sugar
2 tablespoons cornstarch
2 tablespoons unsalted butter

Combine the rhubarb, ½ cup of the wine, and the sugar in a heavy saucepan. Bring to a boil, reduce the heat to low, and simmer until tender, about 10 minutes. Combine the cornstarch and remaining ¼ cup of wine in a small bowl. Stir into the hot rhubarb mixture with a whisk. Cook until slightly thickened, about 1 minute. Remove from the heat and stir in the butter. Serve warm or chilled.

Pumpkin Shortcakes with Winter Fruit Compote

~

Although shortcakes are normally served with juicy fresh fruit, a compote that takes advantage of premium canned, dried, and frozen fruit is perfect for the winter months. If you are a wine harvest buff, use an available variety of fresh grapes such as Cabernet, Concord, or Zinfandel in place of the seedless grapes in early fall. I favor Bargetto fruit wines from Santa Cruz, California, for cooking and macerating the fruits in the Winter Fruit Compote liquid. With their kaleidoscope of shiny, jewel-like colors, Pumpkin Shortcakes are ideal for a winter holiday brunch.

YIELD: 10 shortcakes

2½ cups unbleached all-purpose flour
½ cup light brown sugar
1 tablespoon baking powder
½ teaspoon fresh-ground nutmeg
¼ teaspoon salt

½ cup (1 stick) cold unsalted butter,
    cut into pieces
½ cup pumpkin purée, fresh (page xx) or
    canned
¾ cup milk, buttermilk, or heavy cream
Yellow cornmeal for sprinkling
Winter Fruit Compote, following
Sweetened whipped cream or cold crème fraîche
    for topping

1. Preheat the oven to 375°F. In a mixing bowl, combine the flour, brown sugar, baking powder, nutmeg, and salt. Cut the butter pieces into the dry ingredients with a pastry blender or 2 knives until the mixture resembles coarse cornmeal laced with small chunks of butter. Add the pumpkin purée and the milk, buttermilk, or cream to the dry ingredients and stir just until moistened, adding additional liquid 1 tablespoon at a time if the mixture seems too dry.

2. Turn the dough out onto a clean work surface and gently knead a few times just until the dough comes together. The dough will not be totally smooth. Roll out to a thickness of 1 inch and cut into 3-inch circles, squares, or hearts. Individual shortcakes can be made as small as 1½ inches (the dough can also be formed into 1 large biscuit for a shortcake that can be filled and cut into wedges to serve). Place the individual shortcakes about 1 inch apart on an ungreased or parchment-lined baking sheet sprinkled with cornmeal.

3. Bake in the center of the preheated oven until the tops are brown and firm to the touch, about 18 to 20 minutes. Cool on racks. Serve warm or room temperature.

4. To serve, cut the biscuits in half horizontally with a serrated knife. Place the lower portion of each biscuit on an individual serving plate, and ladle with the Winter Fruit Compote and chilled sweetened whipped cream or crème fraîche. Cover with the biscuit tops. Serve immediately with more compote ladled from the traditional footed serving dish, called a compotier, on the side.

WINTER FRUIT COMPOTE

YIELD: About 4 cups

½ pound dried apricots
1 cup apricot wine
¼ cup sugar
Juice and zest of 1 lemon
1 cup pitted whole dried prunes
One 8-ounce can pineapple chunks in
    unsweetened juice, undrained
One 16-ounce can sliced peaches, drained, or
    2 cups unsweetened frozen peaches
One 11-ounce can mandarin oranges,
    undrained, or 2 fresh tangerines,
    seeded and sectioned
1 cup seedless green or red grapes
1 cup fresh or frozen whole unsweetened
    raspberries
⅓ cup slivered blanched almonds
2 tablespoons chopped candied ginger,
    orange peel, or lemon peel

Place the dried apricots, wine, sugar, and lemon juice and zest in a large saucepan. Bring to a boil, reduce heat, and simmer 20 minutes, uncovered. Remove from the heat and add the prunes, pineapple, peaches, and oranges. Let cool until warm and add the grapes, raspberries, almonds, and candied fruit. Serve slightly warm.

Notes from the Kitchen

~ Ingredients & Basic Recipes ~

~ Almond Paste: Although a good commercial brand of almond paste is available from Solo, homemade almond paste is a good staple to have on hand for baking purposes. Tightly wrapped, it keeps indefinitely in the refrigerator or freezer. Bring to room temperature before using in recipes.

HOMEMADE ALMOND PASTE

1 pound fresh whole almonds, blanched
2 cups granulated sugar
3 tablespoons light corn syrup
1 cup water
2 teaspoons almond extract

Grind the almonds in the workbowl of a food processor, ½ cup at a time, with 1 tablespoon of water dribbled in to help keep the oil down, until finely ground and pasty. In a saucepan, combine the sugar, corn syrup, and water to make a simple syrup. Bring to a boil, cover, and reduce heat to low. Cook 4 minutes, or until the sugar is completely dissolved. Uncover and attach a candy thermometer. Continue cooking until the thermometer registers 240°F. Remove the syrup from the heat and let rest for about a minute. Add the almond extract. Place the almonds in a bowl, beating with a wooden spoon or electric mixer, or process in the food processor, drizzling in the hot syrup until smooth and the mixture forms a ball. It will be soft initially, then stiffen as it cools. Use immediately, refrigerate up to 2 weeks, or freeze. Yield: About 4 cups.

~ Baking Powder: Baking powder is a versatile leavener that makes quick breads rise and creates a light texture. It starts a chemical reaction between two or more ingredients to create carbon dioxide and guarantees consistent baking results. The leavening is first mixed or sifted with the dry ingredients to evenly distribute. It is then combined with the wet ingredients and activated immediately, giving off carbon dioxide gas in the form of bubbles of air. During baking, the flour and egg proteins set with the heat and steam around the bubbles, forming texture. However, do not use this product if you are on a sodium-restricted diet. Many bakers recommend brands that do not contain aluminum, as it has a bitter aftertaste. Rumford is an aluminum-free brand often sold in natural foods stores as well as supermarkets. *Double-acting baking powder* is commonly available on supermarket shelves, a mixture of alkaline and acid ingredients: baking soda (sodium bicarbonate), cornstarch (a stabilizer and dryer), and mono-calcium phosphate, sodium acid pyrophosphate, or sodium aluminum sulfate (some form of phosphate salt). It can be used in combination with all types of liquid ingredients. It reacts twice, once when moistened with liquid and again in the hot oven. Batters made with double-acting baking powder can sit in the refrigerator for days and still be light textured when baked. It is known as *backpulver* in Germany and *levure chimique* in France, and sold in 11-gram packets. *Single-acting baking powder* is leavened with cream

of tartar (crystals of tartaric acid, also known as potassium bitartrate) and reacts only once with the liquid ingredients. Single-acting baking powder is no longer commercially available because tartaric acid is expensive, but the instructions to bake batters immediately after mixing, a necessity with single-acting baking powder, has remained in many recipes. Many bakers find it results in a finer texture and higher volume, so they mix their own (recipe follows) or use a small amount of cream of tartar (usually ½ teaspoon per 2 cups of flour) in recipes. *Cream of tartar* is a naturally fermented leavener, like wild yeasts and sourdough starters, contained in the sediment scraped from the bottom of wine barrels. It is the main ingredient used with baking soda to make single-acting baking powder.

Too much baking powder, especially those containing aluminum sulfate, can leave a bitter aftertaste in the baked good, so exact measures are important. Use the guideline of no more than 1½ teaspoons of baking powder to 1 cup of flour. When double or tripling a recipe, cut back the total amount of leavener by one quarter. For baking at altitudes over 3,500 feet, reduce the baking powder by half the amount to compensate for its ability to expand more quickly at higher altitudes. Baking powder has a shelf life of only 4 months before its effectiveness decreases. Most packages are dated. Test for freshness by placing a teaspoon in a small amount of hot water. If it is fresh, it will fizzle. Quick breads can also be risen by aerating leaveners, such as whole eggs, egg whites, butter, lard, and solid vegetable fats, which produce steam that sets during baking.

HOMEMADE SINGLE-ACTING BAKING POWDER

Combine 1 teaspoon baking soda (alkali) and 2 teaspoons cream of tartar (acid) to substitute for 1 tablespoon baking powder in a recipe's dry ingredients. Bake immediately after mixing. This mixture will not store.

~ Baking Soda: Bicarbonate of soda, an alkali originally known as saleratus in the 1800s, is now made from trona, a natural mineral remaining in evaporated salt lakes, that is converted to sodium carbonate and refined to form the familiar $NaHCO_3$. It is an essential leavener needed to create carbon dioxide gas when acid ingredients such as buttermilk, yogurt, sour cream (lactic acids), citrus, molasses, maple syrup, vinegar (acetic acid), chocolate, cream of tartar, and acid fruits are used. Batters containing baking soda must be baked immediately after mixing for best results. It lends a distinctive flavor to traditional soda breads and darkens baked cocoa-infused batters to a ruddy red. It is often added to recipes just to neutralize the acids, as in sourdough batters. Too much baking soda gives quick breads a soapy flavor with an acidy odor. Modern baking soda is

ground very fine and does not need to be dissolved in hot water before adding to the batter. Store your box of baking soda in a cool, dry place.

~ Baking Sprays: This is a grease-in-a-can product, such as Pam, also available with added flour or with a lecithin-base, such as Baker's Joy. There is also an olive oil-based spray good for savory baking. These vegetable oil–based sprays are invaluable for greasing intricate molds and muffin tins.

~ Blossoms and Leaves: Scented blossoms and leaves of edible home-grown (unsprayed) plants are a real blessing in baking. From decoration to flavorings, using blossoms and leaves is an artistic expression, as well as a flavor enhancer. Use fresh violets, scented geraniums (Pelargoniums), rose or lilac blossoms, anise hyssop, cinnamon basil, a variety of mints, lavender, lemon thyme, sweet woodruff, lemon balm, and orange or lemon blossoms to delicately flavor compound butters and sugars to be used in recipes or sprinkled on top of your quick breads. Following the directions below, use only one type of flavoring per recipe of sugar for the most distinctive, haunting flavors and scents.

HOMEMADE BLOSSOM AND LEAF-SCENTED SUGARS:

In an airtight container, place a bottom layer of about ½ cup of powdered or granulated sugar. Lay a few edible, unsprayed leaves or

blossoms on top of the sugar. Continue to layer sugar and leaves or blossoms two more times, ending with a layer of sugar. Cover tightly and let stand at room temperature 1 week to meld flavors before using. Remove the blossoms or leaves before use. Flavored sugars keep for 3 months. Yields about 2 cups.

~ Brans: A protective outer layer covering the whole grain kernel before grinding, bran is acknowledged for its contribution to nutrition. It provides roughage in the form of soluble fiber and is a plentiful source of minerals. It is a by-product of refined flours during the bolting process that separates the bran and wheat germ from the starchy center after milling. Because brans are rather tasteless, they are used with flours to boost the nutrition and fiber content of quick breads, rather than used exclusively. Brans are high in natural oils, so refrigeration is recommended for freshness. *Wheat brans,* sometimes marketed as miller's bran or unprocessed wheat bran, are a favorite ingredient in quick breads and muffins. *Oat bran* is the outer coating of a hulled oat groat and is a favorite mild-flavored ingredient. *Rice bran* is a ground bran that is thought to be as effective as oat bran as a soluble fiber. *Corn bran* is a good addition to cornmeals made with degerminated meals or in combination with other brans. All brans are credited with lowering blood-cholesterol levels and are available in natural food stores.

~ Buckwheat: Buckwheat is a musky-flavored triangular-shaped grain that when ground into flour makes wonderful pancakes, *blini* (raised Russian-style pancakes), Japanese *soba* noodles, Brêton crêpes, earthy muffins, and quick loaves. It comes both light or dark, with the dark flour having a stronger flavor. It is excellent in combination with oats. Order from Pocono Buckwheat Flour from Birkett Mills, P.O. Box 440, Penn Yan, NY 14527.

~ Butter: Butter tenderizes quick bread batters and doughs. Unsalted butter is recommended for the best results in baking. It has no added color or salt, a delicate flavor, a sweet aroma, and a lower percentage of moisture than salted butter. Whipped butter contains 40 percent air, so it is not recommended for baking unless you measure by weight instead of volume. French *beurre* is known as an excellent flavorful addition to baked goods, and differs from American butter because it is made with matured rather than sweet cream. These butters can be used interchangeably in recipes. Butter freezes well for storage up to 6 months. It can be substituted for margarine because it contains the same amount of fat.

~ Buttermilk and Buttermilk Powder: Buttermilk is a creamy, tangy, cultured low-fat milk product, not the by-product of butter making. It is a tenderizer in quick breads and an excellent ingredient in biscuits and pancakes. Many of the recipes in this book use buttermilk as the primary liquid. If a recipe calls for buttermilk, it can be substituted with 2 tablespoons of lemon juice or vinegar added per 2 cups low-fat milk and allowed to stand and thicken for 5 minutes. Dehydrated buttermilk makes a powder that is very delicious and perfect for baking use, but please mix the powder with the dry ingredients. It is available in supermarkets. Refrigerate buttermilk powder, after opening, up to a year.

~ Caviar and Smoked Fish: Amber-colored American golden caviar is the roe from lake-bred whitefish. Mild-flavored and jewellike in color, it is a real treat on hot buttermilk pancakes with dollops of homemade *crème fraîche,* for a special brunch or midnight supper. It is low in cost compared to imported varieties and freezes well. Smoked salmon from the Pacific Northwest or Maine is excellent, with a delicate, sweet flavor. It is cold smoked over alder chips and worth seeking out for garnishing pancakes and biscuits. Smoked trout is a delicacy, hot smoked with a bit of brown sugar. Use it as an alternative to smoked salmon. Smoked fish is usually available vacuum packed in grocery store meat departments and gourmet food stores. Some markets smoke their own, which will look darker and more rustic than commercial brands. Excellent smoked fish may be ordered from Ducktrap River Fish Farm, RFD 2, Box 378, Lincolnville, ME 04849.

~ Cheeses: Cheeses typically favored for cooking also lend themselves to baking. Cheddar, Swiss, Emmenthaler, Monterey Jack, *chèvre,* Brie, blue, mozzarella, and Parmesan are among the most popular cheeses for baking into batters and doughs. Cheese blends well with other ingredients in a batter, which keeps it from separating or overheating. Soft curd cheeses, such as fresh cottage cheese, cream cheese, and ricotta, add distinctive flavor and moisture to quick breads. When buying cheese, be reminded that 4 ounces of grated cheese equals 1 cup.

~ Chestnuts: Chestnuts are edible after their hard husk and inner skin are removed after cooking. Although classified as a nut, they are very starchy, with a texture akin to sweet potatoes, and can be dried and ground into flour as well as candied, boiled, puréed, or roasted. Excellent Italian or French imported chestnuts are sold frozen, canned, or vacuum-packed. Chestnuts are available as *marron glacés,* whole sugar-glazed nuts, that can be chopped and added to batters with other fruits and nuts; in a sugar syrup; or as *crème de marrons,* a popular imported French paste of candied chestnut pieces with sugar, glucose, and vanilla. The flavor of chestnuts marries well with brandy and sherry. Chestnut pureé is an excellent ingredient in batters or flavorful spreads.

TO COOK AND PEEL FRESH CHESTNUTS:

With a sharp, pointed paring knife, press a slit or X into the flat side of each chestnut. Place in a saucepan, cover with cold water, and bring to a boil. Reduce heat to a simmer and cook, uncovered, for 15 minutes. Remove from the heat. Chestnuts can also be roasted in a 375°F oven in one layer on a baking sheet for 20 to 25 minutes, shaking occasionally for even roasting. After cooking, remove a few chestnuts at a time with a slotted spoon and peel away the outer shell and inner skin with your fingers. The nuts are now ready to be chopped or sieved for use plain in sweet or savory recipes. One pound raw chestnuts yields about 12 ounces or 2½ cups shelled, peeled nuts.

CHESTNUT PURÉE:

To prepare fresh chestnuts as a purée for use in quick breads, place peeled, plain chestnuts in a medium saucepan and cover with fresh cold water or a combination of half water and half milk. Add 1 to 2 tablespoons of sugar, a piece of vanilla bean, and a tablespoon of butter per pound of chestnuts. Bring to a boil, reduce heat, and simmer for about 40 minutes, or until the chestnuts are tender. Drain and cool before puréeing the flavored pieces. (An imported 15-ounce can of whole chestnuts may be substituted for each pound of the prepared fresh.)

~ Chèvre: *Chèvre* is cheese made from goat's milk. It is a rustic cheese that has found its place in the mass market and in the hearts of cheese lovers. It has an appealing acidy tang, is a smooth melter, combines well with other ingredients, and is tremendously versatile in cooking. It is sold from fresh to aged, in creamy to hard textures, and in a variety of shapes, colors, and flavors. For all-purpose uses, choose a domestic chabi or its French counterpart, Montrachet, for light taste and creamy texture. There are many excellent brands of domestic *chèvre* now available from cheesemakers such as Laura Chenel, Cypress Grove, Kendall Cheese Company, and Alpine Chèvre in California; Mozzarella Company, Coonridge, and Sierra Farms in the Southwest; Coach Farm and Little Rainbow in New York; Sheepscot Valley in Maine; and Mt. Capra Cheese in Washington State.

~ Chocolate: Chocolate is an equatorial bean that is roasted and blended with sugar to form solid bars or powdered cocoa. *Unsweetened chocolate* is known as chocolate liquor and contains about 50 percent cocoa butter. It is sold in 8-ounce boxes, with each 1-ounce square conveniently individually wrapped. *Bittersweet and semisweet dark chocolate* contain 35 percent liquor and, depending on the manufactureer, a varying array of milk solids, butterfat, lecithin, and vanillin. American semisweet chocolate is the equivalent of European bittersweet. *Couverture* is a thin-coating chocolate used especially for candy making, dipping fruits, and glazing, but it can be substituted for bittersweet and semisweet chocolates. It melts and spreads beautifully. When using this chocolate in a recipe, use less fat per recipe than for regular dark chocolates, as it contains 39 percent cocoa butter. It is usually available in 10-pound bars from wholesale bakery supply houses. *Sweet dark chocolate* contains 15 percent liquor plus more sugar and other ingredients than bittersweet and semisweet chocolates. *Milk chocolate* has 10 percent liquor and a high amount of butterfat and milk solids. It is very sensitive to heat. *White chocolate* is not a true chocolate, but a combination of sugar, cocoa butter, milk solids, lecithin, and vanilla flavoring. It is extremely sensitive to heat. Good-quality brands of white, dark, and milk chocolate are Lindt, Ghirardelli, Maillard, Callebaut, Tobler, Valrhôna, and Nestlé. Store your solid chocolates tightly wrapped in a cool, dry place up to 6 months. If your solid chocolate develops a thin white surface, known as bloom, it has been stored at too warm a temperature. Bloom is harmless and the chocolate may be used as needed.

Unsweetened cocoa is chocolate liquor that has had some of its cocoa butter pressed out and is then ground to a fine powder. It is a good choice in baking for fat- and cholesterol-restricted diets. Dutch-processed cocoa is alkaline-treated, and therefore darker in color, less bitter, and richer in flavor than nonalkalized cocoa. Quick bread recipes utilizing Dutch cocoa use slightly more baking powder to maintain the proper acid-alkaline balance. When using nonalkalized natural cocoa, such as Hershey's (in the brown can), baking soda is an important ingredient for balancing the natural acids. They can be substituted for each other in recipes, but the flavor and color will be different. Good brands of Dutch-processed cocoa are Dröste, Poulain, Baker's, van Houten, Hershey's European-style (in the silver can), and Ghirardelli. Cocoa keeps indefinitely in an airtight container. Do not substitute instant cocoa powder in recipes, as it is precooked and sweetened. *To substitute cocoa powder for baking chocolate:* Substitute 3 tablespoons cocoa and 1 tablespoon vegetable oil or butter for every 1-ounce square of baking chocolate.

Melting Chocolate: The trick to melting chocolate successfully is to melt it slowly over low heat on the stove-top or briefly in the microwave (directions follow). Whatever method you use, first chop it coarsely for even melting. It burns very easily, so keep the temperature below 125°F. If overheated, chocolate will become grainy and taste scorched. The container in which it is melted must be dry. All types and brands of chocolate melt at different rates and have different consistencies. Semisweet and milk chocolates tend to hold their shape when melted and must be stirred with a whisk or rubber spatula to create a smooth consistency.

In a double boiler, place coarsely chopped chocolate over hot, just below simmering, water. Let stand until melted, stirring occasionally. Because milk and white chocolates are so heat sensitive, after the water is hot, remove the double boiler from the heat and let stand until the chocolate is melted.

In a conventional oven, place the chocolate in a Pyrex or other oven-proof baking dish in a preheated 300°F to 350°F oven. Check every 5 minutes until melted.

In a microwave oven, place coarsely chopped chocolate in a microwave-proof container and partially cover with plastic wrap. Microwave at 50 percent power for 2 to 4 minutes, depending on the volume, until shiny and slightly melted. Stir at 1-minute intervals throughout the melting process until completely melted. Milk and white chocolates take less time than dark or unsweetened.

~ Citrus: For the best flavor, use fresh-squeezed lemon, lime, and orange juices in recipes. Frozen orange and tangerine juices are also very good. Lemons miraculously yield more juice when heated in the microwave for 30 seconds or so. Strained juices can be frozen for later use. An ice cube tray is a convenient way to do this. For a standard ice cube tray, each cube is about 2 tablespoons. *Zests* are obtained from the outer part of the citrus peel, which contains the color and volatile oils, giving quick breads flavor without using a liquid. Remove with a sharp knife, fine grater, zester, or vegetable peeler, taking care not to remove any of the bitter white pith.

~ Coconut Milk: Coconuts are drupe fruits, a tropical member of the family including apricots, peaches, cherries, and plums. When unripe, coconut meat is soft, sweet, and jellylike and can be eaten with a spoon. In place of milk or water in quick breads, for a unique tropical flavor use commercial unsweetened coconut meat juice, known as *Nam Katee* in Thai, available in Asian markets, or cream of coconut, available in supermarkets canned or frozen. To prepare your own milk, choose a fresh coconut, shaking to make sure that you hear liquid inside. The inner liquid is really coconut water, a slightly fermented liquid that is very refreshing.

To open and prepare a fresh coconut: Hold the coconut at the top pole and tap with the blunt end of a large cleaver or hammer, or bake in a 350°F oven for 30 minutes, wrapping it in two layers of thick tea towels before hammering. The coconut will crack open. Drain the liquid. Break the shell into smaller pieces. Insert a strong, small knife between the meat and the shell to remove chunks. Use a vegetable peeler to scrape off the thin inner skin. Chop the meat into small pieces and process in a food processor or use a coconut scraper to shred the meat to the desired consistency.

Homemade Coconut Milk: Combine 3 cups of scalded milk or hot water with 2 cups chopped or coarsely shredded fresh white coconut meat, which contains the fat (or substitute 3 cups unsweetened dried coconut for the fresh meat), soak ½ hour, and purée in a blender for 3 minutes. Let stand at room temperature until completely cool. Strain through 3 layers of cheesecloth in a colander. Squeeze to completely press out all of the liquid. If left to set, the cream will rise to the top. Stir to prevent separating. Rich and creamy, coconut milk is an excellent liquid addition to quick breads in place of milk.

~ Cornmeal: *White* and *yellow corn-meals* come in a variety of grinds, from fine to coarse, and are used for cornbreads, biscuits, shortcakes, and muffins. Cornmeal has a unique flavor and texture, and there is no other grain to substitute for it. *Degerminated cornmeal* has had the germ removed for longer supermarket shelf-life, but for the best flavor, use fresh stone- and water-ground meals. Excellent yellow and white fine fresh ground meals are available from Kenyon Cornmeal Company, Usquepaugh, West Kingston, RI 02892 and Gray's Grist Mill, P.O. Box 422, Adamsville, RI 02801. White water-ground cornmeals and southern-style grits are available from Woodson's Mill, P.O. Box 11005, Norfolk, VA 23517. *Blue cornmeal, maiz azul,* is slightly grainier and sweeter, with more corn-flavor than other colored meals. It makes purple-pink to blue-green to lavender-tinged baked products depending on the type of liquid ingredients it is combined with. It is also known as Hopi blue corn. Muffins and biscuits made with blue cornmeal need a bit more fat per recipe, as it contains about 7 percent less fat than other colored meals. Like yellow and white cornmeals, blue meals comes in a variety of grinds. *Harinilla* is a fine grade of blue corn flour, especially good in pancakes. *Harina de maiz azul* is a lime-treated, coarser grind used especially for tortilla making. It is also very good in corn-breads. Blue corn products are available from Casados Farms, P.O. Box 852, San Juan Pueblo, NM 87566. *Polenta* is the Italian name for a very coarse-ground yellow corn-meal. It also can be bought mixed with wheat germ or buckwheat meal, and, occasionally, ground from white corn. Instant polenta is also available. These polentas may be substituted for yellow cornmeal in recipes, but the texture of the finished product will vary. *Masa harina* is a distinctly flavored, dehydrated yellow corn flour made from dried corn kernels treated with a lime solution (calcium hydroxide). It is used to make tortilla corn doughs. It is ground much finer than regular yellow cornmeals. Blue cornmeal *masa harina* can also be ordered from Casados Farms. Store cornmeals, tightly covered, in a cool, dry place or refrigerate up to 8 months.

~ Corn Husks: Dried corn husks from Mexican field or sweet corn are the traditional wrappings for steamed tamales and tamale pies. They contribute a delicate corn flavor when used as a muffin or quick bread wrapping. Rinse and remove the silks on fresh husks, or buy dried. Soak the dried husks in warm water about 1 hour, or until pliable, for easiest handling.

~ Cornstarch: Ground from the endosperm, or germ, of the corn kernel, cornstarch is used to thicken liquids and is especially nice for thickening homemade syrups and sauces. Dissolve first in a small amount of cold water, or combine with sugar to separate the granules. Cornstarch must be cooked for about a minute, until the liquid becomes thick and translucent in color, stirring constantly to avoid burning and lumping. Cornstarch can also be added in a small amount to unbleached flour to lower the gluten, making a soft cake flour that results in more tender cakes, crêpes, or biscuits.

~ Corn Syrup: Light corn syrup is a translucent, sweet, but bland syrup made from cornstarch diluted with water. Dark corn syrup is more flavorful because refiner's syrup and a slight caramel flavoring are added to the light syrup. A homemade version of dark corn syrup can be made by combining 1 cup of light syrup with 1 tablespoon molasses. Both light and dark syrups are about half the sweetness of honey or granulated sugar. When measuring, use an oiled measuring cup for easiest pouring.

~ Cream: Cream is defined by the percentage of milkfat, also known as butterfat, it contains. Sweet-tasting creams are available in regular pasteurized or ultra-pasteurized, a process done to lengthen shelf life. Heavy cream, or heavy whipping cream, is 36 to 40 percent milkfat, the best for whipping. Whipping cream is 30 to 36 percent milkfat, light cream is 18 to 30 percent milkfat, and half-and-half, a mixture of milk and cream is 10 to 18 percent milkfat. Ultra-pasteurized cream is not recommended for whipping.

~ Dairy: In the United States, cultured milk products such as sour cream, *crème fraîche,* yogurt, buttermilk, ricotta, and cottage cheese are made from pasteurized cow's milk, but in many countries they are also made from yak, goat, sheep, or water buffalo milk. The milk is fermented with a bacteria that transforms milk sugar (lactose) into lactic acid, and it curdles naturally into a thick, creamy, and tangy product. Sour cream, *crème fraîche,* and yogurt can be used interchangeably in baking recipes, although the flavor and textures of the final product will vary. They are also excellent for use as toppings. *Sour cream* is thickened heavy sweet cream that, when added to quick breads, results in a dense, moist-textured bread due to its lactic acid. It is a favorite luxurious addition to all types of quick breads. Low-fat sour cream may be substituted. *Crème fraîche* is made in the same manner but uses a different bacteria. It is naturally low in calories and fat, and contains no stabilizers or preservatives. It can be drained in cheesecloth to make a *mascarpone* reminiscent of the authentic Italian cream cheese. It is a great topping

for pancakes drizzled with honey. *Yogurt* is also cultured from whole, low-fat or nonfat milk, but it is thinner in consistency and more tart in flavor than sour cream and *crème fraîche. Yogurt cheese,* made simply by draining yogurt in cheesecloth, is a low-fat, tangy alternative to mascarpone and excellent as a spread on scones drizzled with honey. It can be substituted with *kefir cheese,* which has the beneficial acidophilus culture added. Do not freeze dairy products.

HOMEMADE CRÈME FRAÎCHE:

YIELD: About 1 cup

1 cup pasteurized fresh heavy cream, 36 percent to 40 percent milkfat, without stabilizers (carrageen) or UHT treatment
¼ cup cultured sour cream or crème fraîche, *commercially produced or from a previous batch*

In a small saucepan, heat the cream to about 80°F. Gently whisk in the sour cream or *crème fraîche* until smooth. Pour into a clean jar or crock and loosely cover. Let stand at room temperature 12 to 24 hours. Although *crème fraîche* tastes best fresh, it can be covered tightly and refrigerated up to 2 weeks. If there is any separation, pour off the liquid.

HOMEMADE MASCARPONE:

Spoon *crème fraîche* into a colander or sieve lined with two layers of rinsed cheesecloth. Place over a bowl to catch the whey. Drain at room temperature for 2 to 4 hours, weighted for a denser texture, if desired. Turn the cheese onto a shallow plate and store covered with plastic wrap in the refrigerator until serving.

YOGURT CHEESE:

Spoon a quart of chilled yogurt that does not contain gelatin or agar agar as a stabilizer into a mesh colander or sieve lined with two layers of rinsed cheesecloth large enough to hang over the sides. Place over a bowl to catch the whey. Drain at room temperature for 1 hour. Loosely tie the corners of the cheesecloth to form a bag and hang on the kitchen faucet to drain overnight, 8 to 12 hours, or until the desired consistency has been reached. The longer the cheese hangs, the firmer the consistency. Turn the cheese into a bowl and season, if desired. To make a savory cheese, gently stir in such additions as salt, herbs, pimiento, roasted peppers, or capers. Sweeten the cheese with chopped fresh fruits, macerated dried fruits, chopped lemon balm or cinnamon basil, spices, or nuts. Kefir cheese, available in natural foods stores, may be substituted. Store, covered in a decorative crock or formed into a mold, in the refrigerator up to 2 weeks.

~ Dried Fruit: Sun- and air-dried fruits, such as golden and dark raisins, apricots, pears, peaches, papaya, dates, apples, prunes, pineapple, and currants, add nutrition, color, and lots of flavor to quick breads. New additions include dried blueberries, kiwifruit, cranberries (also known as crasins), and sweet and sour cherries. Most are available from American Spoon Foods, 411 East Lake Street, Petoskey, MI 49770. Crystallized fruits, such as ginger, pineapple, angelica, and orange and lemon peel, are glistening, sweet alternatives, usually seen around the holidays. Choose plump, moist-looking fruits, as shriveled dried fruits will not become softer during baking. Dried fruits are an excellent alternative to commercial candied fruits in baking. Use sulphured or unsulphured fruits interchangeably, unless a recipe specifies otherwise. To cut dried fruits, sprinkle with a bit of flour from the recipe and chop with a chef's knife by hand or snip with kitchen shears sprayed with a nonstick vegetable spray. Alternatively, pulse with a small amount of flour in a food processor. The light coating of flour will also help keep the fruit from sinking to the bottom of the batter. Before adding to batters, dried fruits are plumped in hot water to reconstitute and regain a softer texture. Do not cover while cooking or softening, to allow the excess sulphur dioxide, used to preserve color and preserve freshness, to evaporate.

~ Eggs: Eggs add a wonderful, golden color, rich flavor and a tender cakelike texture to quick breads. Use large or extra-large A or AA grade eggs. One whole egg can be substituted for two egg yolks and vice versa in baking recipes. Three small whole eggs can be substituted for two large eggs in recipes. One large egg equals ¼ cup liquid measure (about 2 ounces in weight); the white equals 3 tablespoons (about 1 ounce in weight), and the yolk is equal to 1 tablespoon. Two large whites equal ¼ cup and 8 whites equal 1 cup. Egg whites can be frozen in ice cube trays for up to 6 months and defrosted to room temperature before using. The yolks cannot be frozen, as they are predominantly fat. *To separate an egg,* crack it sharply on the edge of a small bowl. Break the shell into two sections. Lightly transfer the yolk, taking care not to break it, from one half to the other, letting the white drop through into the bowl beneath. If any yolk slips into the whites, scoop it out carefully using the jagged edge of the shell. Any yolk left behind will inhibit the whites from being beaten to their full volume. Ninety percent of the commercial egg market is from white leghorn chickens, but brown and blue eggs have a similar flavor and are laid by a variety of breeds. Use duck or quail eggs, if you should have an abundance, to vary color and flavor. All eggs should be at room temperature when added to quick breads. Store in the refrigerator in their carton no longer than 4 weeks.

~ Extracts and Flavorings: For the best flavors, use only pure extracts and flavorings in your baked goods. Vanilla, almond, anise, and citrus are the most familiar distinctive extracts, with their essential flavors preserved in an alcohol solution. The best *vanilla* extracts come from Madagascar and Tahitian beans. For a more concentrated essence, split a quarter of a pod in half lengthwise, scoop out the grainy, black interior, and blend them with the batter ingredients. For a more subtle addition, use vanilla-flavored sugar. *Almond* extract is made from bitter almonds. Avoid imitation extracts, which will taste predominantly alcoholic. *Citrus zests* are grated or slivered from the oil-rich rind of the peel from a variety of citrus fruits. Grate with a fine-textured grater or a metal zester, a tool that has a row of tiny holes to cut and curl fine slivers of zest. Take care not to grate the white pith beneath the skin, as it is bitter. Zests can be steeped in liquids to macerate a few hours for a delightfully fresh, mild-flavored addition to batters or doughs. *Orange- and rose-flower waters* are exotic, fragrant complements, distillations of bitter orange blossoms and rose petals. They originated in Middle Eastern cuisine and were introduced into European baking by the Crusades. Use only a very small amount, as their perfumed aromas are powerful enough to quickly dominate other flavors. For baked goods, the best coffee flavor is imparted by using instant espresso powder.

~ Flour, Unbleached All-Purpose: This is the type of wheat flour called for most in quick bread recipes, and it is the foundation of and main ingredient in American baking as we know it. I prefer unbleached flour, because it has been whitened by natural aging rather than chemical bleaching and is therefore less processed. All-purpose flour is excellent for quick breads and is a combination of high-protein, hard-wheat bread flour (14 percent gluten) and low-protein, soft-wheat cake flour (6 percent to 8 percent gluten) to provide a tender crumb as well as the strength needed to support the quick rising due to chemical leaveners. Unbleached all-purpose flour uses 80 percent hard-wheat flour and 20 percent soft-wheat flour. Enriched flour has added B vitamins and iron. Some cooks recommend using two parts all-purpose flour and one part cake flour for the best-shaped muffins. Regional mills and large milling complexes all have different blending formulas and will often blend their all-purpose flours to meet the needs of their clients. Excellent unbleached flours can be mail ordered from Walnut Acres, Penn Creek, PA 17862 and Arrowhead Mills, Box 2059, Hereford, TX 79045. Southern soft wheat and self-rising flours for biscuit making can be ordered from White Lily Foods Company, P. O. Box 871, Knoxville, TN 37901. Gold Medal, Pillsbury, and Arrowhead Mills are reliable national brands, and Stone-Buhr on the West Coast, Robin Hood in the Mid-west, Martha White in the South, and King Arthur and Hodgson Mill on the East Coast are reliable regional brands.

Measure flours with the "dip and sweep" method: Dip the measuring cup into the flour, filling to overflowing. With a knife or spatula, sweep off the excess to level the top. One cup of unsifted all-purpose flour weighs 5 ounces. Store white flour in a cool, dry, dark place (I use a gallon plastic container with airtight lid), for up to 6 months.

~ Flour, Whole-Wheat: Whole-wheat flour is ground from the fiber-rich whole grain that includes the endosperm, bran, and germ. Each commercial brand is a different grind, each giving a slightly different texture to baked goods. Stone-ground flours are milled with slow millstones rather than huge steel rollers that generate lots of heat and reduce nutrients and flavor. With fine grinds, all the parts of the grain are equally ground; medium and coarse grinds have varying amounts of bran dispersed through the flour, giving a slightly more crumbly texture to baked goods. Whole-wheat flours are denser than white flour, and have a complex, nutty-sweet flavor. They also contain more fiber and overall nutrition than white flours. *White whole-wheat flour* is a strain of wheat with a white bran coating rather than the familiar rust color. It is lighter in taste than other whole-wheat flours and may be substituted exactly for darker whole-wheat flours. *Graham flour* is a different grind of whole wheat that leaves the bran very coarse. Although it is easily substituted with whole-wheat flour, it has a particularly rich, unique flavor not to be missed. *Whole-wheat pastry flour* is ground from whole-grain soft wheat and is excellent in quick breads. It makes for a lighter product than regular whole-wheat flours. The "new" wheats, *kamut* and *spelt* (also known as *farro* or *emmer* in Italy and *dinkel* in Germany) were originally hardy ancient varieties cultivated for centuries in rural Europe. They are now grown domestically in Montana and bakers will find an increasing supply of these flours available. When ground into flours, they can be used as an exact substitute for whole-wheat flours in baking recipes, although their flavors will vary. Whole-grain flours contain a high percentage of oil and should be stored in the refrigerator to protect from rancidity.

~ Herbs and Spices: Use the recently dried or fresh leaves of fragrant herbs for the best flavor in baking. My favorites are tarragon, oregano, basil, dill, rosemary, thyme, and sage. Spices from pungent barks, buds, and roots, such as cinnamon, ginger, nutmeg, mace, pepper, and allspice, are distinctive, exotic flavor additions to all quick breads. Many bakers grind their own spices in an electric coffee mill or by hand in a mortar. Replace dried herbs every 6 months and ground spices every year for the freshest essence. Store *aromates* in a cool, dry place in airtight containers.

~ Honey: Honey is a thick, sweet liquid produced by nectar-gathering bees, and its flavor depends on the flowers from which it was gathered. Usually, light-colored honeys are mild in flavor and the darker honeys are more assertive. My favorites are raspberry, wild thistle, cherry, cactus, and French lavender in addition to the familiar wildflower and clover. I also enjoy cinnamon-spiced honey and flavored creamed honeys, such as Oregon Apiaries' vanilla or blueberry honey *crèmes,* for spreading on biscuits, scones, and waffles. Always investigate your local shops or farmers' markets for a locally produced honey. An oiled measuring cup is the most efficient way to pour honey. For a more pourable consistency, gently warm honey on the stove-top or in a microwave oven for 20 to 30 seconds. Use liquified honey in baking recipes rather than honeycomb or more solid, crystallized honeys, which are better for spreading.

~ Liqueurs and Other Alcoholic Spirits: Distilled spirits add a lavish flavor dimension to quick breads, either as an ingredient infused into a batter or in luscious glazes. The intensely perfumed, firey spirits should be used in small amounts to complement the other ingredients, such as using nut liqueur, rum, or brandy in breads with nuts, for example. My favorite flavor combinations include maple and golden rum; nuts with Frangelico or Amaretto; carrots

or zucchini with brandy; apricots or peaches with Asti Spumante, an Italian sparkling wine; cream sherry with pumpkin; and chocolate-or cream-based liqueurs in glazes. Fruits combine well with corresponding crystal-clear fruit brandies *(eau-de-vie)* or fortified wines, such as raspberry. Two classics to have on hand in the kitchen for all-purpose uses are the imported bitter-orange Grand Marnier and a good brandy, cognac, or Armagnac. Also look for domestic brands of *eau-de-vie,* distilled fruit juices that are about 90 proof, such as St. George Spirits kiwi, cherry kirsch, or quince brandy; Creekside's apple brandy from Sebastapol; Clear Creek Distillery's Oregon Bartlett pear brandy *(poire Williams)* or apple brandy. Bonny Doon Vineyards' Framboise is a delicious blend of macerated fresh raspberries in 17 proof neutral grape spirits. These spirits are good in sauces and for macerating. They enhance all baked goods, preserving their delicate fruit essences and flavor through the baking process.

~ Maple Syrup: If you have never experienced the rich flavor of a pure fancy-grade maple syrup from the northeastern United States and Canada, prepare yourself for a treat. It is at once smoky-sweet, luxurious to the tongue, and a beautiful, earthy-color. After tasting one cornmeal pancake breakfast drizzled with the real thing, you will *never* go back to imitation-flavored sugar syrups. Fancy (also known as Light Amber) is the first of the season, pale and delicate.

Grade A and Grade B syrups (Medium and Dark Amber) are progressively darker and more potent in flavor. Grade A is perfect for all-purpose table use and in cooking. Grade B is quite robust in flavor, but less expensive, and it makes the best baked beans and baked goods. The syrups are good for use as a sweetener in batters, as well as for making toppings, butters, poached fruits, and sweetened whipped cream. Refrigerate after opening and store no longer than 3 months for the best flavor. *Maple sugar* can be bought in cakes and grated for use over sour cream or *crème fraîche* on hot pancakes and waffles. The pressed candies that come in the maple leaf form can also be crumbled or grated for use. *Granulated or powdered maple sugar* is free-flowing and can be exactly substituted for regular granulated sugar. It can also be reconstituted to make maple syrup. *Maple butter cream* is maple syrup that has been reduced to the consistency of a thick spread that looks quite a bit like honey. Try it spread on toast, muffins, waffles, poured over ice cream, or as a frosting for white gingerbread. All maple products are available from The Vermont Country Store, P.O. Box 3000, Manchester Center, VT 05255-3000.

To substitute maple syrup for granulated sugar in a recipe: Use an equal amount of syrup for the sugar called for in the recipe. Add ¼ teaspoon baking soda for each cup of syrup and reduce the measurement of the total liquid ingredients by half the volume.

~ **Milk:** Use fresh whole or low-fat milk for the best flavor in recipes. Ninety-five percent of the commercial brands of milk are from holstein-friesian cows. Excellent jersey and guernsey milks are regional favorites and have a slightly different taste. The milk source is usually marked on the carton. Nonfat milk and reconstituted nonfat dry milk can be used in place of the whole milks, although the powder can also be mixed with the dry ingredients.

~ **Molasses:** Molasses is manufactured from the juice of sun-ripened cane sugar, and it adds flavor, sweetness, and color to quick breads. Use unsulphured light molasses, known as Barbados molasses, for the best flavor. Dark and sulphured molasses are the by-products of the second boiling and much stronger in flavor than the light. Most supermarkets carry a brand that falls between the light and dark. Blackstrap is the most bitter, containing a high percentage of ash and a waste product of sugar refining, and it is not often used in cooking. *Malt syrups* are made from sprouted and fermented barley rice. *Dark Treacle* is a less bitter cane-sugar syrup and popular in British baking. They are mild substitutes for molasses and 25 percent less sweet than other sugars.

~ **Nuts and Seeds:** A recipe's flavor can be altered by the addition of raw or toasted nuts and seeds. My favorite nuts for baking are almonds, hazelnuts, pecans, walnuts, macadamias, pistachios, cashews, pine nuts, and Brazil nuts. Sesame, sunflower, and pumpkins seeds can also be used for extra flavor, texture, and nutrition. Measure nuts in dry measuring cups or by weight. Chop by hand with a good chef's knife, in a nut grinder, or in a food processor, taking care not to overprocess or the nuts will become a paste. Always pay attention to the recipe instructions, as nuts may be chopped in sizes ranging from chunky to quite fine. Coarsely chopped nuts are slightly larger than a raisin, finely chopped nuts are about the size of a currant, coarsely ground nuts look rather like polenta, and finely ground nuts are a powder the consistency of coarse whole-wheat flour. For best results, grind with a few tablespoons of flour from the recipe. Be sure to buy fresh nuts and store in the refrigerator no more than 9 months or in the freezer no longer than 2 years to prevent rancidity.

To toast nuts: Place on an ungreased baking sheet in the center of a preheated 325°F to 350°F oven until golden. Alternatively, shake in a dry skillet over medium heat until golden, a method that is especially good for sesame seeds or rolled oats. They will crisp as they cool. Do not bake nuts to the point that they are dark in color, as they will taste burnt. *To toast nuts in a microwave oven,* place the nuts in a single layer on paper toweling or a microwave-proof plate, uncovered. Microwave at full power for 1 to 4 minutes, stirring twice. The nuts will be golden brown. *Almonds* can be purchased whole with skins, blanched, slivered, or sliced. They are the most important and widely used nut for baking purposes. To toast, bake for 5 to 10 minutes; the sliced almonds cook the most rapidly. To blanch whole almonds, cover with an inch of boiling water. Let stand 1 to 2 minutes. Drain and squeeze each nut to pop off the skin. Dry and recrisp in a 200°F oven for 12 to 15 minutes. *Hazelnuts* are bought whole and may also be marketed as filberts. They have an exceptional flavor in quick breads. Bake for 10 to 14 minutes, or until lightly colored and the skins blister. Immediately wrap the nuts in a clean dish towel and let stand 1 minute. Rub the nuts in the towel to remove the skins and cool. *Pecans, cashews, macadamias* (also known as the Queensland nut), and *walnuts* are soft, buttery-flavored nuts. They can be bought in halves or pieces. Bake 5 to 8 minutes. Macadamias are often hard to locate, but a good source is the Mauna Loa Macadamia Nut Corporation, 1-800-832-9993. *Pine nuts, sunflower seeds,* and *pumpkin seeds* bake in 7 to 10 minutes. *Pistachios,* which are naturally a pale green, need to be shelled, skinned, and oven dried if they are not bought already shelled and salt-free. To remove the skins, in a heat-proof bowl, pour boiling water to cover shelled pistachios. Let stand 1 minute, then drain. Turn the nuts out onto a dish towel and rub off the skins. Place on an ungreased baking sheet and oven-dry at 300°F for 10 minutes. Cool before storing in an airtight container in the freezer up to a year.

~ Oats: Use rolled and quick-cooking oat flakes interchangeably in recipes. They have a creamy consistency and sweet, mild flavor and add lots of fiber to baked goods. The rolled flakes can be ground in the food processor to make a coarse flour. Rolled oats are good in combination with barley flakes.

~ Oils: To tenderize and preserve freshness in a loaf, for general baking purposes use a neutral-flavored cold-pressed vegetable or nut oil, such as sunflower, sesame, soy, or safflower or use a blend. For a more pronounced flavor, a recipe may specify a specific oil, such as corn or olive oil. Olive oils vary greatly in flavor depending on the method of extraction and where they were grown. Italian olive oils are the finest in the world, with a complex and sophisticated flavor. French oils are fruitier, Spanish oils are a bit harsher, Greek oils are very strong, and California oils are hearty. Pressings from unripe olives make an oil with a deep green color, while ripe black olives press into a golden oil. Virgin or pure olive oils are the best for use in these recipes. Save the savory extra-virgin oils for salads and sautéeing. Walnut, hazelnut, and almond oils have a nutty essence that also works well in quick breads. The cold-pressed, domestic varieties are gentler in flavor than the imported ones made from toasted nuts. Since oils are 100 percent fat, they cannot be substituted exactly for butter. Substitute ⅓ cup butter (or margarine or solid vegetable shortening) with ¼ cup oil in recipes.

~ Poppy Seeds: Poppy seeds are a crunchy addition to quick breads and can range in color from a clear slate blue to blue-black, with a corresponding wide range of sweetness. In specialty stores, look for Dutch blue poppy seeds, as they are the highest quality and very sweet. Store the seeds in the freezer to prevent rancidity since, like nuts, they have a high oil content.

~ Pumpkins: The American pumpkin is a member of the large family of winter squash that is ready to eat during the fall months. The meaty flesh is a bright orange and sweetish in flavor. The cooked and puréed meat is an excellent addition to quick breads. Other winter squash, such as Blue Hubbard, Blue Kuri, Delicata, Butternut, Turban, or Acorn, can be prepared in the same manner as the following pumpkin purée and substituted for it in recipes, although each has its own distinct flavor. Commercial canned pumpkin is actually part Hubbard squash, which has a distinct sweet flavor and low percentage of moisture.

FRESH PUMPKIN PURÉE:

YIELD: About 1 pound of raw pumpkin will yield about 1 cup purée

Wash a medium-sized sugar or other cooking pumpkin and cut off the top. Cut in half and then into large cubes, leaving the skin intact. Scoop out the seeds and fibers. Place flesh down in a baking dish filled with about 1 inch of water. Cover and bake at 350°F for 1 to 1½ hours, or until tender. Let cool. Peel off and discard the skin. Purée the pulp until smooth in a blender, food mill, or food processor. Cool, cover, and refrigerate for up to 5 days or freeze up to 9 months.

~ Roasted Garlic: Loosely wrap one or more heads of garlic brushed lightly with some olive or corn oil in heavy-duty aluminum foil. Roast in a 400°F oven for 50 to 60 minutes or until the tip of a sharp knife pierces a clove with no resistance. Unwrap and let packages cool to room temperature. Snip the root end of each clove and, one by one, gently squeeze out the pulp into a small bowl. Alternatively, purée through a food mill. Cover and store in the refrigerator for use in savory recipes or as a spread on crusty bread.

~ Roasted Peppers: Place red, green, or yellow bell peppers over a gas burner, on a charcoal grill, or under a broiler until the skin blisters and blackens. Turn often with tongs to roast evenly. Remove to a clean plastic bag and close. Let stand until cool. Scrape off the skin with a sharp knife and rinse under running water. This method is also suitable for fresh hot chile peppers, but handle carefully with kitchen gloves to protect your skin and eyes from the extremely volatile oils. The flavor of roasted peppers is exceptional in quick loaves, pancakes, and scones and worth the time invested. Roasted red peppers are also available canned, but the flavor is not quite as exciting as fresh.

~ Salt: Iodized rock table salt and fine sea salt can be used interchangeably in recipes. Salt is a flavor enhancer in quick breads, but it is optional.

~ Shallots: The French *éschalote* is a flavor cross between an onion and garlic, has a delightfully delicate flavor, and is used in savory pancake batters and sauces.

~ Sugar: Most quick bread recipes call for regular granulated cane sugar (sucrose) for sweetening, which also makes for a brown crust and tender crumb. *Superfine sugar* is very finely granulated and can be either purchased or made by processing regular granulated sugar in a food processor for 10 seconds. It is known as caster sugar in British recipes. *Coarse sugar* is known as decorator's sugar and is used for toppings. Crushed rock sugar or sugar cubes can also be used to create a sweet-crusted top layer. *Powdered sugar,* also known as confectioner's sugar, is perfect for glazes, sweetening whipped cream, and decoratively dusting baked sweet loaves. It is best used after sifting. To make homemade powdered sugar, combine 1 cup granulated sugar with 1½ teaspoons cornstarch in a blender for 1 minute. This mixture cannot be ground fine enough in a food processor. *Brown sugar* has a moist texture because it is a combination of granulated sugar and molasses. I prefer light brown sugar in my recipes. Dark brown sugar has more molasses added than light brown sugar. It can be used as an exact substitute for granulated sugar or light brown sugar, but the flavor is more assertive. It is important that brown sugar be packed during measuring, as it contains a lot of air. It is known as demerara sugar in British recipes. *Fructose* is granulated high-fructose corn syrup and is often used as an alternative to sucrose. It is the same sugar found in fruits and honey. Because it is easier to digest and absorbed more slowly into the bloodstream than sucrose, it is good for hypoglycemics and diabetics. Fructose is about 60 percent sweeter than sucrose, so adjust amounts downward when adding to recipes as a substitute for granulated sugar.

~ Sun-Dried Tomatoes: Roma tomatoes are the variety used for imported and domestic sun-dried tomatoes available dehydrated and oil-marinated in jars. I find the imported brands more salty to the palate, but many people prefer them to the excellent domestic brands, such as Timber Crest Farms and Mezzetta. Drain marinated dried tomatoes before using. The air-dried tomato slices need to be reconstituted in hot water for about 1 hour, then drained, before using as directed in recipes. Sun-dried tomatoes are very concentrated in flavor, so a little goes a long way. Order sun-dried tomatoes from Timber Crest Farms, 4791 Dry Creek Road, Healdsburg, CA 95448. Timber Crest Farms also mail orders a large variety of top-quality dried fruits and nuts.

~ Syrups: Without a doubt, pancakes and waffles are just not quite right served without a rich, sweet syrup. Besides the incomparable pure maple syrup, there are numerous commercial brands of peach, apricot, raspberry, blueberry, blackberry, and ollalaberry syrups from which to choose. Molasses-based syrups are also popular. Lyle's Golden Syrup, also known as light treacle, is pale yellow and thick, with a honeylike consistency and a unique taste that literally sings of British baking. Pure cane syrup, also known as golden refiner's syrup, is domestically available from C. S. Steen Syrup Mill, Inc., P. O. Box 339, Abbeville, LA 70510. Many cottage industries specialize in fruit syrups, such as Oregon Apiaries' superb honey-berry syrups, available in specialty food stores. This book contains many recipes for outstanding homemade syrups, including whole blueberry and apple cider, that you will find indispensable.

HOMEMADE FRUIT SYRUP

In contrast to commercial brands, homemade fruit syrup is less sweet and the fruit flavor more pronounced, as in homemade jams. The process is very easy and not messy. Enjoy favorite fruit combinations such as boysenberry-raspberry, kumquat-cranberry, fig-orange, apricot-pineapple, or peach-plum. The addition of the pectin is important in this recipe to retain a bright, clear fruit color after cooking.

YIELD: About 1 quart syrup

3½ to 4 cups fresh fruit pieces (such as
strawberries, blueberries, or raspberries;
peeled, stoned, and chopped apricots, peaches,
Santa Rosa plums, purple prune-plums,
or mangoes, peeled, stoned, and chopped;
1 pound kumquats (discard the seeds and
end pieces; the skin is edible); 1 pound
cherries, pitted; or 25 fresh figs)
½ cup fresh lemon juice
One 1¾- or 2-ounce package powdered pectin
1 cup water
1 cup light corn syrup
1 to 1½ cups granulated sugar, or to taste

In a food processor, purée the fruit and lemon
juice until smooth. Place in a glass or ceramic
bowl and stir in the pectin. Let stand at
room temperature 30 minutes. Place in a deep
nonalumimum saucepan and mix in the
water, corn syrup, and sugar to taste with a
large whisk. Place over medium-high heat
and bring to a boil. Reduce heat slightly and
cook until the sugar is dissolved and a candy
thermometer reaches 160°F to 170°F. The
mixture will come to a very low boil and a
thin layer of foam will coat the surface. Skim
off the foam. Cool to lukewarm and pour
into a clean glass storage jar. The syrup will
thicken slightly when cooled and chilled.
Store, covered tightly, in the refrigerator for
up to 4 months.

~ Wild Rice: Delicious by itself or
in combination with other rices, wild rice has
a strong woodsy flavor and a chewy texture.
Wild rice is an excellent addition to quick
breads, scones, muffins, and pancakes. It is
not really a rice, but the seed of an aquatic
grass native to the Great Lakes region.
Known as the "gourmet grain," each brand
of wild rice has its own particular taste,
so if you have experienced a brand that was
too husky for your palate, experiment with
others. For a milder taste use hand-harvested
varieties, labeled on the package and a tell-
tale grey-green in color, which are known
for their delicate flavor. Some wild rice is still
harvested by hand in lakes by Native Americans in the traditional manner, but most
is cultivated in man-made paddies, with
California the biggest producer. Clear Lake
and Sutter County produce good brands
known by their dark, shiny kernels. They are
readily available in supermarkets. Teals Super
Valu, P.O. Box 660, Cass Lake, MN 56633,
is a good source for traditional hand-harvested wild rice, and St. Maries Wild Rice,
P.O. Box 293, St. Maries, ID 83861, is a
good source for excellent, mild-flavored,
paddy-grown wild rice.

TO COOK WILD RICE:

The ideal texture of cooked rice is a personal
preference, so adjust the following cooking
directions to your taste. For a crunchy rice,
cook less time, until the kernels just start to
open. For a tender, fluffy version with the
kernels popped open, cook a bit longer with
about ¼ to ½ cup more water.
YIELD: About 1½ to 2 cups cooked rice

In a medium saucepan, bring 1½ cups water
to a rolling boil over high heat. Add ¾ cup
wild rice. Return to a rolling boil. Cover
tightly and reduce heat to the low setting.
Cook paddy-cultivated rice for 55 minutes,
and hand-harvested rice for 30 minutes,
or until the rice is tender and all liquid has
been absorbed. Set aside to cool. The cooked
rice can be refrigerated up to 3 days or frozen
up to 6 months.

~ Kitchen Equipment ~

~ **Bakeware:** Always use the best-quality bakeware for baking quick breads. Buy in professional kitchen equipment outlets, good gourmet stores, restaurant supply stores, or by mail order. Quality bakeware is a satisfying lifetime investment. The best bakeware is made of heavy-duty aluminum, which makes a big difference in absorbing, retaining, and distributing heat during baking. I also use the disposable/reusable aluminum loaf pans available in the supermarket with excellent success. Chicago Metallic is the stalwart commercial brand of the restaurant industry. If you have a large oven, their popover frames with 20 cups, mini-loaf frames with 12 sections, bread pan straps in sets of four muffin and cluster roll frames with 24 sections, and Mary Ann frames with 12 or 24 sections are top of the line. One of my favorite brands of nonstick pans is Kaiser, a German brand with silicon coating. I especially like their fluted *kugelhof* (also known as *gupelhopf* in Britain or *gugelhupf* in Germany), the scalloped turk's cap molds with sloping, patterned sides and a center tunnel for even baking; the 11-by-4-inch braided loaf pan; the 8-inch square pan with deep handles; and the springform pans. Many springform pans come with an interchangeable section that transforms it into an attractive fluted ring mold. Half-loaf pans, sold in pairs, bake unique, ridged, half-moon-shaped loaves. Other unusual baking pans for your quick breads are miniature loaf pans, heart-shaped terra cotta loaf pans, king-sized crown muffin pans, cast-iron loaf pans, baby bundtlette pans, 1- and 2-quart fluted tin molds with clip lids for steamed breads, and borosilica glass pans that can be used in recipes calling for 1-pound or 2-pound coffee cans (all available from the King Arthur catalog).

Different sizes and shapes give quick breads their unique characters. For the best results, always use the pan size indicated in a recipe, to avoid flat tops or overflowing batters. Fill pans no more than half- to two-thirds full, leaving room for expansion. If substituting another shape, be certain it holds the same volume of batter. Smaller pans need less baking time, so adjust accordingly. Dark finishes and Pyrex brown breads faster, and therefore require a reduction of oven heat by 25°F. Glass, lightweight, or burned bakeware conduct heat in an uneven manner. The following chart gives the *amount of batter* that will fill each pan, rather than the *total volume* of the pan. Excellent mail-order sources for specialty bakeware is the Maid of Scandinavia Catalog, 3244 Raleigh Avenue, Minneapolis, MN 55416 and the King Arthur Flour Baker's Catalogue, P.O. Box 876, Norwich, VT 05055.

Round cake and springform pans (2½ inches deep):
6-inch pan holds 2 cups batter
8-inch pan holds 4 cups batter
9-inch pan holds 5 cups batter
10-inch pan holds 7½ cups batter
12-inch pan holds 9 cups batter
14-inch pan (deep pizza pan) holds 14 cups batter
11-by-1½-inch scalloped Swiss rosette pan holds 4 cups batter
11-by-2½-inch pleated celebration pan holds 8 cups batter
Two 8-inch or 9-inch round pans will fill one 9½-by-13-by-2-inch or 15½-by-10½-by-1-inch rectangular pan

Square Pans (2½ inches deep):
8-inch pan holds 3½ cups batter
9-inch pan holds 4 cups batter
10-inch pan holds 6 cups batter
12-inch pan holds 9 cups batter

Loaf Pans:
4-by-2½-by-2-inch loaf pan holds ¾ cup batter
5½-by-3-by-3-inch loaf pan holds 1½ cups batter
7½-by-3½-by-3-inch loaf pan holds 2½ cups batter
8½-by-4½-by-2½-inch loaf pan holds 3 cups batter
9½-by-5 ¼-by-3-inch loaf pan holds 4 cups batter
11-by-4-by-3-inch braided loaf pan holds 5½ cups batter
One 9 ½-by-5 ¼-by-3-inch loaf pan will fill one 9-inch square pan or one 6-inch charlotte mold
One 8 ½-by-4½-by-2½-inch loaf pan will fill one 8-inch square pan

Half-Loaf Pans:

8-by-4½-by-2-inch half-loaf pan holds
  2½ cups batter

12-by-4½-by 2-inch half-loaf pan holds
  4 cups batter

Heart-shaped Pans (2½ inches deep):

3½-inch individual heart mold holds
  ⅓ cup batter

6 ½-inch heart pan holds 2 ¾ cups batter

9-inch heart pan holds 4 ¾ cups batter

12-inch heart pan holds 9 cups batter

Muffin Tins:

1⅝- to 2-by-¾-inch miniature muffin cup
  holds 2 tablespoons batter

2 ¾-by-1¼-inch standard muffin cup holds
  ⅓ cup batter

3¼-by-1-inch oversized muffin cup holds
  ½ cup batter

Charlotte Molds:

6-inch round mold holds 4 cups batter

7-inch round mold holds 6 cups batter

Tube Pans:

3¼-inch individual *savarin* ring mold holds
  3 tablespoons batter

4-inch fluted bundtlette pan holds
  ¾ cup batter

6-by-1½-inch fluted tube pan holds
  1½ cups batter

6 ¾-inch fluted *kugelhof* mold holds
  3½ cups batter

7-by-6 ½-inch pannetone tube mold holds
  8 cups batter

8-inch fluted bundt pan holds 3 cups batter

8-inch plain tube pan holds 5 cups batter

8 ¾-inch fluted *kugelhof* mold holds
  6 cups batter

10-inch plain tube pan holds 10 cups batter

10-inch fluted bundt pan holds 9 cups batter

10-inch fluted *kugelhof* mold holds
  9 cups batter

12-inch tube pan holds 16 cups batter

Two 9 ½-by-5 ¼-by-3-inch loaf pan or one
  9½-by-13-by-2-inch loaf pan fill one 10-
  inch tube pan

~ Baking Sheets: An important
piece of equipment for baking scones, biscuits, and any free-form quick bread, a stan-
dard-size, good-quality aluminum baking
sheet is 10 by 15 inches with a ¾- to 1-inch-
high rim. Half-sheet cake pans are 12 by 18
inches and are available in restaurant supply
stores. Chicago Metallic and Leyse Toro are
the best brands of professional heavy-weight
aluminum. Baking sheets are also available
in air-cushioned and nonstick types.

~ Cake Tester: A straight, firm
wire with a looped end for grasping that is
inserted into the center of a loaf or muffin to
test for doneness. If the tester pulls out clean,
the quick bread or cake is done baking. If
it has batter or some crumbs attached, bake
another 5 to 10 minutes and then retest
with a clean tester. Toothpicks, thin knives,
and bamboo skewers can be used in the
exact manner.

~ Cheesecloth: Cheesecloth is
an inexpensive, porous, lightweight, finely
woven natural cotton gauze designed for
wrapping foods to maintain their shape, or
for straining liquids. It is an essential piece
of equipment in a well-stocked baker's
kitchen: It drains homemade cheeses, molds
multi-layered cheese tortas, wraps mulling
spices and herb bouquets, and slowly soaks
fruitcakes and quick breads in spirited
essences. Cheesecloth is available in supermarkets and cookware stores.

~ Cooling Racks: Wire or wood
cooling racks come in a variety of sizes and
in round, square, or large rectangular shapes.
They are used to slightly elevate hot baked
goods to allow for even circulation during
cooling, preventing sogginess.

~ Electric Mixers: All quick
breads can be made with the aid of a heavy-
duty electric mixer, as they are powerful and
efficient machines. They come with an aluminum mixing bowl, a whisk for whipping,
a flat paddle for general beating, and a dough
hook for yeast breads. I use a Kitchen Aid
stationary model K45. Small hand-held
or old-fashioned stand mixers are not strong
enough for most quick bread doughs and
may quickly overheat. Use them for small
jobs, such as whipping cream or egg whites.

~ Food Processor: The food processor is a very efficient kitchen tool, especially for grating, grinding, and puréeing foods. It has a plastic workbowl that holds 4, 7, or 10 cups of dry ingredients, and is fitted with a sharp steel blade. The speed of the blade is controlled by pulsing or a quick whirl. The blade should be handled with care and never be touched or disassembled until the machine is at a full stop. The problem with most processors is that overprocessing occurs very quickly, creating a very fine purée. However, when used properly, this is a machine the baker will greatly appreciate. I use a Robot Coupe, which is made by the French company that originally manufactured Cuisinart. Information on the Robot Coupe food processor is available from European Home Products, 1-800-225-0760. If you do not own a processor, the mandoline is the traditional hand tool that does many of the same shredding jobs.

~ Measuring Cups: In the United States, the standardized measures for calibrated nested dry-ingredient measuring cups are in ¼-, ⅓-, ½-, and 1-cup capacities. They are the most accurate for dry measuring of flour and sugar. They are available in stainless or plastic sets. Measuring cups for liquid ingredients have a lip for easy pouring and graduated amounts marked on the cup. They are available in glass or plastic. Please use the dry measures for dry ingredients and the liquid measures for liquids, as they are not interchangeable.

~ Ovens: It is essential that your oven thermostat be calibrated to the proper temperature. Also, for some reason, a clean oven bakes best. Whatever pans are used, especially with baking sheets, there should always be a minimum of 1 inch of space around them to allow for heat circulation around all sides for even baking. Stagger baking sheets on separate racks when more than one is in use, with the bottom pan doubled to protect the bottoms from browning too quickly. When baking several pans at once, stagger them so there is space between the pans. Rearrange pans halfway through baking, if necessary. Always preheat the oven for 15 minutes before baking, since batters will react poorly in cool ovens. Use an *auxiliary oven thermometer* to be sure your thermostat is accurate. Use heavy-duty insulated *oven mitts* for secure handling of hot pans. I especially like larger mitts designed for barbecue cookery for the best protection of the wrists and lower arms. Many bakers prefer *convection ovens* for baking, which circulate the heat with a fan, providing an even temperature throughout the oven without the heat variables common in a standard oven. These are popular in professional bakeries, but the professional models bake differently than home models, and bake much more evenly. If you bake in a convection oven, quick breads are apt to bake more quickly and dry out, so reduce the oven temperature by 25°F to 50°F and reduce baking times by 10 to 15 minutes. Please consult the manufacturer's literature accompanying your oven for precise directions. Bread will rise, but not brown, when baked in a microwave oven, and baking times will vary according to the power of the oven.

~ Pancake Griddles: If you make pancakes regularly, consider investing in a griddle specifically designed for the job. Griddles are also good for cooking tortillas, eggs, French toast, blintzes, and homemade English muffins. *Electric griddles* as well as waffle irons with a reversible grill/grid are very popular as backups to stove-top cooking. Many professional ranges used in home kitchens come with an optional family-sized steel griddle attachment built into the top of the stove. *Stove-top griddles* are usually a thick, flat round or square with a shallow rim from 9 to 14 inches in diameter. For larger quantities, there are rectangular or oval griddles to fit over two burners, often made of black heavy cast aluminum or soapstone. *Soapstone griddles* are made of nonporous, acid-resistant greyish stone that retains heat and needs no greasing. They are aesthetically rimmed in a thin band of copper with small handles. They are available in 10- and 12-inch rounds and 9-by-13-inch or 10-by-20-inch oval shapes from Vermont Soapstone Company, Box 168, Perkinsville, VT 05151. They are a lifetime investment and cost no more than a good saucepan. For how to season your pancake griddle, see Techniques.

Specialized pans used to create uncommon pancakes include individual 4-inch blini pans; crêpe pans with flat bottoms of seasoned rolled steel, in sizes from 5 to 8½ inches; shallow 11- to 15-inch-diameter Breton crêpe pans for thin buckwheat crêpes; and the cast-iron *plett* for making seven 3-inch, thin-battered Swedish pancakes or *blini* at the same time. Nonstick coated skillets or sauté pans need to be used with care as they cannot withstand the high heat needed for pancakes and the coating can disintegrate over time.

~ Parchment Paper and Waxed Paper: Parchment paper is a nonporous, silicone-treated paper used for lining pans and preventing sticking. Pans do not need to be greased if parchment is used. It is available in rolls in most supermarkets. It is not the same as waxed paper, which is coated with paraffin and highly flammable.

~ Pastry Brushes: Flat or round pastry brushes with plastic and soft natural bristles are available in a variety of sizes from ½ to 3 inches wide. They are indispensable for applying glazes, greasing pans, and dusting doughs.

~ Pastry Scraper: The all-purpose pastry scraper is made of metal or flexible plastic. It is a rectangular blade with a wood or plastic handle, and is used for scraping work surfaces clean, as a straight edge for cutting dough, or as a spatula, bowl scraper, or spreader. I label it a hand extension, because it does many jobs the outer edge of the hand can perform.

~ Pastry Wheel and Dough Cutters: A pastry wheel, made of metal with a wooden handle, is used for easy cutting of dough by rolling along on a work surface. Hand-held metal cutters come in various simple shapes with a raised handle. They are made in the shapes of the playing card suits, as well as hearts, rounds, squares, and triangles, and are used to form quick dough breads, such as biscuits and scones, into individual decorative shapes. Also look for special shapes, such as a half-moon. Pastry wheels and metal cutters both come with smooth or zigzag edges.

~ Rolling Pins: I use a 28-inch, heavy, ball bearing–loaded hardwood rolling pin made by Rowoco for its smooth, even rolling action. Since a rolling pin is perhaps one of the most personal staples in a cook's *batterie de cuisine,* choose one that feels right for you. They are available in a variety of shapes and sizes. I never use marble or ceramic models, as I find their qualities are overrated and they are too small in size.

~ Ruler: For general pastry and quick bread making, keep a flat metal ruler or retractable tape measure in the utility drawer for measuring doughs when cutting and shaping, as well as for checking pan sizes.

~ Serrated Knife: A long knife with a saw-tooth edge that makes a clean cut through delicate breads and pastries without tearing or squashing. Use an 8-inch blade, and always use an easy back-and-forth sawing motion when slicing breads. A fiddle bow bread knife is a serrated blade set into a fiddle bow–shaped frame, which acts as a guide for uniform slicing. Handmade cherry-wood fiddle bows for left or right-handed slicers are available from The Wooden Spoon, P. O. Box 931, Clinton, CT 06413.

~ Spatulas: Spatulas are another indispensable staple kitchen tool, used for scraping and mixing doughs. Made of flexible rubber and plastic, they come in a variety of shapes . The large, oversized spatulas, used extensively by professional bakers, are a wonderful a tool. Hard plastic spatulas are made especially for use with the food processor. Metal icing spatulas are for frosting but are also excellent for spreading doughs evenly. Wide metal or heat-proof plastic spatulas are useful for removing pieces of coffee cake or loosening baked goods and transferring them to serving dishes.

~ Timer: A kitchen timer to remind you that there is something in the oven is invaluable, even to the most seasoned baker. They are available in good kitchen and hardware emporiums.

~ Waffle Irons: Modern electric waffle irons are designed to simultaneously cook both honeycomb-shaped sides of a waffle fast and evenly. Models specifically form waffles in the shapes of rectangles (which break into two 5-by-6-inch waffles), rounds (a 6½-inch round that breaks into four sections), squares (which breaks into four 3½- to 4½-inch small squares), or lobed rounds (a 6¼-inch round that breaks into five individual hearts). Irons are usually made from cast aluminum with plain or nonstick grids in regular and exaggerated Belgian styles. Stove-top nonelectric models with heatproof handles make four 3½-inch squares for both waffle styles. The plain grids need to be seasoned before use, but the nonstick, easy-release surfaces are so efficient, they eliminate the need for seasoning. It is important to grease both grid types before pouring in the batter to save yourself from the ordeal of prying the waffle out of the maker and subsequent messy cleanup. On electric models, built-in thermostats signal when the iron is hot, usually about 7 minutes after turning it on, as well as when the waffle is done, after about 4 minutes. Many models have the grids permanently set into their frames, but others snap out for easy washing and reversing to form a flat griddle for grilled sandwiches and pancakes or *pizelle* Italian cookie molds. All models carry 1- to 3-year warranties and are easily available in hardware, department, and cookware stores. Good brands include Black and Decker, Rowenta, Toastmaster, Oster, Nordic Ware, and Vitantonio. For information about how to season your waffle iron, see Techniques.

~ Whisks and Other Utensils: Whisks are an important part of a properly equipped kitchen. They range in dimension from finger-sized, for beating one egg yolk, to 12-inch balloons, for beating liquid batters and egg whites. Use stainless steel with a metal or wooden handle for best agility. Wooden spoons, metal spoons, heatproof plastic spoons, zesters, graters, ladles, a pizza cutter, biscuit cutters in a variety of sizes, and a good pair of kitchen shears are also good basic elements in a well-equipped kitchen.

~ Techniques ~

~ Blanching: Fruits or vegetables are immersed briefly into boiling water, usually about 30 seconds to 1 minute, to set the color, remove the raw taste, or allow for easy removal of the peel from fruits such as tomatoes or peaches.

~ Creaming: When a recipe calls for creaming, room temperature butter or some type of solid fat is beaten with a wooden spoon, whisk, electric mixer, or food processor, alone or with sugar, until soft and light in texture or, in professional terms, until emulsified and aerated. Creaming is important for proper leavening in quick bread recipes.

~ Folding: Folding is the technique used for combining dry ingredients with liquids or beaten egg whites to form a batter, without deflating the lighter mixture. The heavier ingredients must always be on the bottom and folded with a large spatula to the top until no streaks are visible. With a spatula, cut through the center of the batter down to the bottom. With a twist of the wrist, pull under the mixture and then pull over the top. Do this repeatedly, gently, and fast to maintain the batter's foamy consistency. This technique is used for pancake, waffle, and some muffin batters to lighten the texture or, as in the case of egg whites, to act as a secondary leavening agent.

~ Glazing: A glaze is a shiny, thin layer poured onto quick breads, coffee cakes, or muffins. Glazing adds a counterpoint of flavor and texture to the finished product. Beaten eggs, melted chocolate, sugar syrups, melted jam, or thinned powdered sugar are favorites.

~ Light Baking: The recipes in this book all use fresh ingredients, lots of different whole grains and stone-ground unbleached flours, high-fiber fresh fruits and vegetables, cold-pressed vegetable oils, and a minimal amount of sugar, but they can be further adapted for today's healthier lifestyle and special diets by using less fat, sugar, salt. Quick breads are naturally rich in fiber and complex carbohydrates; unbleached all-purpose flour contains about 9 to 13 grams of protein per cup. To lower cholesterol, for each whole egg in a recipe, substitute 2 egg whites or a commercial egg substitute equivalent to 1 egg. To increase fiber, substitute up to a few tablespoons of bran, oat, whole-wheat, or other specialty flour for an equal amount of all-purpose flour. All-purpose flour can be substituted with exact measures of whole-wheat pastry flour. Substitute reduced-calorie margarine for unsalted butter. Salt can be reduced by half or eliminated. Low-fat, low-calorie flavor enhancers include herbs, spices, and extracts. Eliminate any alcoholic spirit, if necessary, and substitute with fruit juice. In many cases, high-fat dairy products can be substituted with nonfat yogurt, instant nonfat dry milk powder, nonfat or 1 percent buttermilk, evaporated skim milk, low-fat cottage cheese, Neufchâtel cream cheese, part-skim ricotta cheese, and low-fat sour cream. Sugar can be cut back by one third the total amount in most recipes. Unsweetened fruit juices, apple or pineapple juice concentrate, puréed fruit, fructose, honey, and low-calorie syrups can also be used as alternative sweeteners. Experimenting is the key to finding the right flavors and textures for your tastes and needs.

~ Macerating: To place fruits in a liquid to soften and absorb flavor, such as soaking dried fruit in an alcoholic spirit or fruit juice. Macerating is often confused with marinating, which refers to tenderizing and flavoring meats.

~ Puréeing: To purée fruits and vegetables, use the old-fashioned hand-crank machine known as a food mill, fitted with interchangeable fine, medium, and coarse discs used for puréeing. The 5 ½-inch-diameter model is all purpose. It is a good tool for straining raspberries. Foods can also be puréed in a blender or food processor, the conical sieve known as a *chinois,* or by forcing through a mesh sieve with the back of a spoon. For puréeing whole garlic and pieces of onion or shallot, the other tool not to be without is a garlic press.

~ Seasoning a Waffle Iron or Pancake Griddle: New, uncoated electric and range-top waffle irons or griddles require seasoning to prevent batters from sticking during baking. New equipment will come with the manufacturer's instructions for the best results. In case they don't, or if you need to reseason, follow these directions: Preheat the iron or griddle to medium-high heat. Brush the entire surface, coating all grids with vegetable oil. Heat the griddle or close the iron and heat just until smoking. Remove the griddle from the heat, or open the iron, and let stand until completely cool. Wipe the griddle or iron clean with a soft cloth or paper towel. The griddle or waffle iron is now ready for use. Discard the first set of waffles baked. If the waffles stick, clean the grids carefully with a damp cloth and reseason.

~ Sifting: Flour, cornstarch, or powdered sugar is aerated, leaveners are evenly distributed, and lumps are removed when sifted through a mesh sieve. Recipes will specify this step, if necessary.

~ Unmolding: To prevent sogginess, quick batter breads must be turned out of their hot pans after baking to cool on racks If a quick bread sticks, use a knife around the edges to loosen, or avoid the problem by lining pans with pieces of parchment paper.

~ Whipping: Whipping is the process of incorporating air into a mixture by beating in a vigorous circular motion with a whisk or an electric mixer until fluffy. However, if ingredients such as cream are overbeaten, the protein walls will break down, making butter and whey out of the cream. When flavoring whipped cream, add about a tablespoon of liqueur or extract per cup of cream *just* as the mixture starts to thicken, rather than at the beginning. Use fine-grained sugars, such as powdered or superfine, for sweetening whipped cream, since granulated sugar can stay gritty. A good rule of thumb here is keep it clean, keep it cold, and keep an eye on it during the beating process. In beating egg whites, it is very important that the bowl and beaters be dry and squeaky clean, free from any fat, which will inhibit the whites from reaching the proper consistency.

Calendar of Fruits, Vegetables, and Grains

The baking of quick breads depends heavily on the seasonal availability of fresh fruits and vegetables. Although many batters and doughs can be made to include dried, frozen, and canned fruits, nuts, and flavoring essences (such as bananas, chocolate, lemons, limes, liqueurs, and extracts) that are available year-round, using fresh produce is a great way to enjoy and celebrate the seasons. Also, preserves and syrups made from over-ripe fruit, stewed dried fruits, and poached and sautéed fresh fruits are sumptuous additions to pancake or waffle meals and shortcake desserts.

In addition to fresh produce, other important quick-bread ingredients are the flours and grains that are the foundation of the batters. In studying the types of wheat grown in the United States and Canada, it is interesting to note that the texture and flavor of different flours vary according to the variety of grains used as well as where and by what method they were grown. The large grain-growing farms are situated primarily in the Midwest, with the surrounding regions growing smaller crops, many of them organic. The high-quality strong wheats from the High Plains are exported throughout the world and are used in a variety of excellent products, such as Italian dry pastas. Cornmeals have a variety of subtle flavors, textures, and unique colors, also depending on the soil and temperature conditions of where they were grown. As with all your other quick bread ingredients, buy grains and flours fresh. Grains that are milled and shipped directly after harvest are the most flavorful. Please note that grain harvests listed on the Calendar may vary a few weeks from year to year, as crops ripen depending on yearly rainfall and other weather conditions.

Shop at local produce stands, local flour mills, reliable mail-order sources, farmer's markets, natural foods stores, and good supermarkets for the best selection of fresh produce, flours, and grains. The list below, reflecting West Coast peak seasonality, can be used as a guide to choosing your ingredients for baking. Please note that the produce is usually available for a few months.

~ January: Navel oranges; Red Cuban bananas; Ruby Red grapefruit; kiwifruit; papayas; fresh dates; apples; pears; carrots; end of the fresh coconuts

~ February: Fairchild and Satsuma tangerines; Minneola tangelos; Ruby Red grapefruit; blood oranges; apples; fresh Barhi, Medjool, and Deglet Noor dates; pears; rocket; asparagus; artichokes; broccoli

~ March: Hawaiian pineapples; carambola star fruits; blood oranges; grapefruits; pomelos; the first purple passion fruits from New Zealand; beets; asparagus; sorrel; spring greens; Mexican red and purple garlic; violets; Vermont maple syrup harvest

~ April: Meyer lemons; rhubarb; the first strawberries; pears; unsprayed roses; asparagus; baby spinach; Chantenay carrots; Valencia oranges

~ May: Blackberries; ollalaberries; the first high-bush blueberries; guava; mangoes; the first papayas; kiwifruit; avocados, rhubarb; strawberries; lavender; borage flowers; nasturtiums; the first Tartarian cherries; fresh morel mushrooms; end of the organic Maine potatoes

~ June: Blenheim, Moorpark, and Royal apricots; mulberries; red currants; Royal Ann, Bing, and Great Lakes sour Montmorency cherries; passion fruits; fresh Italian prunes; pink-fleshed and strawberry guavas; clingstone nectarines; first crop Black Mission and Calimyrna figs; Gravenstein apples; the first clingstone peaches and plums; mangoes; muskmelons; wild lowbush blueberries; huckleberries; tomatillos; home-grown basil and tarragon; garlic; Washington barley harvest; Kansas white winter wheat harvest

~ July: Oregon blueberries; loganberries; boysenberries; first crop of dried apricots; Bing and Lambert cherries; muskmelons; nectarines; passion fruits; red currants; plums; red and yellow raspberries; freestone and white peaches; Green Gage plums; strawberries; pawpaws; watermelons; zucchini; summer squash; tomatoes; peppers; table corn; fresh green chile peppers; California garlic harvest; Canadian rye harvest; Midwest, Washington, Oregon, and New York soft winter wheat harvest; dill; herbs in bloom; *Roasa rugosa* rosehips

~ August: Berries; muskmelons; nectarines; freestone and white peaches; the first dried apricots; passion fruits; crab apples; Santa Rosa and Burbank plums; red and yellow raspberries; Thompson seedless and Champagne grapes; Cardona and Amarilla prickly pear fruits; fresh Italian prune harvest; zucchini and yellow summer squash; lemon cucumbers; tomatoes; red, green, and yellow sweet bell peppers; sweet white and yellow table corn; Midwest oat harvest; North Dakota and Colorado millet harvest

~ September: The first homegrown Rome Beauty apples and Red Bartlett pears; late strawberries; late crop figs; Asian pears; local Concord and Muscat grapes; wine harvest; melons; loquats; lemons; late summer squashes and tomatoes; pumpkin and sunflower seeds; California passion fruits; peppers; table corn; Mission and Ascalano olives; Minnesota, Idaho, and California machine- and hand-harvested wild rice; organic Maine potatoes; Canadian, North Dakota, and Montana hard spring and durum wheat harvest (the *best* for breads and pastas); New York soft spring wheat harvest; New Mexico white corn harvest; Oregon oat harvest; Nebraska popcorn; Colorado quinoa harvest; California San Joaquin Valley white, red, and durum wheat harvest; North Dakota buckwheat harvest

~ October: Pomegranates; coconuts; Asian pears; Hachiya and Fuyu persimmons; apples; pears; prickly pears; guavas; fresh walnuts, almonds, and hazelnuts; quince; pumpkins; winter squash; sweet potatoes and yams; raisins; wild mushrooms; Hawaiian macadamias; New Mexico red chile harvest; New Mexico yellow, red, and blue corn harvest; California white, brown, and variety rice harvest; Rhode Island Narragansett White Cap corn harvest (best for johnnycakes)

~ November: Maine, Canadian, and Northwest cranberries; sweet potatoes and yams; butternut squash; Red Anjou and Comice pears; Marsh white and Ruby Red grapefruit; kumquats; Hawaiian macadamias; fresh chanterelles; first Arizona and New Mexico piñon nut harvest; Southern and Southwest pecan harvest; California and Southwest pistachio harvest; fresh imported Italian chesnuts; fresh Washington chestnuts

~ December: Mandarin oranges; tangerines; tangelos; apples; cranberries; navel oranges; first fresh Coachella Valley dates; Napa cabbage; Persian and Key limes; domestic Manzano and Brazilian bananas from Southern California; imported and domestic sweet chestnut flour

~ Index ~

~ Recipe Index ~

~ Table of Equivalents ~

The exact equivalents in the following tables have been rounded for convenience.

US/UK

oz = ounce
lb = pound
in = inch
ft = foot
tbl = tablespoon
fl oz = fluid ounce
qt = quart

METRIC

g = gram
kg = kilogram
mm = millimeter
cm = centimeter
ml = milliliter
l = liter

LIQUIDS

US	Metric	UK
2 tbl	30 ml	1 fl oz
¼ cup	60 ml	2 fl oz
⅓ cup	80 ml	3 fl oz
½ cup	125 ml	4 fl oz
⅔ cup	160 ml	5 fl oz
¾ cup	180 ml	6 fl oz
1 cup	250 ml	8 fl oz
1½ cups	375 ml	12 fl oz
2 cups	500 ml	16 fl oz
4 cups/1 qt	1 l	32 fl oz

WEIGHTS

US/UK	Metric
1 oz	30 g
2 oz	60 g
3 oz	90 g
4 oz (¼ lb)	125 g
5 oz (⅓ lb)	155 g
6 oz	185 g
7 oz	220 g
8 oz (½ lb)	250 g
10 oz	315 g
12 oz (¾ lb)	375 g
14 oz	440 g
16 oz (1 lb)	500 g
1½ lb	750 g
2 lb	1 kg
3 lb	1.5 kg

OVEN TEMPERATURES

Fahrenheit	Celsius	Gas
250	120	½
275	140	1
300	150	2
325	160	3
350	180	4
375	190	5
400	200	6
425	220	7
450	230	8
475	240	9
500	260	10

LENGTH MEASURES

⅛ in	3 mm
¼ in	6 mm
½ in	12 mm
1 in	2.5 cm
2 in	5 cm
3 in	7.5 cm
4 in	10 cm
5 in	13 cm
6 in	15 cm
7 in	18 cm
8 in	20 cm
9 in	23 cm
10 in	25 cm
11 in	28 cm
12 in/1 ft	30 cm

Equivalents for Commonly Used Ingredients

Raisins/Currants/Semolina

¼ cup	1 oz	30 g
⅓ cup	2 oz	60 g
½ cup	3 oz	90 g
¾ cup	4 oz	125 g
1 cup	5 oz	155 g

Long-Grain Rice/Cornmeal

⅓ cup	2 oz	60 g
½ cup	2½ oz	75 g
¾ cup	4 oz	125 g
1 cup	5 oz	155 g
1½ cups	8 oz	250 g

Grated Parmesan/Romano Cheese

¼ cup	1 oz	30 g
½ cup	2 oz	60 g
¾ cup	3 oz	90 g
1 cup	4 oz	125 g
1⅓ cups	5 oz	155 g
2 cups	7 oz	220 g

All-Purpose (Plain) Flour/Dried Bread Crumbs/Chopped Nuts

¼ cup	1 oz	30 g
⅓ cup	1½ oz	45 g
½ cup	2 oz	60 g
¾ cup	3 oz	90 g
1 cup	4 oz	125 g
1½ cups	6 oz	185 g
2 cups	8 oz	250 g

Whole-Wheat (Wholemeal) Flour

3 tbl	1 oz	30 g
½ cup	2 oz	60 g
⅔ cup	3 oz	90 g
1 cup	4 oz	125 g
1¼ cups	5 oz	155 g
1⅔ cups	7 oz	210 g
1¾ cups	8 oz	250 g

Rolled Oats

⅓ cup	1 oz	30 g
⅔ cup	2 oz	60 g
1 cup	3 oz	90 g
1½ cups	4 oz	125 g
2 cups	5 oz	155 g

Brown Sugar

¼ cup	1½ oz	45 g
½ cup	3 oz	90 g
¾ cup	4 oz	125 g
1 cup	5½ oz	170 g
1½ cups	8 oz	250 g
2 cups	10 oz	315 g

White Sugar

¼ cup	2 oz	60 g
⅓ cup	3 oz	90 g
½ cup	4 oz	125 g
¾ cup	6 oz	185 g
1 cup	8 oz	250 g
1½ cups	12 oz	375 g
2 cups	1 lb	500 g

Jam/Honey

2 tbl	2 oz	60 g
¼ cup	3 oz	90 g
½ cup	5 oz	155 g
¾ cup	8 oz	250 g
1 cup	11 oz	345 g

Credits

~

Joyce Oudkerk Pool, Amy Nathan and Carol Hacker would like to thank the following people for all their help:

Nan Bullock: Food Styling Assistance

Melissa Hacker: Assistant Prop Stylist

Joe Maggiore: Photo Assistant

Gumps' San Francisco for their exquisite props.

Palecek Imports for props.

Gardiner Hempel for props.

The text of this book was set in Garamond No. 3 types
with display heads set in Caslon Open Face.
Composition by On Line Typography, San Francisco.
The cover and interior were designed by
Gretchen Scoble, San Francisco.

It was printed and bound in Japan.

~